HOW TO
TEACH HANDWRITING

A Teacher's Manual

BY

FRANK N. FREEMAN

Professor of Educational Psychology, The University of Chicago
Author of The Teaching of Handwriting, Psychology of the
Common Branches, How Children Learn, etc.

AND

MARY L. DOUGHERTY

Instructor in Education, Johns Hopkins University

HOUGHTON MIFFLIN COMPANY

BOSTON   NEW YORK   CHICAGO   SAN FRANCISCO

The Riverside Press Cambridge

ACKNOWLEDGMENTS

THE authors acknowledge the courtesy of the following publishers who have allowed the reprinting of copyright selections:

Houghton Mifflin Company, for permission to include selections from Alice and Phœbe Cary, Emerson, Holmes, Lucy Larcom, Longfellow, Lowell, Frank Dempster Sherman, Celia Thaxter, and Whittier.

Charles Scribner's Sons, for selections from Mary Mapes Dodge's *Rhymes and Jingles*, Eugene Field's *Poems*, Robert Louis Stevenson's *A Child's Garden of Verses*, and Henry van Dyke's *Poems*.

Harper and Brothers, and *The Christian Herald*, for poems by Margaret Sangster.

The Macmillan Company, for poems by Christina G. Rossetti.

The Riverside Press

CAMBRIDGE · MASSACHUSETTS

PRINTED IN THE U.S.A.

PREFACE

Two mistakes of an opposite nature have been made in teaching writing. The first mistake is to expect writing to grow up incidentally without giving the child any specific training in the writing act. The child can learn after a fashion to write with little or no special training, but the quality of his writing is much better when he has had suitable training.

The second mistake is to suppose that teaching writing is some strange mysterious process which can be mastered only by special teachers who have had a large amount of technical training. Writing is no more difficult to teach than the other subjects in the school. Writing is badly taught by the grade teacher, when she attempts to teach it, simply because she has had no training at all in preparation for teaching it.

Writing can be taught by the grade teacher and there are strong reasons why it should so be taught. Writing is an activity which the child performs in much of his school work besides his writing lesson. It is necessary that all the writing be done properly, and it is the grade teacher who must see that it is properly done. When the grade teacher teaches writing, she will feel responsible for the quality of all the child's written work — otherwise not.

If the grade teacher teaches writing, she must have the necessary equipment. This equipment is of two sorts, pedagogical and technical. The teacher must know the principles which govern the process of learning to write and must have a grasp of the methods which grow out of these principles. This is the pedagogical equipment. In addition to this the teacher must have a certain amount of skill in writing in order to be able to teach it. This is her technical equipment.

The importance of the teacher's pedagogical equipment has been grossly underestimated and it has been almost totally neglected. The importance of technical equipment has been commonly overestimated, but nevertheless it has commonly been neglected also. In the small number of cases in which teachers have been trained, the emphasis has been almost wholly on the development of skill in writing.

The aim of this manual is to enable the teacher to get the pedagogical equipment she needs and to furnish the detailed exercises for her use together with such explanation as will enable her to use them intelligently.

The teacher will need to spend time in the preparation of each lesson, particularly in the beginning. This preparation should include a study of the directions, and practice in writing the exercises. It is necessary that the teacher should *show* the class how to write the exercises by writing them on the board. To do this properly the teacher must have a reasonable amount of technical skill and a thorough knowledge of the timing, and all other details, of each exercise.

In the first part of the manual the chief pedagogical and psychological principles which govern the learning process in writing are presented in concise and simple form. This discussion is based in part upon experimental studies of writing, particularly the studies made in the laboratory of the University of Chicago by motion-picture photography and allied methods, and described in the monograph entitled *The Handwriting Movement*, by F. N. Freeman, Supplementary Educational Monograph, Department of Education. In this study, the writing movement of a large number of good and poor writers was photographed and analyzed. From this study of actual cases the characteristics of good writing were determined as described in the first part of this manual.

As the result of this study certain broad principles have emerged as being the most important, and these are made the foundation of the present method of teaching. Among the most important of these is correct position, a fluent and easy sideward movement of the hand across the page, and the proper organization of the movement with reference to time, which we may call the rhythm of the writing. The principle which was found not to deserve the emphasis which has been given it in recent years in American penmanship is the arm movement in forming the letters. This is distinctly subordinate in importance to the other principles which have been mentioned.

In addition to these principles, which are derived directly from the experiments on writing, certain principles of effective practice in the development of skill of movement are applied. Among these is the need of sufficient repetition of a specific act, with the attention concentrated upon its improvement. Another principle is the distribution of these repetitions throughout several periods. A third is consistency, which is accomplished in writing by the correlation of penmanship with other subjects of study. This is emphasized throughout the course.

The manual also makes use of the results of widespread surveys of writing in the public schools, and discusses in a systematic but concise way the pedagogical principles which govern the teaching of the subject.

In the second part of the manual the general principles which are laid down in the first part are applied in a full series of exercises for the first six grades. These exercises are described and illustrated in sufficient detail to be taught from the manual. The exercises are arranged in the form of daily lessons.

A prominent feature of the exercises is their organization into a definite sequence, based on certain clearly defined principles. The principles govern the order in which the letters are practiced, the choice of words, the speed at which the writing is done, the characteristics on which attention is focused, etc. In general, only those letters and words are used in the exercises which have been previously practiced.

A distinctive characteristic of the course is the emphasis which is laid on the adoption of a special set of aims for each grade. This is necessary in order to adapt the work to the capacity of the pupils at different stages of maturity, and in order to build progressively on what has gone before. It is also necessary to provide fresh stimulus and interest to the pupils in a subject which otherwise merely repeats monotonously the same exercises year after year.

The course assumes that the mass of pupils can learn to write in the six years of the coming elementary school. This is done, can be done, and must be done if the teachers of writing are to escape the imputation of gross inefficiency.

CONTENTS

PART I

INTRODUCTION — GENERAL PRINCIPLES OF INSTRUCTION IN WRITING

PART II

DAILY EXERCISES BY GRADES

HOW TO TEACH HANDWRITING

PART I

INTRODUCTION — GENERAL PRINCIPLES OF INSTRUCTION IN WRITING

CHAPTER I

THE PLACE OF WRITING IN THE CURRICULUM

THE USES OF HANDWRITING

WRITING is important, first, as an instrument in school work. It is of value as a means of keeping a record of the information which the pupil has gained or the judgments which he has formed. It counteracts the forgetfulness which makes us lose the information or ideas which we have once had. The habit of taking notes and of summarizing what is read is a means both to the better recollection of what has been studied and to its preservation in completed form for future reference. To this type of record should be added the record of the results of experimental work.

Writing is useful, in the second place, as a means of organizing thought and making it definite. Francis Bacon referred to this value when he said, "Writing maketh an exact man." One may speak in an indefinite and hazy way and the indefiniteness may not be so clearly noticed as when his thoughts are represented in writing. Writing helps the organization of thought by enabling one to have before him at the same time the different points which he is endeavoring to present. Without the help of writing it is difficult to keep in mind the different aspects of a subject. These two uses appear in the subject of written composition.

The pupil writes compositions in the school largely because the teacher recognizes this as an excellent means of clarifying his thought. This can be done most effectively when the pupil is in the mental situation of addressing an audience.

The most frequent use of writing for communication with others is correspondence, which takes the form of personal or business correspondence. This is one of the earliest and most continuous uses of handwriting and constitutes the best single ultimate motive of universal application. Of a somewhat similar kind is the preparation of written work which is to be handed in to the teacher.

The conservation of the results of experience in records which are systematically kept and filed in such form as to be readily accessible is one of the most important kinds of technique which the pupil can learn. As the student advances in his school work he will also find it necessary to take notes of spoken lectures. The facility with which he can do this will greatly influence the amount which he is able to gain from such lectures.

In all these cases the degree of the usefulness of the writing will depend very largely upon the ease and fluency with which the pupil can write, as well as upon the legibility of the written record. There is no question that the efficiency of a student is influenced very considerably by the facility with which he can write.

The value of writing to the adult may also be divided into the two aspects of keeping records, and of expressing thoughts to others in correspondence. If the adult has not a thoroughly good mastery of the art of writing, he will avoid the use of writing in keeping records or in correspondence, and when he does write, the difficulty of the process will cause loss of time and the distraction of attention from the thought which he desires to express. Furthermore, the poor quality of the result will make the record difficult to interpret, or will produce an unfavorable reaction in the reader.

When we come to the vocational use of writing, we find it to vary all the way from the infrequent incidental use, such as that to which it is put by the carpenter who keeps a record of his orders and his job, to that of the addressor whose sole business is to write. The vocational use of writing is, of course, being greatly reduced by the typewriter, but there are still numberless commercial employees who use it very frequently. An example of the intermediate use is to be found in the case of the store clerk who is required to make a record of his sales. In this case the ease and legibility of the writing is an important element in individual efficiency. It is not necessary to go into detail to recount the frequency with which writing is required in commercial life. It is an evidence of its importance that it is emphasized in the training of commercial students which is given in commercial courses or in commercial schools. We shall find when we discuss the standards of writing that it is necessary to distinguish between the standards which are desirable for everybody and those which should be set up for the student who is to prepare for a vocation of a commercial type.

WRITING STANDARDS — FINAL STANDARDS

We may distinguish two types of standards in a school subject which is taught throughout the grades. In the first place, we have to consider the standard which the pupil should reach at the end of his school career. In the second place, we should consider the standard which he should attain at each stage in his progress

toward the final goal. We may consider, first, the final standard.

The final standard in writing has to be determined on the basis
of two sets of facts. First, we should consider the demand for writing in the life in the school or in after life, and, second, we should
consider the ability of the child and the amount of time and effort
which it is necessary to spend in order to reach a given standard.
So far as the demand is concerned, we need concern ourselves only
with the demands of after life. The demands of the school are not
greater than these. We may consider, first, the demands of life
upon writing, and, second, the ability of the pupils as shown in surveys of their writing ability.

Some investigation has been made of the demand both of vocational life and of common life upon instruction in writing. A ques-
tionnaire [1] sent to fourteen commercial firms in Chicago, which
included correspondence schools, department stores, mail-order
houses, packing companies, etc., indicated that the writing should
be at least as good in form as score 60 on the Ayres Scale. Four of
the fourteen demanded a score of from 70 to 90. When asked
whether a quality of writing better than that which was considered
essential was desirable, all the firms answered in the affirmative.
The desirable quality ranged from 70 to 90, eight of the firms speci-
fying the highest quality on the Ayres Scale. In regard to speed,
eleven of the fourteen indicated that it was important. One only
answered that it was not; two replied that it was moderately important.

The number of employees represented by these firms was seven-
teen hundred, and the answers may be taken as fairly representa-
tive of those firms which employ clerical help. We may summarize
the returns by saying that the writing should be at least as good as
60, and that better writing is desirable. With reference to speed
the writing should be fluent.

In another study [2] the writing of over a thousand adults was
scored in order to find the quality of the writing which adults find
necessary or desirable to maintain. The occupations which were
represented numbered thirty-four, and may be taken as fairly rep-
resentative. Among those persons who used writing mainly for
correspondence the average of the various groups was somewhat below 60 on the Ayres Scale. Among those who made particular use
of writing in their vocation, such as addressors and accountants, the
average ranged about 70. The conclusion arrived at in this study

[1] Frank N. Freeman, "Minimum Essentials in Handwriting." *Fourteenth Yearbook of the National Society for the Study of Education,* pp. 72, 73.

[2] L. V. Koos, "The Determination of Ultimate Standards of Quality in Handwriting for the Public Schools," *Elem. Sch. Jour.* 1918, xviii, 423–46.

was that 60 is an adequate standard for those who use writing for correspondence and other general uses, and that 70 is an adequate standard for those for whom writing is an important function in their vocation.

We have next to consider what standards the child is capable of reaching with an ordinary amount of training. A survey of the writing from schools in over fifty cities [1] reveals the fact that the average quality was 62.8 upon the Ayres Scale, and the average speed 73 letters a minute, at the end of the eighth grade. Under present conditions, therefore, the standard of 60 in quality and 70 in speed is easily obtainable by the end of the elementary school. We shall have to consider in a later section whether a still higher degree of efficiency should be demanded, not by securing a higher degree of excellence, but by securing it at an earlier period in the school. We may anticipate the later discussion here to the extent of saying that it is probably not unreasonable to expect that this standard should be attained by the end of the sixth grade. This grade is coming more and more to be recognized as the culmination of the period of general training which all children have in common. At the beginning of the junior high school there will come a differentiation of the type of work taken by different groups of children. At this point those who are to prepare particularly in commercial work might continue their special practice in writing, while those who are to continue the more general type of training might well discontinue it.

Standards have thus far been spoken of as though they were to be expressed by the average performance of a class. There is an entirely different way of expressing a standard which measures efficiency in a more direct way. We may set up as the goal for attainment in a grade a certain quality and a certain speed, but the attainment of this standard quality and speed is measured not by the average attainment of the class, but by the percentage of the pupils who reach the norm or the standard. This is after all the kind of measure which is most satisfactory. If the average of a class comes up to a certain point, this means that approximately half the class is below the norm. The average is brought up by the superiority of the other half. The efficiency of the lower half of the pupils is not counterbalanced by the superiority of the others, in so far as the needs and demands of the poor writers are concerned.

There has been comparatively little experimentation done by this method of measuring the attainment of a class. We should undoubtedly have to make a lower standard if we insisted that a large proportion, say 80 per cent or more, of the pupils should attain it.

[1] Frank N. Freeman, "Minimum Essentials in Handwriting," *Fourteenth Yearbook of the National Society for the Study of Education*, p. 6.

We might perhaps set 10 points below the average as a minimum standard for all the pupils to attain. In the later section on "Principles of Learning," specimen record forms will be shown on which can be kept the proportion of pupils of a class who attain to a standard. The raising of this percentage ought to be one of the most direct aims of the teacher and of the class.

GRADE STANDARDS

In addition to a final standard we must also have grade standards for the guidance of teachers throughout the stages before the final grade is reached. The following standards, derived from widespread tests [1] of the writing of children in the elementary school, may be laid down.

GRADE STANDARDS IN WRITING

GRADE	FORM			SPEED
	Ayres Scale	Thorndike Scale	Freeman Scale	Letters per min.
II	35	8.5	11	30
III	39	9.3	12.5	44
IV	46	10.2	14.5	51
V	50	11.0	16	60
VI	57	11.9	18	63
VII	62	12.7	20	68
VIII	66	13.5	21	73

In order to measure the attainment of the pupils for the purpose of comparing it with a standard, careful tests must be made. The methods of making such tests have been worked out by experimentation and are described at the end of the next chapter.

[1] Frank N. Freeman, article in the *Fourteenth Yearbook*, cited above.

CHAPTER II

STANDARD TESTS AND SCALES

Uses of Tests

One of the most useful innovations in the field of handwriting has been the development of methods of measuring the writing by means of which the attainment of different classes and schools can be compared. For the most effective work, a definite aim is necessary. It has been found by experience that an ordinary examination, or the marks which are given to the pupil on the ordinary percentage basis, are exceedingly unreliable. Until the introduction of scales, therefore, the teachers have had no means of finding out in any exact way whether they are attaining a satisfactory standard or not.

The pupil also needs to know whether he is writing as well as he should, and whether he is making satisfactory progress. The score which can be given him as a result of a careful test and the grading of his papers by a scale enables him to trace his progress from time to time, and in this way stimulates and encourages him. The pupils have been found competent to measure their own writing with sufficient exactness to serve as a stimulus and as an index of their progress.

The second value of tests and scales to the teacher is found in the means which they furnish for the comparison of the effectiveness of different methods of teaching or of learning. The same teacher in different years may try somewhat different methods, and may trace the progress of her classes by giving them careful tests and thus comparing the two methods. Broader comparison of the same sort may be made between schools, or groups of schools. In this way we have an instrument for the scientific determination of the comparative values of methods or devices. Some of the methods which are described in this manual were tested in this way.

Still another use can be made of scales when they are so designed that they give not simply a single score, which represents the quality of the pupil's writing as a whole, but when, on the other hand, they analyze the quality into several elements. When this is done we can say what the nature of the pupil's deficiency is, and can direct his effort toward overcoming some special difficulty. For example, it may be found that the slope of his letters is irregular, and that this is his worst fault. If this is the case, he can gain much more from his practice, when he attempts to overcome this particular fault, than when he works with only a vague general aim in mind.

Kinds of Scales

Various kinds of scales have been devised. These scales may be distinguished, in the first place, according to the element of the writing which they attempt to measure. The Ayres Scale,[1] for example, is designed to measure the legibility of the writing. In order that it may measure this characteristic, the specimens on the scale were chosen by measuring the speed with which they could be read. It is found, however, that the scores which are obtained by the use of the scale depend rather upon the general form of the letters and the words than upon the ease with which they can be read. The Thorndike Scale[2] is based upon beauty, legibility, and character; that is, the judges who picked out the specimens for the scale were instructed to keep in mind these characteristics. Other scales simply attempt to measure general appearance or form.

Some scales have been put upon the market which profess to measure not only the objective characteristics of the writing, but also the means by which the writing was produced, such as the character of the movement, or the position of the hand, or the element of speed. It is unwise to attempt to include such elements as these because they are not a part of the form of the writing itself. They might be measured, but they would have to be measured by observing the pupil rather than by looking at his writing. Speed should be measured as an entirely separate element, and then, if it is desired, the score can later be combined with the score in form.

In the next place, scales may be classified according as they call for judgment which is based upon a general impression, or upon an analysis of the writing. In using the first type of scale one may give the specimen a score by comparing the general impression which the writing makes upon him with the general impression made by the different specimens on the scale. This is a type which is represented by the Ayres Scale and the Thorndike Scale, and the great majority of other scales which have been published. The analytical scale, on the other hand, calls for an examination of different points of excellence in the writing separately. This scale is represented, for example, in the Freeman Scale. One is called upon in using this scale to grade the writing in uniformity of slant, and of the alinement of the top and bottom of the letters, in letter formation, in spacing, and in the quality of the line. Such a scale gives

[1] Leonard P. Ayres, *A Scale for Measuring the Quality of Handwriting of Children.* Russell Sage Foundation, *Division of Education.*

[2] E. L. Thorndike, "Handwriting," *Teachers College Record*, March, 1910.

five separate scores, which then may be added to make a combined score.

Another distinction is between the universal scale, which is intended to be used to grade papers from all levels in the schools, and a grade scale, intended to be used only in a particular grade. The universal scale has the advantage that it will show by its scores the comparison in the standing of the pupils all the way up the grades. It is, however, difficult to use a scale which is made up of specimens from the upper grades with the papers of children in the lower grades. Few grade scales have been designed, but there will undoubtedly be further development in this direction in the near future.

Finally, there is a distinction between general scales which are intended to be applied to any locality and local scales which are made from specimens written by the pupils of a given city or locality. The advantage of a local scale is that the type of writing upon the scale is similar to the writing of the children which is to be measured by it. The writing of pupils throughout the cities is coming to be so similar in type, however, that the disadvantage of general scales is not great.

The general impression type of scale is somewhat easier to use than the analytical scale, and for the purpose of a general comparison of the writing of a class or of an individual pupil with the standard, it is a satisfactory instrument. For the further study of the writing of the pupil, with the aim of helping him to see the faults of his writing and to direct his efforts particularly to overcoming those faults, an analytical scale is useful.

In order that the use of a standard test may give reliable results, it is necessary to use care in giving the test and in scoring the papers. The methods of doing this have been carefully worked out, and the teacher may, by a little practice, and with attention to the directions which are given below, secure reasonably accurate results.

METHOD OF CONDUCTING A HANDWRITING TEST

1. Give the pupils some preliminary practice in writing the words which they will write in the test so that they can write them freely from memory. In the second and third grades use some suitable rhyme, as:

> The rain is raining all around,
> It falls on field and tree,
> It rains on the umbrellas here
> And on the ships at sea.

In the fourth to the eighth grades use the names of the numerals (not the figures), one, two, three, etc., practicing up to thirty.

2. Be provided with a stop-watch or watch with a second-hand.

3. See that the pupils are ready with pen and ink (or pencil in the grades in which pens have not been used) and paper.

4. Instruct the pupils substantially as follows:

"We are to have a test (or game) to see how well you can write. To write well means to write rapidly and also to make it look well. We are going to write what we have been practicing. [Make sure the pupils know what this is.] You will start when I say 'Begin' and stop when I say 'Stop.' Be sure to keep writing all the time till I say 'Stop.' [If this is the first test, give a trial or two in starting and stopping on other paper than that which is prepared for the test.] Remember, write well and rapidly and keep on writing until I say 'Stop.'"

5. See that everybody is ready, start the watch, or wait till the second-hand is at zero, and say "Begin."

6. Keep watch of the pupils and start going again any that may stop.

7. Note the watch carefully and say "Stop" exactly at the end of two minutes.

8. Glance about and stop any pupils that may continue.

Scoring the Papers

The speed may be quickly and accurately scored by the following procedure:

1. Make a scoring copy by writing out the text and placing above each word the number of the letters in the text up to the end of that word.

2. Note the last letter the pupil has written and give him provisionally the corresponding score by referring to the scoring copy.

3. Read through the pupil's copy to see that it is correctly written, and add or deduct any letters he has inserted or left out.

4. Divide by two in order to get the score in terms of letters per minute.

The form may be scored by following the directions which accompany the scale which is used. In general, some practice is needed before scoring can be done accurately.

Records of Attainment

The purposes for which any measurement is made are best attained when a permanent record is kept of the measurements. This record serves as a basis of comparison for the attainment of a class at different times, and also for the attainment of the individual pupils. There should, therefore, be records for the class as a whole and records for the attainment of each pupil. Such records as these are more effective stimuli to the pupil than are buttons or certificates, or other evidences of attainment given by an outside authority.   The pupil knows definitely the meaning of such records as these.   Moreover, by means of them he can trace his progress and not merely know that he has attained a certain level at a given time.   The pupil is intensely interested in watching the rise of his progress curve.   Record blanks may be prepared by each pupil. This constitutes an excellent exercise and initiates the pupils into the meaning of the graphs.   If preferred, the forms may be duplicated and given to the pupils.

After each test, each pupil should indicate his scores by short marks on the appropriate vertical lines on the individual record blanks for speed and form.   The percentage of pupils who have reached or exceeded the norm for the grade should also be indicated on the class record blanks, the first indicating the percentage of the children who reach the norm in speed, the second indicating the percentage who reach it in form, and the third indicating the percentage who reach it in both form and speed.

The units for scoring on the record blank for form correspond to the units of the Ayres Handwriting Scale (Russell Sage Foundation).   If some other scale is used, the units which it employs should be substituted.   The units of the speed record are letters per minute.

In order that the pupils may have a record of the particular features in which their writing is strong or weak, directions are given in this manual for grading by the analytical scale.

CHAPTER III

PRINCIPLES OF LEARNING

Position of the Body and Arms

Certain positions in writing are better than others, because they are more favorable to good writing, to easy and fluent movement, and also because they are better for the health of the child. Studies of physiology and of hygiene have indicated that a position which compels the child to sit habitually in a bad posture produces curvature of the spine, congestion of the blood in the lower part of the trunk, and other physical defects. Such a position is also bad for the eyes. There is not space in a manual of this sort to give the reasons for all the directions which are presented. These reasons are described in more detail in other writings.[1] The directions for good position will be given here without any attempt to justify them in detail by reference to their scientific evidence.

The writer should sit facing the desk squarely. His seat should be of such height that his feet may rest flat on the floor and the thighs be parallel to the surface of the seat. The desk should be of such a height that when the child is sitting erect and the arms rest on the desk, the elbows will be two or three inches from the body. The feet should project under the desk slightly in order that the child may sit back in the seat without being compelled to lean forward in order to rest his arms upon the desk. The child should sit back in the seat and should sit reasonably erect. The head should be held reasonably erect and not inclined much to the one side or the other. Slight variations in position are to be admitted since entirely unvarying posture is very hard for the child to maintain, but he should not maintain any habitual posture which is markedly different from the one which has been described.

The arms should rest easily on the desk, but should not support the weight of the body to any great extent. The forearms should be inclined toward one another so that the hands are near together. The left hand should be used to hold the paper, and to move it either upward or to the side when the adjustment of its position is necessary.

The paper should be situated directly in front of the child and so inclined that the bottom edge makes an angle of about thirty de-

[1] Frank N. Freeman, "Principles of Method in Teaching Writing Derived from Scientific Investigation," *Eighteenth Yearbook of the National Society for the Study of Education*, part II, 1919, pp. 11–25.

grees with the edge of the desk. This brings the line of writing nearly parallel to a diagonal line from the lower left-hand corner of the ordinary school desk to the upper right-hand corner. It may be desirable to draw this diagonal with chalk in order to help the child to keep his paper in the proper position until he has formed the habit.

With the paper and arm in the position described, the sideward movement of the forearm will carry the pen along the line of writing without any shifting backward and forward. This movement is then made by the rotation of the forearm about the elbow, or about the point on which the forearm rests on the desk. This sideward movement is one of the most important in the entire activity of writing, and it should be very easily and readily made.

The forearm should rest about three quarters of its length on the desk. As the pupil writes down the page, it will be necessary, in order to avoid having the forearm project too far off the desk, to move the paper upward every few lines of writing. This may be readily done with the left hand without much loss of time.

Position in Left-Handed Writing

A word may be said at this point in regard to left-handed writing. There is a certain small but definite proportion of people who are strongly left-handed. For such persons to write with the right hand is much more difficult than to write with the left hand, and there is a good deal of scientific evidence to indicate that, for such persons, writing with the right hand frequently produces difficulties or defects in speech. If a pupil is strongly left-handed, therefore, he should be allowed to write with his left hand.

The reason that left-handed pupils have so much difficulty in writing is that they are given no help in adapting conditions to their peculiar needs. When a left-handed pupil attempts to write with the paper in the position for the right hand, as he ordinarily does, the situation is very awkward for him. If we apply the same principles that have been laid down for the right-handed pupil, we will place the paper so that it tilts thirty degrees to the right rather than to the left. This will put it in such a position that the left hand will move along the line of writing when the left arm is turned about the elbow. We shall touch upon the modification to be made in the slope of left-handed writing in discussing the topic of slant below.

Hand Position and Pen-Holding

The hand should be held with the palm turned down until the wrist is not far from level. It may deviate as far as forty-five degrees without prejudicing the writing, but with children it is well to be on the safe side and require that the wrist be not tilted as far as this. It is not well, however, to insist upon the rigid requirement that the wrist be held level.

The reason that the wrist should not be turned much to the side is that this position prevents the hand from sliding easily across the paper. To make this sliding movement easy, the hand should rest upon the third and fourth fingers. The best position is probably one in which the fingers slide upon the nails. They may also slide upon the first joint of the little finger. In any case the hand should not rest upon the side, or upon the base of the hand. These positions make it difficult to keep the hand moving sideward while the letters are being formed.

The pen should be grasped easily and lightly, in a position which is natural to the form of the hand of the individual writer. The thumb and first finger should not be drawn in or tightly pressed against the penholder. The first finger should rest nearer the point of the pen than the thumb. It is well to test the looseness of grasp occasionally by drawing the pen from the child's fingers and seeing how much resistance is offered.

It is not necessary to insist that the penholder cross the knuckle, as was formerly required, or that it point to the shoulder or the right ear. Experts sometimes hold the penholder in the depression between the thumb and the forefinger.

Some persons write well with the pen between the first and second fingers, and it may be desirable for an adult who does a large amount of writing to use this position as a means of relief, but it is better for the child in the grades to use the prescribed position.

In general it is desirable that the child should be consistent in the position which he adopts and in the form of his movements. It will be necessary for him to vary slightly in order to find the best method, but his variation should not be capricious. Undue variation in the method of performing an act of skill prevents the habituation of the act.

MOVEMENT

We may distinguish between two aspects of the writing movement. The first has to do with the composition, which refers to the character and relationship of simpler movements which make up the complex coördination. The second has to do with the nature of the changes in the speed or the rhythm of the writing. We shall first discuss the composition of the movement.

COMPONENTS OF THE MOVEMENT

The movement may be considered from two points of view. The first concerns the side-to-side progression of the hand across the

page while the letters are being formed. Experimental analysis
has shown that this is one of the most important aspects of the writing movement. Exercises will be given which are designed especially to develop this movement. In fact these are the only purely
formal movement exercises in the course. When this sideward
movement is not properly carried out the hand becomes cramped
and the letters cannot be easily formed. Furthermore, if it is not
carried on continuously and regularly, the slant and shape of the
letters are likely to be irregular.

This sideward movement, as has already been said, is made by
swinging the forearm about the elbow or the resting-place of the
arm on the table. This is a movement which is very easily made
alone, but it is difficult to combine with the production of the letters. The most common fault is the alternation between the writing
of the letters and the progression of the hand. The difficulty comes,
then, in learning to combine the two. Specific exercises are also
given to facilitate this combination of sideward movement and letter formation.

As the arm movement is adapted to carry the hand sideways
across the page, so the fingers are adapted for the greater part of
the formation of the letters. This is contrary to the common view,
but experimental evidence shows very clearly that the arm movement is not well adapted, in the case of the great majority of persons, for the formation of the details of the letter. It is a large,
comparatively slow movement, and not particularly well adapted
for the production of minute forms. It requires a great deal of
practice to develop, and, while after it has been developed it results in smooth, regular writing, it is not suited to the majority of
public school children. Careful measurements have shown that
the majority of children who have been trained in its use employ it
very little in their ordinary writing. Even expert writers use the
finger movement to a greater or less extent.

That the arm movement is not conducive to rapidity is shown by
the fact that there is no correlation between the speed of writing
and the amount of arm movement which is used. The child will
naturally fall into the use of the arm to a slight degree in making
the up-and-down strokes, if he develops a free sideward movement of the arm and hand. It is not necessary, however, to talk
to him about this or to give exercises which are designed directly to
produce it. He may be allowed to use his fingers as much as he is
inclined, provided he maintains the proper position, the freedom
of sideward movement, and ease of grasp. These may be secured
without the extensive and strenuous arm movement drill which is
common.

RHYTHM

An aspect of the writing, which has not received much attention because it is difficult to observe, has been shown by experimentation to be very important. This is the organization of the movement in respect to its timing. We ordinarily refer to this aspect when we speak of the rhythm of a movement. The timing of the handwriting movement, however, is not characterized by a definite and uniform rhythm. The movement is divided into units, as in the case of a uniformly rhythmical movement, but these units are not of equal length. They are adapted to the complexity and length of the stroke which is to be made. In the early stages of the development of the movement, we use a uniform rhythm in order to give the child a start, but as the movement becomes more delicately adjusted to the requirements of the letters, the duration of each stroke becomes slightly modified.

The rate at which the count for the exercises is given is adjusted to the ability of the pupils of successive grades. The rate which is prescribed for each grade is such that the pupil in following it will write at the standard rate for that grade.

Some pupils will be able to adapt themselves to a faster rate when the writing in concert is abandoned in the latter part of the year, and other pupils may find it advantageous to write at a somewhat slower rhythm. These individual adjustments can be made after the pupils have become accustomed to rhythmic writing through the class exercises.

The good writer as contrasted with the poor writer breaks the entire movement into units or strokes. These units are not separated by complete pauses, in most cases, but by a slowing down of the movement. Thus the movement proceeds by a succession of alternate flights and rests.

A unit ordinarily corresponds to a double stroke, an upward and downward, or a downward and upward stroke. Each of these units is made with a gradual increase in speed toward the middle, and a gradual decrease toward the end. The speed decreases when the stroke changes abruptly in direction. Thus the *m* is a succession of three strokes, each composed of an upward and downward stroke. The stroke slows down somewhat on the curve at the top and is retarded more decidedly still when the direction of the movement is sharply reversed at the bottom. The poor writer either does not slow down at the places where there is a radical change in the direction of the stroke, or he slows down at those places where it is not appropriate.

Each of these units is made in regular fashion. If we compare the movement of a good writer upon successive units which produce similar letter forms, we find that the speed changes are always similar. The poor writer, on the other hand, is inconsistent, and may vary considerably the type of speed changes in making a succession of similar letter forms.

The division of the writing into units is promoted by counting. The counting, however, must be done in such a way as to be suited to the letter forms which are being made. Furthermore, the child must be shown how to adapt his strokes to the counting in detail. Mere counting rapidly while the child writes along, without having learned how to apply the count to each individual letter, is of little use. One of the most prominent features of the exercises which are given later, therefore, consists of the careful analysis of each letter, and of instructions as to how the count should be adapted to each letter.

This requires careful study on the part of the teacher and of the pupil. The teacher should show the pupil, by writing on the board, just how the count is applied to the letter. The pupil should then practice until he is able to do it as the teacher has done it. The counting, of course, is recognized as an intermediate stage in the practice. After a time the pupil will become independent of it. Its purpose is to develop the organization of the movement into units, and to develop the free and fluent writing of the letters by a succession of impulses.

Since one unit of the count ordinarily corresponds to a double stroke — an upward and a downward — the beat may come either on the upward or the downward stroke. It is usual to give the count on the downward stroke. In this manual, however, the count is given on the upward stroke. The chief reason for this is that the upward stroke in slanting writing carries the hand forward along the line. This forward movement needs to be emphasized, and placing the count on the upward stroke serves to do this. The only important exception to this rule is to be found in the count used on some of the capitals.

The adoption of a favorable position and the development of a movement organized into units, as has been described, will promote the development of one of the most important features of a skillful act. This is a moderate relaxation of the muscles. The muscles, of course, must have a certain amount of tension, but the tension is very commonly too great. The tension is naturally greater in the earlier stages of learning than later on, but the practice should be so directed that it may be overcome as rapidly as possible. A steady and regular succession of movements and pauses is one of the best means of promoting this desirable relaxation.

PRINCIPLES OF PRACTICE

REPETITION

The fundamental principle of practice in learning an act of skill is repetition. Repetition, of course, may merely habituate the wrong way of performing the act, if the act is not done properly, or if the attention is not so directed as to bring about improvement. But improvement cannot take place without repetition. Discussion in handwriting lessons should be distinctly supplementary to practice by the pupil. The greater part of the writing period should therefore be spent by the pupil in actually writing. Some of this writing may consist in writing the same words or exercises over again, and some of it may consist in writing new words or exercises, but the rule which should be remembered is that the pupil should be actually writing the greater part of the time.

ATTENTION ON IMPROVEMENT

In order that practice may be effective, the child should constantly watch the results of his efforts and strive in some definite and specific way to improve his writing. This improvement is most effectively and quickly brought about by giving attention to the form of the writing itself. We shall see that the child may profit, to some extent, by thinking of his position, or of the method of making the movement, but this is entirely subordinate to his effort to bring about some definite change in the form of the letter.

One of the best methods of securing the pupil's attention to his writing, with sufficient attention to details to make for progress, is to have him grade his writing. The attention which he gives when he compares his writing with the scale, in order to decide what score it shall have, calls his attention to imperfections and to those parts on which improvement should be made. The more detailed the examination is, the better. For this reason a scale which has several parts, each to be applied in judging one feature of the writing, is the most helpful. Thus the child may be led to examine, first, the uniformity of slant, then the uniformity of alinement, the letter formation, the spacing, and the quality of line, in succession, and can try to improve in one specific element at a time.

It is well to have the pupil practice continuously for some length of time upon the improvement of some specific feature. Thus he may spend a week upon uniformity, a week upon spacing, and so on. Practice which is directed to the improvement of some specific element in the writing is like shooting at a target with a rifle, while practice in which the aim is merely general improvement is like shooting with a blunderbuss, which scatters the shot widely in the hope that one of the bullets may hit the target.

While it is important that the pupil should practice with very concentrated attention upon the improvement of the appearance of his writing, some attention may be given also to certain features of his position and movement. We sometimes say that an act of skill is done in good form. We mean by this that the position which is assumed is the one which has been found to be the best, and that the movement is carried out in a general way in the manner which is recognized to be the best. Thus, in serving a tennis ball, the left foot should be placed in front of the right foot. In making a golf stroke, the right hand, in right-handed players, should be placed below the left hand. While the golf stroke is being executed, the head and body should not be moved. Such general features of a movement as this can readily be observed, and can be taught by means of instruction and imitation.

There are certain features of this sort in the writing movement which can be acquired through instruction and imitation. The hand should be held in the position which has been described above, the movement across the page should be free and easy, and the grasp of the pen should be light. Such matters as these can be emphasized by the teacher. However, the carrying out of the execution of the movement must be learned by the pupil through practice, with his attention fixed upon the result. When the result is better than he has been producing before, he knows that the movement is successful. He then repeats the movement in the attempt to secure the same success. This process of trial and success is the method by which he learns to execute a movement, after he has adopted the accepted position.

Emphasis on Speed and on Quality

In directing the pupil's practice the question arises whether it is better to encourage him to aim at speed at the beginning and gradually develop accuracy of letter formation, or whether it is better to aim at a high degree of accuracy at the start and gradually increase the speed. The answer to this question differs in different kinds of learning. In those activities in which the pupil may be shown exactly how to make the movement and make it correctly from the start, a high degree of accuracy should be maintained throughout the training. This is the best method, for example, in typewriting. In this case the errors which the pupil makes retard his progress. In writing, however, it is impossible to secure much accuracy at the start and maintain anything like the desirable degree of fluency of movement. When accuracy is over-emphasized, the pupil resorts to a different sort of movement from that which he will have to make later on. He in this way fails to get the feeling of the movement which corresponds to the form of the letters. He improves in such an act of skill as this by trying more or less blindly. At first his writing is crude. If his attention is ever on improvement, however, he learns gradually, by noting when he fails and when he succeeds, to produce better and better letter forms.

With reference to speed, two extremes in procedure are also found. One extreme is to require of the child as great or nearly as great speed at the beginning as will be expected of him in the end. This is as great a mistake as the attempt to secure extreme accuracy from the start. When the writing is too rapid, the pupil is unable to control the stroke. His letters are badly scrawled and he forms the habit of being satisfied with very poorly formed letters and words. Fluency can be secured with a movement of moderate speed and the sacrifice in accuracy can be avoided. Many tests have shown that the general control of movement is less in the young child than in the older child or the adult. The deficient control should be recognized and the conditions made easy for the child in every way possible.

AUTOMATIZATION

When the writing habit has been completely formed, it is automatic: that is, the writer executes without paying much attention to the position, to the details of the movement, or to the letters. The mind is then left free to give attention to the meaning of what is being written. To gain this advantage we must choose a type of movement which can be allowed to become automatic without a too excessive amount of practice. If too difficult or artificial a type of movement is taught, the child does not use it in all his writing and it therefore does not become automatic. This is one of the chief objections of the arm movement style of writing as taught in the elementary school. In order that a movement may be automatized, the style should not be changed capriciously. Fashions in the form of letters or freakish methods of holding the pen sometimes attack a school. These should be resisted.

A further obstacle to consistency is fatigue. When one has been performing a certain act long, he becomes tired, and without knowing why feels the desire to perform the act in a different way. This produces a kind of variation which does not produce progress, but rather breaks down the habit which is being formed. The avoidance of this fatigue is desirable and necessitates comparatively short periods. We shall consider the periods of practice in the next section.

PERIODS OF PRACTICE AND REVIEW

For the reasons just mentioned it is necessary that the period of practice in writing should not be too long. It can, of course, be longer with older pupils than with younger ones, since the more accomplished we are in an act the longer we can perform it without fatigue. A comparison of the results obtained in schools where different amounts of time are given to drill in writing indicate that the progress secured with ten or fifteen minutes of practice a day is equal to that obtained by a much longer period. While the adult may secure forced improvement by intensive practice, the acquirement of the art of writing by the primary and intermediate child requires a longer stretch of time. The attempt to force it by long periods of practice does not secure corresponding returns.

The other feature of the distribution of time is the length of time between practice periods. There has been no opportunity to compare different intervals between practice periods on a large scale. The common practice is to hold one practice period a day. The analogy with forms of learning in which different intervals have been compared would seem to indicate that one period a day is a good arrangement. If pupils require more than the ordinary practice, it is probably better to give them two periods of ten to fifteen minutes each in a day rather than one period of thirty minutes. In the grades up to the fifth or sixth, one period a day is in all probability better than a period every other day.

The principle of distribution of practice applies also to the individual exercises. A particular exercise can be learned more economically by spreading the practice over several days than by concentrating it all on one day. By the distributed arrangement the pupil's interest is kept at a higher pitch and he profits from the advantage of reviews. For this reason the present course utilizes the methods of short practice on each exercise in a given period and frequent review.

What shall we set before the pupil as the aim and goal of his efforts? The common practice, of course, has been to use a copy whether in a copy-book or on copy-slips. The thing which the pupil is to aim at is the production of letters of a certain form. It has already been said that the most prominent aim in the child's mind should be the production of good letter forms. This can be done in two ways — first by setting before him ideal forms, and, second, by leading him to examine his own writing and to distinguish between his own successful and unsuccessful attempts. Certainly the examination of the standard form should be supplemented by a very large amount of self-analysis on the part of the pupil. This procedure is repeatedly advised in the following exercises.

The Model of the Teacher's Writing

In the exclusive use of a copy an element of the writing is neglected which has been found by experiment to be very important.

This element has already been mentioned in discussing the speed changes of the writing movement. The movement of the pen should be organized into a series of units. This cannot all be conveyed to the pupil by simply putting before him a copy. It can be done only by showing him the actual writing process. For this reason it is necessary for the best results that the teacher should show the pupil how to write, and not merely show him a perfect copy. The case is like that of learning to handle any tool. The teacher shows the pupil how the tool is to be handled and the pupil learns a great deal from watching the expert perform the act. The teacher should be sufficiently expert to demonstrate on the board the manner of performing the letters. The stimulus should then include the teacher in the act of writing as well as the copy.

Assuming that we have set a copy before the pupil, what should the style of writing be? The history of the development of writing and the analysis of the movement show that it should have a moderate but not an extreme slant. If the paper is tilted thirty degrees, the downward strokes will deviate about thirty degrees from the vertical, and will hence make an angle of about sixty degrees with the base line. The letters should be plain without flourishes, and such as can be easily written. In this course the style of letters adopted by the National Association of Writing Supervisors is used with slight modifications in unimportant details.

Movement Exercises

There are two important types of movement exercise used in this course. The first of these has for its purpose the development of a fluent and well-coördinated sideward movement of the hand and arm. A comparison of good and poor writers shows that the sideward movement is very important. In order to carry on this movement, the hand has to be held so that it slides freely. This sideward movement is promoted by a swinging side-to-side stroke. It is also promoted by writing the letters spaced widely apart. Both of these exercises are used freely in the present course.

The second device which is prominent in this course is that of counting. There are two ways of counting. The first is not specifically adjusted to the particular letters which are being made. Frequently the counting is done chiefly for the formal exercises such as ovals or the up-and-down stroke. When the pupil comes to write the letters the count is not carried over to them. In the present course very little counting is done except when the letters are actually being written, and the count is so adjusted to these that the pupil makes each part of the letters in the time which is suited to its form and the movement by which it is made. Each letter has its characteristic rhythm, and can be divided into parts.

Each of these parts may be made to a single count or beat. Every time a new letter or combination of letters is introduced, the manner of counting which is suited to these letters or combinations is indicated, and the pupil is to be drilled in writing to the count before he writes these letters independently. This writing to count is bound to be somewhat artificial, but it is intended to be only a transition stage which has for its purpose the development of rhythmic writing. After the pupil has learned to organize the writing movement into units and to make each one with a single sweep of the pen, he is then given latitude in the exact time which he devotes to each part of the letter.

No attention is given in this course to formal drills for the development of the arm movement. The familiar ovals and up-and-down strokes are not used. As has already been said, the development of arm movement is not recognized as being an important aim of the teaching of writing. This is the reason why these drills are not used. The other use of the drills, the develop-ment of a fluent and rhythmical movement, is attained more directly and more effectively, it is believed, by the use of the count upon the letters and words themselves. It is well known that the practice of formal drills does not carry over satisfactorily to the writing of letters. Therefore, such formal drills are reduced to a minimum in this course.

The Use of Tests and Records [1]

It is necessary to make tests of the attainment of each pupil in the class at regular intervals and to keep records of the results of these tests, for several reasons. The teacher should have as definite data as possible by which to follow the progress of the class as a whole and of each individual pupil. This is necessary in order that he may know whether the methods which he is using are producing satisfactory results or whether they need to be altered. These records also furnish the indispensable means by which the super-visor can judge of the success of the teacher. In addition to these uses, it stimulates the pupil's effort to watch his progress as it is represented in his progress curve. A class as a whole, also, is energized by watching its own progress from month to month.

Adaptation to the Age and Maturity of the Pupil — the Needs of the Young Child

A serious defect in many courses in writing is the failure to adapt them to the limitations and the capacity of the younger pupils. For many years the dominant handwriting methods gave almost

[1] See pp. 8, 9, and 10 for directions concerning the conduct of tests and the forms for keeping records.

exactly the same drill to first-grade pupils as to those in the eighth grade or in the commercial school. There has frequently been an almost total lack of adjustment to differences in natural skill and development of these younger pupils and of the older children. There has been marked increase in recent years in modifying the demands to suit these younger pupils. The grade standards which have already been given indicate that the demand should be progressively higher as we go up the grade. We must neither require so great speed nor so high a degree of accuracy in the young child as in the older one. This is an obvious adaptation to the younger child's lesser degree of control. Another way in which the burden is lightened for the younger child is by giving him materials which are easier to handle. The chalk and blackboard are much easier to use than pencil and paper, and the pencil and paper are easier than the pen and paper. Large writing with a coarse pencil is easier than finer writing with a smaller pencil or with a hard pencil. The way in which new difficulties and higher requirements are gradually introduced is shown in detail in the plan for the succeeding grades which are given in the exercises.

LOWER AND UPPER LIMITS OF INSTRUCTION

A special problem in the adaptation of writing to the maturity of the pupil concerns the best time for beginning and the best time for ending the teaching of writing. Some educators have believed that the child should not learn to write until the second or third grade. At the other extreme is the practice of the Montessori method which begins the practice of writing in the kindergarten period. There is no sufficient reason why writing should not begin as early as this, provided it is adapted to the capacities of the young child by the methods which have been already referred to. On the other hand, writing as it has often been taught in the primary grades is not suited to the child below the third or fourth grade. The place at which writing should begin depends altogether, then, upon the character of the writing which is taught.

The question regarding the upper limit of instruction in writing concerns, first, the standard which should be attained, and, secondly, the degree of efficiency of writing instruction which we should demand. It is the opinion of the writers, based upon surveys of writing of various cities, and experiments in teaching writing, that the regular writing drill which is designed to be carried on by the majority of pupils of the class should be completed in the sixth grade. By this time the pupil will have had at least three years of practice with the materials which he will use permanently. During these three years he possesses a reasonable degree of natural manual skill. He should certainly, by this time, if his training in writing has been at all consistent and effective, have laid the foundation of his handwriting habit. While it is desirable to continue to watch over his writing to keep it up to standard, he should, as a result of the natural maturing which takes place in succeeding years, be able to develop a settled habit in handwriting without specific drill.

The case is different, of course, both with the pupils who need to write especially well to prepare for the demands of a particular vocation and for the pupil who is naturally very deficient in manual skill. These two groups, for opposite reasons, may need continued writing drill beyond the sixth grade. It has been demonstrated, under ordinary public school conditions, however, that the large majority of the pupils can attain the final standards which have been laid down by the end of the sixth grade. It should not be necessary to prolong training in such a definite and specific habit as handwriting for more than six years. If it is necessary, the methods of teaching writing should surely be subjected to careful examination as to why they are not more efficient. We do not need to argue the point merely upon theoretical grounds. Actual experience has shown that six years is ample time in which to develop the average child's handwriting coördination. This course, therefore, is organized to cover only the first six grades.

INDIVIDUAL DIFFERENCES

The general principles of learning to write have been described in the foregoing sections. These general principles apply to the practice of all individuals. In their application, however, it is necessary to allow for variations in the manner of writing to adapt it to the peculiarities of individuals. In the first place, there are differences in the nature of the writing coördination.

POSITION

The position which is natural for one individual differs somewhat from the position which is natural for others. No two persons are exactly alike in the proportions and structure of the hand. If a group of persons are asked to extend the fingers, it may easily be observed that the relative length of the different fingers varies. In some, for example, the index finger is longer than the third finger and in the others it is shorter. In some, the middle finger projects out farther from the two adjacent fingers than in others. The length of the thumb in comparison to the fingers differs in different persons. These are merely illustrations of the general fact of variation. It would be very surprising if these differences did not make desirable variations in the manner of holding the pen.

Mode of Writing

In addition to these structural differences, there are variations in the natural mode of activity of different individuals. This may be observed, for example, in the habitual posture and manner of walking. In many cases the child's habitual posture may be observed to resemble that of one of his parents or grandparents, indicating that it is an inherited and, therefore, natural mode of action rather than accidental. We must have due respect for these fundamental variations and must allow sufficient scope in all standard requirements to permit of their expression. In the preceding description of standard position and of the mode of writing, the statement was sufficiently broad to permit of considerable individual variation.

The teacher should make a careful study of each child early in the development of his habit in order to assist him in adapting the general requirements to his individual needs. In doing this, care should be taken to distinguish between variations which are fundamental to the child and those which he adopts upon mere caprice. He should be encouraged, after he has found the mode of writing which suits him best, to practice consistently in this manner and thus to develop a habit which has permanence and is at the same time adapted to his needs.

Differences in Ability

Besides these differences among individuals in the manner of writing, there are differences in ability. It is a matter of common observation that some children are naturally poor writers and others naturally good writers. These differences are found to exist in every subject of instruction which has ever been measured, and they are almost incredibly large. If we examine the scores in the speed and quality of writing of all the fifth-grade children in a school system, we shall find individuals who write more poorly than the average first-grade child and others who write better than the average of the eighth grade. An idea of these individual differences may be gathered from a table which shows the results of the test in the fifth grade of a certain city.

This is a so-called distribution table. In it each pupil is given a position according to the speed of his writing, on the one hand, and of the form or quality, on the other. His position in the vertical rows will be determined by the speed. Thus, if his writing is at the rate of from 60 to 69 letters a minute, he will be placed somewhere in the horizontal row to the right of those numbers which appear in the left-hand column of the table. The score in quality will determine which vertical column his record will appear in.

Thus, if the score in form is 50 to 55, his tally will be placed in the column under these numbers. Each number in the table indicates the number of pupils whose writing has a particular combination

SPEED	FORM							
	Ayres Scale Scores							
Letters per minute	20 and 25	30 and 35	40 and 45	50 and 55	60 and 65	70 and 75	80 and 85	90
100 and above......	3	4	5	2	5	1	—	—
90–99..............	1	4	9	6	2	—	—	—
80–89..............	3	10	20	29	27	14	2	—
70–79..............	7	16	30	31	42	8	3	—
60–69..............	2	22	38	32	37	12	1	—
50–59..............	8	13	29	32	40	12	5	1
40–49..............	4	5	17	14	22	11	7	—
30–39..............	1	1	1	2	4	1	1	—
20–29..............	—	—	—	1	1	—	—	—

of scores in form and speed. Thus we find that, of the pupils who write from 60 to 69 letters a minute, there were 32 whose form was graded from 50 to 55. These pupils represent the average ability in both speed and form. The pupils who are represented at the left-hand side of the table write with poor quality, those at the right-hand side with good quality. Those who are represented toward the bottom write slowly and those at the upper part rapidly. The pupils at the lower left-hand corner write poorly and slowly; those at the upper left-hand corner poorly and rapidly. Those at the upper right-hand corner write well and rapidly; those at the lower right-hand corner well and slowly.

We see from the table that we get nearly all combinations within the fifth grade. This tremendous variation makes the problem of teaching such a class of pupils a complex one. It is almost as though we were teaching pupils selected from several different grades. In fact, we might select pupils from the fifth and eighth grades who would be much more nearly alike in writing ability than those of an unselected fifth grade.

BALANCE BETWEEN FORM AND SPEED

Many problems are raised by such a condition as this. One of them, for example, grows out of the relation between form and speed. Take the three pupils who write more rapidly than one hundred letters a minute and yet whose form is graded 25 or below. It appears that these pupils sacrifice form or quality to speed. If they wrote more slowly, it is conceivable that they might also write considerably better. These pupils, by reducing their speed to 70 letters a minute, might be able to raise the quality to 40 or 45. A similar statement would apply to the pupils who write very slowly and very accurately. Take, for example, the one who wrote 30 to 39 letters a minute with a score in quality of 80 to 85. Such a pupil could well be encouraged to write somewhat more rapidly even at the expense of quality. The probability is that with the appropriate drill the pupil could be trained to maintain a more advantageous balance between these two elements of the writing.

Even if we succeeded in overcoming the one-sided development of the pupils who write with high speed and poor quality, or with low speed and unusually good quality, there would be widespread differences in the ability of the various pupils of a grade. These differences would be represented by the position along the diagonal line running from the lower left-hand to the upper right-hand corner of the table. If the pupils were all grouped along this line, they would all be well balanced in reference to the relation of speed and quality of their writing, but those toward the left hand would write very poorly and those toward the right hand very well. The practical question is, what should be done with the pupils who differ so from one another in their writing ability?

MINUTER DIFFERENCES

While the abilities of the various pupils of an instruction group may fall within a narrow range, there will still be important individual differences which must be observed in the instruction of these pupils. It was said in the first paragraph on individual differences that the structure and natural type of coördination between pupils varied. As a consequence, each person has what may be called an individual style of writing, a style which is best suited to his physical and mental make-up. This style forms what is called the character of his writing. Each pupil should be allowed or even encouraged to develop a characteristic style. This style is not something to be intentionally adopted by a pupil, but is something which he falls into naturally when he writes freely, without thinking particularly about the details of his writing. It is something which comes to a pupil when his habit has become somewhat automatic and he can withdraw his attention from the details of form or movement. Investigations have shown that there is often a resemblance between the writing of the child and certain of his ancestors. It is of the characteristics in which such resemblances are found that we are now speaking.

Another somewhat more definite individual characteristic is the rhythm of the writing. The writing of some persons, like their movements in general, is rather abrupt. The individual strokes are made rapidly and with considerable pauses or changes in speed. This type of rhythm ordinarily results in an angular style of writing.

The movement of other persons is more even and uniform in speed and their writing is likely to be rounder in style. Another difference in rhythm is in the natural rate of writing. It is a matter of common observation that some persons move rapidly in general and others slowly. This difference in natural rate may be observed also in writing. While it is necessary in class exercises to use a common rhythm, this common rhythm is bound to do certain violence to both the extremely slow and the extremely rapid writers. We must, therefore, permit these extreme cases to find their own rhythm in individual practice.

Another difference with respect to rhythm is the relative ease with which different pupils can conform to any rhythm. A careful photograph of writing movements has shown that some individuals, when asked to make a series of simple writing strokes, make them in regular rhythm, while others do not. Since rhythm is such an important element in good writing, pupils who are deficient in this aspect of the movement must receive special help. When a class exercise in making rhythmical strokes is given, it will be found that the majority of the pupils can follow the rhythm fairly easily. A few, however, will never attain it in the class exercises alone. It is necessary to give those special individual help. It may be that there are a few rare cases who are so deficient that it is hopeless to attempt to develop rhythmical movement in them. We should not despair, however, of any individuals until they have been given considerable special help.

There are other particular elements of the writing in which individuals will need special help. Some pupils' writing will be irregular in slant and in alinement. They need to give special attention to this quality. In others the arrangement of the spacing on the page will require special attention. Some meet special difficulty in the form of particular letters and others in the smoothness and evenness of the line. Assistance should be given to each individual pupil at the particular point where he needs it most.

Methods of Dealing with Individual Differences

It was mentioned incidentally above that the exceptionally good or exceptionally poor pupils of a grade should be given different treatment from the majority of the pupils. Just what adjustment should be made will depend upon the circumstances of the particular school or system, but certain general suggestions may be made for the meeting of this problem. First, with reference to the exceptionally good writers. The course which is here described is based upon a six-year elementary school.

There are many pupils at the end of the fifth grade who write better than the average pupil at the end of the sixth grade. If these pupils are selected by means of a careful test, they are found to be able to do without further writing instruction. It is necessary, of course, to make an occasional test to be sure that these pupils maintain their standard. It would be safe to select the upper fifth of the class on entering the sixth grade and to excuse them from writing drill.

The pupils who write very poorly may be treated in one of two ways. They may either be given extra drill as they pass through the lower grades, or their handwriting drill may be continued beyond the sixth grade. The latter method is probably the one which would be easiest to administer. The device has been used in the high school by the organization of special classes for drill in writing without credit. It is probable that if careful attention were given to the grading and instruction of these pupils throughout the grades, it would not be necessary to give them further drill beyond the eighth grade, in an ordinary system, or in the junior high school.

When we have thus eliminated pupils at both extremes, we shall still have a group which differs widely in ability. The better pupils of this group will be equal in ability to the pupils of lower ability in the next grade above them, and the poorer pupils in the group will be able to write no better than the better pupils of the grade below. Experiments have been made in grouping together pupils from two or three school grades according to their writing ability. This makes the ability of the pupils of the writing section more even and makes their instruction somewhat simpler. Where the school program allows for this reclassification, it is advisable to make it.

It is not advisable to group together pupils of very widely differing grades. While it is true that many pupils of the fifth grade do not write better than the second-grade pupils, their style of writing and the kind of drill they need is very different. We should, therefore, not group together pupils from widely different grades on the basis of the quality of their writing. It is quite permissible, however, to combine the groups from two or three successive grades.

The assumption which is made is that the majority of the pupils can learn to write satisfactorily in six years. At the end of this time the pupils who are likely to require writing for use in commercial life may receive additional instruction. The others need every encouragement to maintain a good standard.

We may summarize the plan which has been suggested for organizing handwriting instruction to suit individual differences as follows: The average pupil should complete his regular handwriting instruction by the end of the sixth grade. The exceptionally good writer may be excused at the end of the fifth grade. All these pupils should be tested occasionally, however, in order to be sure that they maintain a satisfactory standard. The exceptionally poor writers should be given additional drill, continuing their instruction to the eighth or ninth grade. The pupils of the large average group in two successive grades can advantageously be grouped in sections according to their writing ability.

Suggestions regarding individualized instruction are made from time to time in the exercises, particularly in the fifth and sixth grades.

Correlation of Writing with Other Subjects

Some of the ways in which writing is correlated with other subjects have already been mentioned. A few additional remarks may here be made.

The problem of correlation between writing and other subjects arises because of the fact that writing is an independent subject of instruction. This is necessary in order to make opportunity for the specific drill required to develop facility in writing. It is not sufficient to treat writing as incidental to the other work in the school. The child needs to have his attention called to the requirements of the writing itself. If this is done incidentally to the study of some other subject, the child's attention is divided. If his attention is not given to the improvement of his writing at all, the child fails to become a good writer.

The correlation with other work is carried on in two ways. First, although instruction in writing is given in a separate period, the child should be required to apply the methods which he learns in the writing period to all his written work. This can probably be best accomplished by requiring a definite standard of neatness in all his work. It is also desirable, while the child is developing certain necessary habits of position, that some attention be given to the maintenance of these habits in the other subjects.

The second type of correlation consists in introducing into the writing lesson practice in those forms of work which the child requires in his other work. Mention has already been made of the arrangement of the work on the page, and of correct forms in correspondence and in number work. It is possible that other types of correlation than are here suggested may profitably be arranged. Where the writing instruction is given by the same teacher as instruction in other subjects, this correlation is particularly easy to carry out. Where there is a special teacher of writing, there should be close coöperation with the teachers of other subjects.

External Physical Conditions

Writing-Desks and Chairs

The first set of conditions which are important for writing

concerns the desk and the chair. The chair, in the first place, should be of the right height. It should be of such a height that the child's feet rest on the floor, and high enough to bring the thighs into a horizontal position.

The desk should be at such a height that when the child is sitting erect with the forearms resting on the desk, the elbows are about three inches from the body. If they are much farther than this the desk is too high and if the upper arm hangs close to the body while the forearms are on the desk, the desk is too low.

The position of the seat and the desk on the floor should be such that the edge of the seat projects slightly, two or three inches, under the edge of the desk. This produces what is called minus distance. If the seat does not project under the desk, the child is forced either to lean forward or to sit on the edge of the seat. If the seat projects too far under the desk, the child cannot sit erect, but must bend the upper part of his trunk backward.

The top of the desk should slope somewhat toward the child. This brings the top and the bottom of the paper more nearly at equal distance from his eyes, and avoids the tendency to bend the head forward which the flat-top desk produces. In the primary grades also the sloping desk makes it easier for the child to use a large free movement which is intermediate between the movement which is used at the blackboard and the developed writing movement.

LIGHTING

The amount and arrangement of the lighting is important for the child's health. The light should come from the left side or from above or from a combination of the two. This illuminates the writing and avoids a shadow from the hand on the writing.

The amount of lighting should be about equivalent to five-foot candles. This is the amount of light which would be thrown on a page by a five-candle-power lamp one foot away. It is approximately the amount of light which would be cast by a forty-candle-power lamp three feet away. With ordinary daylight there is frequently less than this amount of illumination, on the dark side of the room. It is necessary whenever the day is not bright to secure as much light as possible on the dark side by raising the shades to their full height. If artificial illumination is provided, this should be used on dark days. In the construction of buildings provision should be made, either through greater window area than is provided by the ordinary standard or through artificial illumination, to give more than the usual amount of illumination on the dark side of the room.

CHAPTER IV

SUMMARY OF PRINCIPLES ON WHICH THE COURSE IS ORGANIZED

ADAPTATION TO AGE

1. THE size of the writing is gradually reduced from the first grade to the sixth. The width of ruling used is as follows:

	GRADE					
	I	II	III	IV	V	VI
Width in inches	1	5/8	1/2	1/2	3/8	3/8

2. The speed of writing required is increased throughout the grades and corresponds approximately to the average speed found in comprehensive surveys of children's writing. The standard is raised slightly above this average in the intermediate and upper grades.

3. The requirement in quality of writing is raised throughout the grades corresponding approximately to the results of surveys.

4. The materials — pencil or pen, blackboard, rough paper or smooth paper — are adapted to the maturity and skill of the child.

5. The vocabulary used in the exercises of each grade consists of the words common in the spoken and written language of children of that grade.

6. The successive exercises which introduce new letters or combinations are introduced more slowly in the lower than in the higher grades. The length of time required to introduce all the letters in the successive grades is as follows:

	GRADE					
	I	II	III	IV	V	VI
Time in weeks	22	20	19	18	13	10

7. The exercises of each grade are presented in language and with types of illustration suited to the grade in question.

8. Correlated material is adapted to the grade.

9. At the beginning of the exercises for each grade is a section in which is given a definition of the objectives for the grade, a description of the character of the movement to be expected and an account of the materials and method used.

CONTENT OF THE EXERCISES

10. The vocabulary used in the exercises is carefully selected by the aid of investigations to determine the words used and needed by children.

11. The words in the exercises of the early part of the year contain only letters already practiced.

12. In the early part of the year sentences are constructed of words already practiced. The sentences correspond to the child's experience and mode of expression.

13. Thorough practice is given on numerals.

14. Toward the end of the year connected discourses, such as proverbs and poems, are given.

15. Common abbreviations and titles which are likely to be used in writing are included in the exercises.

16. Correlated material from other subjects is introduced and the teacher is advised to make use of additional correlated material adapted to local conditions.

ORGANIZATION OF THE COURSE

17. The general plan of organization is spiral. The letters of the alphabet are introduced in approximately the same order in the successive grades, but the level of difficulty is raised each year by the methods indicated above under the heading "Adaptation to Age."

18. The letters are classified on the basis of the type of movement which is used in making them, and letters which are made by a similar movement are introduced in close succession.

19. Adequate repetition is secured on each letter or combination of letters. Few repetitions of an exercise are required in a given period of practice, in order to avoid monotony, but each exercise is reviewed frequently.

20. Letters of similar form are presented in near succession or brought into the same lesson by reviews, and attention is called to their likeness.

METHOD

21. A reasonable standard position is taught and insisted upon until it becomes habitual.

22. The fluent sideward movement of the hand is particularly emphasized and developed by special exercises.

23. The combined movement of the arm or hand and fingers is recognized as the natural one.

24. The rhythm of the movement, adapted to the individual letter forms, is cultivated.

25. Rhythm is developed by writing to count, which is carefully adjusted to the make-up of the letters and words.

26. The rate of count in each grade is chosen so as to agree with the speed of writing in that grade.

27. The teacher is required to demonstrate the rhythm by writing the exercises on the board.

28. Perfection of form is brought about by self-criticism.

29. Self-criticism is carried on by the child first by comparison of different specimens of his own writing, later by analytical comparison with a scale.

30. The effect of self-criticism is enhanced by the use of permanent records of attainment.

31. Provision is made for the adaptation of training to individual abilities and needs through allowance for variation in (a) details of position and movement, (b) rhythm, and (c) amount of drill.

CORRELATION

32. The writing drill is correlated with other work of the school by practice in the writing period on such projects as (a) the arrangement of compositions on the page; (b) the arrangement of arithmetic problems; (c) the use of conventional forms of correspondence; and (d) some practice in writing without lines.

33. The teacher is encouraged to introduce other correlated material.

34. Care is taken to provide that the skill attained in the writing period carries over to other subjects, first, by adopting a natural mode of writing, and, second, by grading the writing which is done outside the writing period.

PART II

DAILY EXERCISES BY GRADES

CHAPTER V

EXERCISES FOR GRADE ONE

OBJECTIVES

Content. At the end of the first year the child should have some practice in writing most of the small letters and most of the capitals and the digits, and should be able to reproduce unhesitatingly all but the more difficult forms and those which are confusing because they are similar. He should be able to write independently such words as the following: [1]

a	an	am	and	at	be
boy	cat	can	do	dog	go
he	her	him	in	I	is
it	man	me	my	no	of
on	or	ran	run	see	she
the	to	up	us	we	you

He should be able to write numbers from *1* to *50* in columns, either in series or in random order, and either from copy or dictation.

Movement. At the end of the first year the child should have developed a motor control characterized as follows: a fluency of twenty letters a minute, fairly continuous lateral movement of the hand coördinated with movement on letters, reasonably standard habits of position. A variation from standard position is allowable in this grade in that the use of the whole arm without rest may be encouraged if the desks slant so as not to compel an awkward, uncomfortable position.

MATERIALS AND METHODS

Materials. Large dodger or dull-finish wrapping paper. Large size pencil. Those called by manufacturers "Beginners' Pencil" are good. The size of the writing should be three-eighths inch for the small letters. The writing for the first year should be, so far as practicable, on the blackboard, because this gives greater en-

---

[1] This list of words is the list assigned to first grade by Pearson and Suzzallo in *Essentials of Spelling.* They are in Courtis's 100 per cent list for the second grade (given in *Teaching Spelling by Plays and Games*), and were given in lists from five first-grade teachers as words which first-grade children should be able to write at the end of the year.

couragement to large movements and because in writing large letters fewer delicate coördinations are required. For writing at desks the following methods are to be used.

Methods. *A. Position.* Facing desk; paper in front at an angle of about thirty degrees to the edge of the desk; arms in symmetrical position, either resting on the desk, or hanging free for whole arm movement; hand turned over to the right not more than forty-five degrees; pencil grasped lightly with fingers slightly curved, the index finger below the thumb.

B. Types of exercises. 1. Rhythmic drills to develop free movement and muscular coördination. These may be motivated by the child's pleasure in the rhythmic activity.

2. Writing words or sentences for which the child has some need, as, each child should write his own initials and later his own name, signs for a store or other play project, season's greetings, invitations, record of activities. The motivation here rests upon the child's need for the means of expressing or recording his ideas, and the aim in this work is to relate writing directly to the child's life so that, as definite drills are introduced, he will understand something of their purpose and value.

C. Standards and criticism. The presentation of a standard to a child of this grade is of doubtful value, but the teacher's knowledge of it should influence her suggestions to the child. Suggestions as to slant, relative size of letters, and certain points in letter formation may be made from time to time as given in the grade outline. But it should be remembered that the chief aim in this grade is the development of coördinated movement and too much attention to details will delay this development. Crude results may be regarded as satisfactory at first if the movement is free and rhythmical.

FIRST MONTH.   FIRST WEEK

LESSON 1

(A short talk somewhat like this is a good way to begin the course. It should be suited to the class. If the writing is done at the blackboard, the procedure must be modified to meet this condition.)

"We all want to learn to write well, so that when we write letters or stories our friends can read them. We can write well and make hard work of it, or we can write easily and well. I am going to show you how to write so that it will be easy to write, and then you will be glad to do it. First, we must sit straight, hips back in the seat, feet flat on the floor." See that all are doing so. "Put the paper in place at an angle of about thirty degrees to the desk line." This will have to be demonstrated to the lower grades. "Put both arms on the desk and let them rest there easily. Make runners of your two little fingers. Let them carry the whole hand sliding back and forth on the paper." Use no pencil for this. "Go all the way across the paper. Do it as I count — one-two, one-two, one-two, one-two. Again. One-two, etc. Can you keep just with my count? Are you sliding on your runners? Is your wrist raised just a little so as to form a bridge? Now, again. One-two, one-two," etc. "Take pencil; hold it so." Show correct position and be sure the index finger is on top of the pencil, not on the left side, and that the thumb is higher on the pencil — farther from the point — than the index finger. See that every child's position is correct this first time and every time. It will take less time in the long run if insisted on at the first and every time. *Place* each pencil right, where it is necessary. Above all things do not get impatient with the child who does not get the position right. They all want to.

"Now can you use your runners with the pencil? Try as I count. 'Way across the paper, but do not write yet. Ready. Slide. One-two, one-two, one-two, one-two.

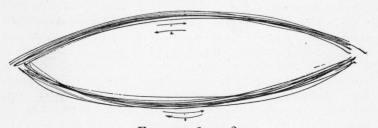

ExERCISES 1 AND 2

"Now I will show you something to write." Give Exercise 1, the over-curve.

Say as you make it on the board:

To and fro, sway the trees,
Bending in the passing breeze.

"Now you may do it just as I did." Repeat the verse as they write. "You may say it as you write. Again." This is sufficient for the first exercise. If there is more time, vary it by letting part of the class do it at the board while others do it at their seats.

These first exercises are for the purpose of accustoming the pupils from the first to the correct position of the body, arms, hand and paper, and to correct pen-holding, and to begin the formation of the habit of sliding the hand along the line as the letters are being formed. Attention should be directed particularly on these phases of the writing activity until they become habitual.

Lesson 2

"Sit straight. Hips back. Feet on the floor. Arms on desk. Can you place your paper right? Good." Do not neglect commendation when possible to give it. "Without pencils use your runners — going all the way across the paper. Ready. Slide. One-two," etc. "Did you keep the time?" Repeat four times. "Now pencils. Is your position like this?" Be sure that it is. "Now slide, but do not write. Ready. Slide. One-two," etc. "Look." Write on the board Exercise 1, saying the verse. "You may write it. Ready. Write. 'To and fro,'" etc. "Did you keep the time? Once more. 'To and fro,'" etc. "Now we have made the tree-tops. Do you like to swing 'way up into the tree-tops among the leaves? Look, I am going to swing up." Give Exercise 2, the under-curve.

While making the curve say:

> How do you like to go up in a swing,
> Up in the air so blue?

"Now you may swing up into your tree-tops. Ready. Write. 'How do you like,'" etc. "Make the tree-tops again. Are your runners ready? Is your pencil right? Are you holding it loosely?"

Exercise 3

Test a few by pulling it from the fingers. "Ready. Write. 'To and fro,'" etc. "Let's swing up to the tree-tops. 'How do you like,'" etc. "Now we will slide another way. I will show you how." Give Exercise 3, *i*. "Make long slides so that you can put only three on a line. Try again. See how I count." Put it on the board with count. Notice the count is on the forward stroke. "Ready. Write. One-two, one-two." Repeat several times to your count by voice, and watch hands for position, looseness of grasp, and sliding on runners. Commend as much as possible. Quietly change the positions that are wrong.

Here the element of letter formation in very simple form is combined with the forward movement. The form may be very crude at first in order that the forward movement may not be hampered. The form should be gradually improved as the forward movement becomes established. The count is given on the forward stroke so as to emphasize the forward movement.

Lesson 3

Give specific directions as to position as in the last lesson. Use Exercises 1, 2, 3, with voice count, and be particular to see that the position is kept.

Exercise 4 requires still greater control and finer coördination of the forward movement and the letter formation, but much crudity of form is still to be expected. By this time, if there is really freedom of movement, you will be inclined to be disturbed by disregard for base line and proper height of letters. Let it go for the present. Work *only* for position, freedom of movement, and correct time.

EXERCISE 4

Give Exercise 4, *u*. "Let us make two of the down slants close together. Yes, it makes *u*. Make long slides so that you can put only three on a line.

EXERCISE 5

"Now look. Make this once more." Give Exercise 3, *i*. "I will make it taller." Give Exercise 5, *t*. "You may try it. Watch the count. Have you the right position?" See that they have, but quickly. "Now. Ready. Write." The count should be given for each exercise, but from this time the teacher will find the count on the written exercise instead of in the directions for the lesson.

LESSON 4

"Take position. Show me how your runners slide. Pencils." Review with rhyme Exercises 1 and 2, putting them on the board first with the rhymes. Review Exercises 3, *i*, 4, *u*, and 5, *t*, with count.

The review exercises should each be given once or twice. Don't make drudgery of the work by too long repetition of an exercise. Don't expect perfection at first. Go back to it often.

EXERCISE 6

"Look, I am going to put two exercises together." Give Exercise 6, *it*. Write it two or three times on the board. "Now you may write it. Ready. Write. Again. Ready. Write. Again. You may dot the *i*'s and cross the *t*'s." Count for this. "Once more. Ready. Write."

The variation in height of strokes here requires still greater control. In counting for this, emphasis should be put on the second count, which is on the tall stroke. Otherwise there is a tendency to make this stroke short. The teacher should be sure to practice this and every exercise in her preparation of the lesson so that she can demonstrate it to the class.

LESSON 5

"Take a clean sheet of paper. We have been practicing all the week. To-day we are going to write all our exercises. Remember the most important part is the way we do it. Paper right, feet right, up straight, hand on runners, pencil loose. Without writing, slide your runners all the way across the paper. Ready. Slide. One-two, etc. Hold your pencil right. Everybody ready. Watch." Put on the board Exercises 1 and 2 saying rhymes. "You may do this. Be sure you swing all the way across the paper. Don't let your tree-tops come too low. Ready. Write. 'To and fro,'" etc. "Now for the swing. Ready. Write. 'How do you like,'" etc. Make this exercise twice. Then put on the board Exercise 3, *i*, and have the children do it to count. Do the same with Exercises 4, 5, and 6.

This set of papers should be kept for comparison from time to time with later work. There are two purposes in this — the children will be encouraged by evidence of progress and their spontaneous comparison of the work will be the first step in the development of critical judgment.

SECOND WEEK. LESSON 1

"Take correct position. Show me how to hold your pencil. Hand on runners. Let us make the tree-tops. Ready. Write. 'To and fro,'" etc. "Now the swing. Ready. Write. 'How do you like,'" etc. "I want to show you a new exercise." Give Exercise 7, *e*. Make it a second time. "Notice the count. Now

EXERCISE 7

you may write. Ready. Write. How many swing all the way across the paper? Let's try it again. Ready. Write. Did you keep the time better then?"

Review Exercises 3, *i*, 4, *u*, 6, *it*. Then have the children write Exercise 7, *e*, again three times. The teacher should put all work on the board first.

The back of this letter should be nearly or quite straight. Call attention to this and have the child aim to make it so, but do not emphasize a matter of form at this time to an extent that will lessen the freedom of movement.

LESSON 2

"Position." Be sure it is good.

Review Exercises 1, 2, 3, 4, 6. Then show Exercise 7, *e*, again. "Ready. Write. Again. Ready. Write. We will put three of our exercises together. Look." Give Exercise 8, *tie*. Make the

cross and dot on count too. "Ready. Write. Now dot the *i*
and cross the *t*. Did you get the right time? Are your runners in
place? Without writing slide once. Ready. Slide. Now write
again this exercise." Give Exercise 8. "Ready. Write."

EXERCISE 8

Here we have shortened the swing, though there is more than is used in
the word when written naturally. The gradual shortening of the swing is
for the purpose of developing muscular control. Care should be taken to see
that the movement is still free and does not become cramped in grasp
of pencil or in movement. The purpose in introducing a return to the
sliding movement in the midst of the lesson is to emphasize the need of free
movement and so help to establish the habit.

LESSON 3

Follow instructions on attention to position and method.

Review Exercises 1, 2, 3, 4, 6, 7, 8. The early ones are kept up
for the sake of automatizing the free forward movement. If done
to count and attentively, once for each exercise is enough when they
have been in use for a week. Have Exercises 6, 7, 8 written three
or four times each.

"Look carefully. See if you can tell how what I put on the
board is different from this — Exercise 7, *e*." Give Exercise 9, *l*.

EXERCISE 9

If this seems too difficult when first given with the single count,
it may at first be written with a count for each down-stroke as well
as for the up-strokes. This helps to make the down-stroke straight,
but if the children write it correctly, the first method is better.

LESSON 4

Review Exercises 1 and 2, once. Review Exercises 3, 7, and 9, *l*,
each two or three times. Now review Exercises 6 and 8. "Next

EXERCISE 10

we will write this." Put on the board with count, Exercise 10,
let. "You may write. Ready. Write."

If time permits, review Exercises 6, 7, 8, each once. Be sure that the class keeps the swing and that three words fill the line. Still encourage the rather long swing. If, however, the children write it naturally with a free movement and letters of right size, do not force the separation of the letters by the long swing.

LESSON 5

"Take clean papers. Position. Without writing slide on your runners. Ready. Slide. One-two, etc. Now, holding your pencil right and keeping on your runners, write." Give Exercises 1, 2, 3, 7, 9, 6, 8, 10. Exercises 6, 8, 10, should be written twice each.

After these papers have been collected to keep for comparison, give practice on the exercises which have not been so well automatized. The children may make frequent comparisons between sheets of their work written at different times, but the first papers should be kept for comparison showing the development of the child throughout the year.

THIRD WEEK. LESSON 1

Review Exercises 1, 2, with rhymes. Review Exercise 4, *u*.

EXERCISE 11

Give Exercise 11, *tut*. Count as shown on the written exercise, as always.

Here the change in the height of the same kind of stroke is the element that develops control in the movement.

LESSON 2

Show Exercise 11, *tut*, and have the class write it two or three times. Review Exercises 6, *it*, 8, *tie*, 10, *let*.

Give Exercise 12, the digits, *1, 2*.

EXERCISE 12

"Every one needs to know how to make figures well. To-day we will see how many of us can learn to make two figures well." For beginners show an object, as one ball, one book, etc. "How many balls have I? I will write it here, *1*. Now you may write it. Now let us say it keeping time as we write, *1, 1, 1, 1*." Show two objects of a kind. "How many books have I? This is the way to write it, *2*. Look at it carefully. Make it in the air, following my hand. Notice how the back curves. Now let us all write it. Do it again as you count. Now let us make *1* and then *2* this way, *1, 2, 1, 2.*"

Lesson 3

Give Exercise 12, *1, 2*, writing them three times. Review Exercises 6, 8, 10. Give Exercise 13, digits, *3, 4*.

Exercise 13   Exercise 14

The fact that *3* when made well is very much like two circles made together may help the children to get the form. Be sure to keep the count here, as the establishment of free rhythmic movements in making with the figures may carry over with profit to all other work in number. See that the lines of *4* are made in the right order, the single down-stroke last.

Lesson 4

Review Exercises 12, 13, digits. Then review Exercises 3, 4, 7, 9.

Give Exercise 14, digit *5*. It is very important in making all of the digits that the child acquire from the beginning the image of the correct form and the habit of making the strokes in the right sequence and direction. In making the *5*, see that the down-stroke and the curve are made first and the horizontal line last. "Notice carefully how I make the *5*. See how we count. Show me where we begin. What is the last stroke we make? Now you may make it. Watch the count."

Lesson 5

"Take clean paper." Give the preliminary swing for limbering before writing. For this week's record write Exercises 3, 4, 7, 9, 12, 13, 14, and 8, 10, 11.

Fourth Week. Lesson 1

Give Exercises 1, 2, swinging only half the page instead of the whole page.

Give Exercises 3, 4, 7, 9, lessening the swing so as to make two or three groups to the line according to the width of the paper. Be very sure that the swing is not lost in shortening it and that the hand really slides on the runners. This is far more important just now than emphasis on correct form.

Notice that here, for the first time, we definitely suggest to the children the shortening of the swing in the process of gaining control. It has been permitted before in words, but not definitely encouraged. Here the important thing is to insist that no loss of freedom shall result.

LESSON 2
Have the children write Exercises 10, 11, making two or three groups to the line. Review Exercises 12, 13, 14.

LESSON 3
Give Exercises 1, 2, half-line swing. Review Exercises 6, 8, 10. Review Exercises 3, 4, 7, 9, on the short swing.

LESSON 4
Give Exercises 1, 2. Review Exercise 10, *let*.

Now review the digits, writing them first in order, then each one four times in a column, being sure that the column is kept straight, then write them consecutively in columns four deep as shown:

1	5	4	3	2
2	1	5	4	3
3	2	1	5	4
4	3	2	1	5

Aside from the practice here on making the figures, the aim is to begin definite training in correct column writing of figures.

LESSON 5
"Take clean paper." Note position and give preliminary swing. Write with short swing Exercises 1, 2, 3, 4, 7, 9, 6, 8, 10, 11, 12, 13, 14, writing all the words without joining them.

SECOND MONTH. FIRST WEEK
Introduce the metronome for count instead of voice. Fifty beats is suggested for the beginning. Determine on the rate that your class can use easily and record it.

The introduction of the metronome to give the rate has two different purposes. It sets the teacher free to inspect and give suggestions to individual children. It gives an absolutely regular beat for a continuous period such as is not possible with the teacher's voice. Also it makes possible the definite determination of the rate to be used at a particular time and the increase of the speed in a systematic way. The idea is to try somewhat different rates and settle on one to which the child responds comparatively easily.

LESSON 1
The exclusive use of the short swing after it is introduced is likely to lead soon to loss of freedom in the movement before it has become an established habit. For this reason we introduce frequently the long swing.

It is better also to use voice count on new work until the children become accustomed to taking the time from the tick of the metronome; otherwise the child will soon learn to disregard the metronome.

Review with long swing Exercises 3, *i*, 4, *u*, 7, *e*. Then give each with the short swing. Begin each new exercise this week with voice count and rather slowly.

Review Exercise 9, *l*. "See how I change this." Give Exercise 15, *b*. "How is this different?" (Final stroke and the second

EXERCISE 15

up-stroke curves back.) Call attention to the curve just opposite the crossing point, but with a gateway left between. Practice Exercises 9 and 15 alternately, calling attention to the likeness and the difference. Notice the count of Exercise 15. There is a distinct pause at the sharp turn before the last stroke. This also occurs in the letters *o*, *w*, and *v*. Call the attention of the children to this in the *b* and make it evident in the writing. It has been found to help both form and rhythm.

LESSON 2

The metronome is to be kept all the week at the rate settled on in the first lesson. Remember that position is all important.

Review Exercises 1, 2. Then review Exercise 15, *b*. Review Exercise 11, *tut*. Give Exercise 16, *but*. Have the children write

EXERCISE 16

several lines keeping exactly to count. If there is trouble in this, write it on the board several times, having the class listen to the metronome while watching. The importance of the teacher's actually writing the exercise to the count and doing it over and over cannot be overestimated. The children will soon get the idea. Review the digits, *1–5*.

In *but* we have the first instance of a connecting stroke between letters, which does not touch the base line. It is necessary to call attention to this and to show just how the connection is made. Write it several times, counting and let the children find just what count comes on the connecting stroke. Call attention to the drop of the connecting stroke a little below the top of the *u*. This will aid in the alinement later.

Lesson 3

Review Exercises 7, 15.   Give Exercise 17, *be*.   Review Exercises 8, 10.   Review Exercises 12, 13, 14 (digits).

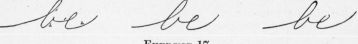

Exercise 17

The joining of the *b* and *e* in Exercise 17 gives a little added difficulty in the fact that, unless the connecting stroke is dropped a little, the child is likely to make the *e* considerably higher than it should be.   This is a very common mistake with children.   The time to correct a fault is before it is made.

Lesson 4

Give Exercises 1, 2, with half-line swing.   Review Exercises 3, 4. Give Exercise 18, *a*.   "Notice that this letter is closed at the top and we slide way over.   See the top does not turn down at all.

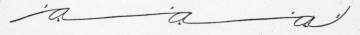

Exercise 18

Look again."   Write it to the count.   "Class.   Ready.   Write. Again."   Then alternate Exercises 9 and 15 a few times.

This is the first time that attention has been definitely called to form. Here we are concerned with a detail of form that is naturally related to free movement.   A continuous upward movement is freer than one which is retarded by a downward hook at the end.   This downward movement is avoided when the child, having the idea of the forward movement in his mind, exerts enough force in the movement to carry the hand straight ahead.

Lesson 5

Be sure that the writing is with the metronome.   "Take clean paper.   Practice the slide without writing."   Give Exercises 12, 13, 14, one line of each.   Give Exercises 9, 18, *a*, 15, 16, 17, one or two lines as paper permits.

After these papers are collected, review Exercises 6, 8, 10, 16, 17, as time permits.

Second Week

Set the metronome at 52.   Be sure to keep the time.   Note the holding of the pencil and see if it is right.

LESSON 1

Review Exercises 3, 4, long swing, twice each. Notice the long swing is given again to ensure freedom of movement. Review Exercises 7, 18.

Give Exercise 19, *at*. Practice several times and then give Exercise 20, *all*, and practice it several times.

Review Exercises 16, *but*, 17, *be*.

EXERCISE 19   *EXERCISE 20*

LESSON 2

Review Exercises 15, 18, 9. Give Exercise 21, *ball*. Give Exercise 22, *a*. Review the digits *1–5*. Give each alone and

EXERCISE 21

EXERCISE 22

practice three or four times before giving the next. Keep the writing with the metronome.

In *ball* again we have the connecting stroke which does not touch the base line. It is higher than in the connection with *u*, as it goes with only a slight dip to the top of the *a*. The word *a* is introduced separately from the letter exercise to call definite attention to the word, which sometimes troubles children when it stands alone. In the first and second grades when writing *a, d, c, g, q, o*, a preliminary up-stroke is used. This brings the first count on the up-stroke as in the case of the other letters, and so makes it easier for the children.

LESSON 3

Give Exercise 18, *a*, with a good swing and position. Give Exercise 23, *d*. Notice that it is the same as Exercise 18 except that

EXERCISE 23

the up-stroke is longer. Review Exercise 15, *b*. Give Exercise 24, *bad*.

Call attention again to the connecting stroke between *b* and *a*. Show the count and see that the placing of the stroke is understood.

EXERCISE 24   EXERCISE 25

LESSON 4

Give Exercises 1, 2, one half-line swing. Give again Exercises 23, 24, three or four times with the metronome. Review Exercises 7, 17.

Give Exercise 25, *bed*. Recall the study of the connecting stroke between *b* and *e*. Be sure that it drops low enough so that the *e* is not higher than the lower part of the *b*.

LESSON 5

"Take a clean sheet. Keep the writing with the metronome. Practice the slide first." Write Exercises 15, 18, 23, 24, 25.

THIRD WEEK. LESSON 1

Review Exercises 3, 4, with long swing twice each. Review Exercises 7, 9, 15, 23, with speed increased to 56.

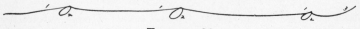

EXERCISE 26

Give Exercise 26, *o*, first at 52 and then at 56. Give Exercise 27, *to*.

Remember the reason for returning to the long swing and do not shorten it where it is given. In Exercise 26, *o*, call the children's attention to the fact that this is another letter like the *b* which does not go down to the base line before joining another letter. Encourage them to get this right in this exercise, making the connecting stroke come about as low as when the *b* connects with the *u*.

EXERCISE 27   EXERCISE 28

LESSON 2

Review Exercises 23, *d*, and 26, *o*. Exercise 28, *do*. Alternate Exercises 27, 28.

Give Exercise 29, digit *6*. Introduce this digit in connection with a group of objects of this number. It is comparatively simple to make, but it should be made the right way from the beginning. Even one wrong performance may lead to confusion. Ask a child

6 6 6 6 6

to show you the place of beginning and which way to turn. Have the children make it in the air to get the feeling of the right movement.

LESSON 3

See that the hand position is good. Review Exercise 4, *u*, long swing.

EXERCISE 30

Give Exercise 30, *w*. Call attention to the likeness and difference between these two exercises. Have the children write a group of each with long swing.

Give Exercise 31, *we*. Review Exercise 17, *be*, and call attention to the joining. Practice Exercises 17 and 31 in alternation.

EXERCISE 31

The *w* is almost like *u* except for the final stroke. The last up-stroke curves a little toward the preceding stroke, but the first-grade child will do well if he makes it like the *u* and adds the connecting stroke. Call attention, too, to the fact that here we have another letter where the connecting stroke does not touch the base line. "What are the others?" If the class does not know the names of the letters, they can show on the board *b* and *o*. Give Exercises 15, *b*, and 26, *o*, and let the children note the likeness.

LESSON 4

Review the digits *1–6*. Give Exercises 32, *7*, and 33, *8*. Practice each digit alone and then in succession.

7 7 7 7 7

EXERCISE 32

8 8 8 8 8

EXERCISE 33

Introduce *7* and *8* as you have the other digits. It is assumed that the children have some idea of the significance of the digits. Here the objects are used to give meaning to the writing.

LESSON 5

"Take clean paper." Give free limbering swing without writing, pencil held loosely. Give Exercises 22, *a*, 24, *bad*, 25, *bed*, in succession — *a bad bed;* then give Exercises 10, 17, 6, in succession — *let it be.* Give the digits *1–8*.

The writing of these words in succession gives the first idea of context writing. While one is only a phrase and the other is not a written sentence because it lacks the capital and period, each does express an idea and helps to give a motive to the work in the child's feeling that what he is doing may be of some use.

FOURTH WEEK. LESSON 1

Take time to-day to compare the papers with those written the first Friday. Let each child see his own papers together and notice the improvement. The improvement may be in lightness or regularity of line, in regularity of slant, in keeping to the base line, in making all *a*'s and *d*'s stay up at the top. We may call this an improvement even though these exercises did not appear in the first sheet, because this is something the children have learned to do. Ask the class to see how often they have kept the letters just on the base line, if ruled paper is used. Suggest that this week we try to do that especially. If there is more time, clinch this suggestion by practicing.

Review Exercises 27, 28, 31. Then increase the metronome to 56 and review Exercises 19, 20, 21. If unruled paper is used, the children may still notice how well they have succeeded in keeping the writing straight.

Notice the form of the suggestion, "See how often you have kept your letters on the base line." This is far better than, "See what letters are wrong." It calls attention to that which the children should repeat and directs their effort toward accomplishing the desirable result rather than on the avoidance of the undesirable one.

LESSON 2

Set the metronome at 52. Review Exercises 27, *to*, 30, *w*, 31, *we*. Give Exercise 34, *two*.

EXERCISE 34

After writing it several times, give Exercise 35, *9*, and Exercise 36, *10*. Always write the exercise on the board enough times to make sure that there is no difficulty about the time. Give the numbers *1–10*.

In the word *two* we have between *w* and *o* what is frequently called by the children the "bridge" connection. Compare this with Exercise 31, and let them write them in alternation — *we two*. This gives another idea of context writing. There may seem too much material in this lesson. Do not crowd the children. It is better, however, to have them write only a short time on a single exercise and review it frequently than to give a continued drill on one exercise. The reason for this is that in long-continued practice on one exercise the child is apt to repeat mistakes which have been made by chance, and so confirm them. In practice which is distributed through several periods the child is apt to vary the mistakes, since they are not emphasized, and to tend toward habituation of the correct forms and the movement habits which are stressed at each repetition.

LESSON 3

Review Exercises 18, *a*, 26, *p*.

Remember to give each new exercise slower at first. Give Exercise 37, *c*. Compare this with Exercise 18. Notice particu-

EXERCISE 37

larly that *c does* turn down at the top in distinction from the *a*. Call attention to the hook, and see that it is made in this swinging exercise.

Review Exercises 6, 8, 10. Mix in more practice of Exercise 37, *c*, so as not to use it continuously enough to encourage carelessness. Compare *c* especially with *a* and get the children to make the difference in writing. After several lines of practice with self-criticism, give Exercise 38, *cat*.

EXERCISE 38

In this exercise are given together the two letters which are being compared, *c* and *a*. Have the children think about this, and if they have difficulty lessen the speed of the metronome, write the

word on the board several times and then have the children write it
at the lower rate.

Lesson 4

"Show me your position." Review the digits. Give Exercises
16, 17, 19, 22. Give again Exercises 37, 38.

Have the children write Exercises 22, 38, continuously — *a cat.*

Until some capitals have been practiced, the children should not
write a sentence, but these combinations of words which give ideas
are a helpful preparation for sentence writing.

Lesson 5

"Take clean papers." Give a preliminary swing. "Let's try to
keep exactly on the line" (or, "to write straight," if the paper is
unruled), "exactly with the metronome, and in perfect position
to-day."

Give Exercises 22, 24, 25, 27, 28, 31, 34, 38, one line of each.
Collect papers. Practice the numbers *1–10.*

Third Month. First Week

During the first two months we have studied eleven of the small letters.
Most of the emphasis has been placed on the forward swing and rhythm.
The class should now begin to show some effect of this in freedom of move-
ment.

We shall now try to gain some degree of control that will lead to better
alinement, but this must be acquired so gradually as not to interfere with
freedom of movement. We shall study more of the small letters and begin
studying the capitals. Please remember that position, freedom of movement, and rhythm are the important things.

Lesson 1

Review Exercises 1, 2, half-line swing with rhyme. Be sure that
the work is done with a free swing. The arm may touch the desk or
be carried a little above. Be sure that it is not in a position that
will cause strain or fatigue. For this work set the metronome at
56. For other work set the metronome at 52 except with new
exercises which should be given at a slower rate.

EXERCISE 39

Review Exercise 9, *l.* "We will take another exercise much like
this. See. It has a long straight line like *l,* but goes below the
line." Give Exercise 39, *f.* "What must we remember about it?"

(To keep the back straight.) "Yes, and here we must remember to keep the stem straight."

Call attention by question to the fact that the cross and the closing point are not together and point out the location of each.

"Now you may try it. Ready. Write." Have it written several times, asking for self-criticism. "How many closed it at the line? How many crossed it halfway between the line and the top?"

LESSON 2

Review Exercise 20, *all*. Give Exercise 40, *fall*. Review Exercise 22, *a*. "Now we will make a capital *A*. See just how I count it so that you can do it, too." Give Exercise 41, *A*.

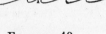

EXERCISE 40   EXERCISE 41

After having written it yourself, send several to the board to write it while the class counts for them. Notice that here and in some of the following exercises the count begins on the down-stroke. In general where the first count is on the down-stroke, there is a half count lost between the capital and the first small letter.

Review Exercises 19, 20, using capital *A* — *At*, *All*.

LESSON 3

Review Exercises 30, *f*, 40, *fall*. Review Exercises 19, 20, using capital *A*. Write the name of any child which begins with *A*. Let all practice it.

The children will enjoy learning to write the names of any classmate and this may arouse the desire to write their own names. The name of any child may be written on the board if the child wishes to write his own, but no drill should be given on any that does not begin with a capital already practiced.

LESSON 4

Review Exercises 26, 29, making the swing so that two groups can be written on the same line. Set the metronome for this at 56. Give Exercise 42, *of*.

EXERCISE 42

This is the first exercise where *o* is followed by another letter. Here the joining of the *o* with the *f* should be approximately at the top of the one-space letters so the connecting line should be nearly horizontal.

Review Exercises 30, *w*, 31, *we*. If any teacher finds too little work this week, she should review some of the swinging exercises. Less work is given intentionally, as it is rather difficult. Both the connecting stroke and the letter *f* present difficulties.

Lesson 5

"Take clean paper." Give the free swing without writing. Use 58 beats for all work to-day. Give Exercises 37, 38, 39, 40, and 19, 20, with capitals.

Second Week. Lesson 1

Review Exercises giving the numbers *1–10*. Use good free swing. Set the metronome at 54. Give the numbers *10, 20, 30, 40, 50, 60, 70, 80, 90, 100*, in column form. Emphasize the importance of keeping the units column in line. Draw a light vertical line if necessary to emphasize this. Having learned to write the nine digits and the number *10*, the children can write all the tens to *100* — not from memory, but by practicing writing *one, naught, two, naught*, etc.

When numbers are to be written in column formation, it is very important that the children should be shown how to do it correctly and that they be required to do it so thereafter in all such work.

When writing numbers in a column, each number should be separated from the number above it by a distance equal to one half the height of the figures. The columns corresponding to the different orders — units, tens, hundreds — should be separated by a space equal to the width of the figures.

The importance of attention to this from the first and all the time lies in the fact that correct column placing of figures has been found to increase the accuracy of computation.

Placing these numbers in columns will help to do two things for the children — to give them an idea that the sequence of tens is the same as the sequence of digits and to impress on them the need of accuracy in writing numbers in columns. Much of the inaccuracy in arithmetical computation in the upper grades is due to incorrect column arrangement. This is a matter of writing, not of mathematics, and if the correct habit is formed from the first, much trouble will be avoided.

Lesson 2

Review Exercise 41, *A*. Give the name of any child beginning with *A*.   Give Exercise 43, *m*.   Call attention to the curved top. "How many curves?   Count as we write, one-two," etc.

EXERCISE 43

Give Exercise 44, *me*.   Give Exercise 45, *am*.

EXERCISE 44   *EXERCISE 45*

Remember that in this grade we make an initial up-stroke on the *a* to simplify the writing for the child by keeping the first count on the up-stroke. This will be changed in the later grades in the interest of economy so that unnecessary strokes will be omitted in beginning letters.   If a child without suggestion drops the initial up-stroke and keeps a rhythmic move-ment, it should not be criticised.   Such a step taken voluntarily is probably an evidence of maturity, but it is better not to force it on the children here.

LESSON 3

Review Exercises 43, 44, 45.   Give Exercise 46, *n*.   "See how this is different from the *m*."   (Only two curves.)   "Count as you write."   Give Exercise 47, *can*, and Exercise 48, *in*.

EXERCISE 46

EXERCISE 47

EXERCISE 48   *EXERCISE 49*

In Exercise 47 and other exercises where *m* or *n* is preceded by another letter, there is especial need of care in getting the over-curve at the begin-ning of the *m* or *n*. The tendency is to give a straight line or slight under-curve which results in a sharp turn at the top instead of a rounded turn.

LESSON 4

Review Exercises 44, 45, 47, 48.   Give Exercise 49, *and*, and Exercise 50, *man*.

EXERCISE 50

Call attention to the number of curves. Count with the writing. Review the writing of tens to one hundred in column form.

Lesson 5

"Take clean paper." Give Exercises 41, 19, and 20, with capitals. Then give Exercises 44, 45, 47, 48, 49, 50. Write the tens to one hundred in a column at the left of the paper.

Third Week. Lesson 1

Set the metronome at 54 this week. If there is time to review old exercises not mentioned, set the metronome at 56 for them. Review Exercises 49, *and*, 50, *man*. Give Exercise 51, *no, an, on*.

EXERCISE 51

These words require much the same movement, but are sufficiently different to prevent the monotony which comes from drill on a single form. Give one at a time until they are understood and then give them together in differing order until the children are able to write them with comparative ease. Do not forget that it is ease and freedom of writing that we care about more than perfection of letter formation. We still expect crudeness there.

Lesson 2

Review Exercises 22, 23. Show Exercise 52, *g*. "How is this like the two we have just written? Yes, the first part is the same.

EXERCISE 52

Now I will write it again. Notice the lower part. Do you see how straight I make the down-stroke? Which way do we turn? Make just the straight down-stroke and the up-stroke. Can you add this to the *a*'s you have made so as to make *g*'s? Do so. Now trace over the whole letter. What shall we remember about the top?" (Keeping up.) "Now you may write. Listen to the metronome. Ready. Write."

Give Exercise 53, *go*.

EXERCISE 53   EXERCISE 54

Lesson 3

Review Exercises 22, 23, 28, 52, 53. Give Exercise 54, *dog*.

Call attention to its likeness to Exercise 28, *do*. This exercise repeats Exercise 28, but requires the new step of adding the *g* and joining it to the *o*. Call attention to the fact that since *g* is like *a* the connecting line will be the same as where one of the letters with "bridge" connection joins the *a*. Do not forget that in the count we pause at the top of the *o* before the connecting stroke.

Lesson 4

"To-day we shall have a new capital." Show Exercise 55, *E*.

EXERCISE 55

"Has any one a name that begins this way? Yes, Edith's name does. Now shall we write it? Look again to see the time." Show it again several times. Then let the children try it and show it again. "Ready. Write." If there is time, review Exercise 41, *A*, and the names with it.

Lesson 5

To-day compare the work done on last Friday with that done on the first Friday of the second month; that is, after the first comparison. Call the child's attention to improvements. Do not emphasize failures. Is the slant more regular? Is the line more even? Find letters that look better than before. Such questions cause the child to discriminate between the right and wrong forms, but give his effort a positive rather than a negative direction.

Fourth Week

A test will be given at the fifth lesson this week for which the teacher should prepare by looking up the directions on page 8 and teaching this week the verse to be written.

Set the metronome at 56. The work this week will be in the nature of a review without the child's being made conscious of it. We shall make phrase combinations of the exercises wherever possible. Are you watching position carefully all the time? Keep the work exactly with the metronome. Try to have it on the base line, or approximately straight if unruled paper is used.

Lesson 1

Give Exercise 56, *A dog and cat.*

a   d   o   g

and   cat

EXERCISE 56

This is the first exercise given which requires more than one line to write. It is the time to teach the child to estimate his space so that he will not crowd the last word, but will write on the next line what does not properly belong on the first line. One of the problems of arrangement in letter-writing and composition comes from the tendency to reduce the writing at the end of the line so as to squeeze on as much as possible. Many problems of upper-grade work would not exist if the child were taught right from the first. It is easier to form a right habit than to reform a wrong one.

LESSON 2

Give Exercise 57, *we can fall.*

we   can

fall   we

EXERCISE 57

LESSON 3

Give Exercise 58, *let me do it.*

LESSON 4

Give Exercise 59, *tie a bad dog.*

In these three lessons there are two things to be gained. First, the child sees a reason for learning to write. What he has learned to write will actually make a sentence. Second, he is having drill on writing in context form, instead of in columns as in the old-style copy-books, and so gets drill in the estimation of spacing for words and lines.

LESSON 5

The work to-day is to be graded. Put on the sheet first the

heading — Full Name, Age, Grade, Date. The teacher should have this heading ready before class time. Then give the two-minute test as directed on page 8, using the test verse for Grades 1–3. Be sure to follow the directions for this. Do not use the metronome for this two-minute test. Then, either below this or on the other side of the paper, write, with the metronome at 56, Exercises 56, 57, 58, 59.

It is assumed that the first-grade children will not be tested on writing at the beginning of the year. At this time it is worth while to give a regular test and grade it by the Standard Chart for the sake of making a comparison at the end of the year.

Fourth Month.   First Week

It is desirable all through the year in this grade to give as much work as possible on the board. While this is desirable, the amount is left to the discretion of the teacher. It is important that, as the children become used to the method and write with some speed with the metronome, they do not neglect proper position. Notice especially the hand position. Keep the "runners" (the third and fourth fingers) in the proper position. It has been found helpful to tell the children in the lower grades that the little finger is the drum-major and must walk ahead and lead the procession. Any device to help them to remember is suitable.

Lesson 1

Set the metronome at 56. Review Exercises 9, 46. Give Exercise 60, *h*. "How is this like the letter *l*?" (First stroke same.) "How is it like the letter *n*?" (Last stroke same.) Let

Exercise 60

the children see this definitely by erasing the last part of the *l* and finishing it to make *h*, and by erasing the first part of the *n* and putting in its place the loop that makes it *h*. Let the children do this. Call attention to the fact that when made in this way the first down-stroke and the second up-stroke follow the same line for only a little distance above the base line. The crossing of the loop comes opposite the top of the one-space part. If these things give the child trouble, as they often do, allow him to construct an *h* as suggested above, and then trace it in time to the metronome, first slowly, then faster. This is the most difficult exercise that has

been given.   With the variations suggested it can be used for the
entire period without becoming monotonous.

LESSON 2

Give Exercise 61, *he*, *the*.   These are to be given one at a time.

he   the

EXERCISE 61

The word *he* is to be given first because *h* is the initial letter.
Have the children write tens to one hundred as before, writing
one, naught, two, naught, etc., in columns.

LESSON 3

Give Exercise 62, *him*.

him   him

EXERCISE 62

The letter *h* is a particularly difficult one, so much review is needed.
Let the children study their work finding the best and making several like
it.   Change from one exercise to another to avoid weariness, but keep the
emphasis on the *h*.

LESSON 4

Review Exercise 41, *A*, and Exercise 55, *E*.   "We are going to
make a letter that is somewhat like both of these, but different.
Notice it carefully."   Give Exercise 63, *C*.   "Make *A* three times
with the metronome at 56.   Ready.   Write.   Now see how I write
this, *C*.   Watch the count.   Look once more.   Now you may write
it.   Listen to the metronome.   Ready.   Write.   Do you keep with
the metronome?   Try again.   Was that better?"   These statements and questions suggest the kind of comment that is desirable.
Spend little time talking about the work.   As in all acts of skill,
practice is essential.   Only see that the practice is with attention
and self-criticism.

LESSON 5

Have the children take clean paper.   Write the names.   Some of
the children may now be able to write their own names.   If so,
encourage them to do it.   So long as the teacher has to write the
names, it will be well to prepare the papers before school time.
Have the children write the tens to one hundred in a column at the

left of the paper. Then write Exercises 41, 55, 63, one line of each, and Exercises 58, 59.

After these papers are collected, allow each child to write his own name. Show those whose names begin with capitals not yet practiced how to write them. Arouse much pride in writing the names well.

SECOND WEEK. LESSON 1

Set the metronome at 56 for new work, and 60 for review.

Review Exercise 63, *C*. Give Exercise 64, *Can*. Give Exercise 65, *Can we fall?*

EXERCISE 63

EXERCISE 64

We give no words in sentence form which the children have not already practiced. Let the children write each word separately first, recognizing the fact that they know it. Then write the sentence on the board and have it read. "Notice this mark at the end, *?*. Have you ever seen it before? Where is it used?" They may remember it from the reader. Practice the interrogation mark, making it with the metronome — *?*. Then write the question.

LESSON 2

Review Exercises 58, 63. Give Exercise 66, *O*. "Notice how much this new letter is like the one you have written. Look again.

EXERCISE 66

What shape is it?" (Almost round, but not quite.) "Now if **I** write it with this exercise (58), it will give us a sentence." Give Exercise 67, *O, let me do it.*

Familiarity with a few forms is important in the establishment of right habit. Notice how previously used work is repeated with some variation to add new interest.

Call attention here to the difference between the punctuation of Exercises 65 and 67. "Is the mark at the end the same? No! Here we have only the period because we are not asking a question." The children are not expected to give the names *period* and *interrogation mark*, but the teacher should use their correct names when she refers to them. Children pick up a good deal by unconscious imitation.

Lesson 3

Review Exercises 41, *A*, 55, *E*, 63, *C*, 66, *O*, and write the names of all children which begin with any of these letters. If there is more time, give the words *of* and *on*, beginning them with capitals.

Lesson 4

"To-day we are going to have a letter which is not much like any letter we have had. See if any one can tell what it is."

Give Exercise 68, *p*. "Notice how straight the down-stroke is."

EXERCISE 68

Retrace it for emphasis. "Notice the last part. Watch as I make it again. It makes a little loop and comes back to the line, does n't it? I will write it once more so you will be sure of the count. Now you may write it. Ready. Write." (With the metronome at 56.)

If the children have trouble, set the metronome slower. After a few lines have been written, give Exercise 69, *up*. "Be careful of the time and see how well we can do this."

EXERCISE 69

It is assumed that the teacher is all the time watching position and not allowing the formation of any habit of cramped or strained position. The position will not be perfect, but so long as the child does not deviate persistently in any one direction and his muscles are not tense, his position is satisfactory.

Lesson 5

"Take clean papers. Write name." Set the metronome at 56. Give Exercises 65, 67, 68, 69.

After papers are collected, let the children write the tens to one hundred once. Then let them write *20*. Have them count to *30*. Suggest writing these numbers. In column write *20, 21, 22,* etc. Call attention to the fact that the numbers in the units column follow the order of the digits.

THIRD WEEK. LESSON 1

Review Exercise 67. Give Exercise 70, *let me up.*
Use this for phrase drill and then give Exercises 41, 55, 63, 66.

LESSON 2

Give Exercise 71, *y.* "Notice carefully as I write this again.

EXERCISE 71

See if you can tell what two letters it is like. What is the first part like?" (Last of *n.*) "And the second part?" (Stem of *g.*) "Remember we must make this long down-stroke straight. Watch again and notice the count." Write it several times counting with the metronome at 56.

The child may be interested to discover that, if made right, *y* makes a good inverted *h.* It is exceedingly important to get regular slant. This is more important now than any other element of form, and it is largely dependent on the free rhythmic quality of the writing, as rhythmic movement tends toward uniformity of slant.

Give Exercise 72, *my.* Note that the first stroke of the *y* is like the three *m* strokes, but that the round turn after the *m* gives a slightly compound curve to the first stroke.

EXERCISE 72

LESSON 3

Review Exercises 71, 72. Give Exercise 73, *boy, you.*

EXERCISE 73

In *boy* we have the difficult "bridge" connection twice.   Call attention to this.   Emphasize the count, which pauses at the point before the bridge in both *b* and *o*.   "Make the writing large and be sure to close the *o*.   Notice the count as I write it again.   Now you may write.   Ready.   Write."

In *you* call special attention to the slant of the down-strokes. "Are they the same?   Could they be used for car-tracks?"

LESSON 4

Give Exercise 74, the *s* swing, and 75, *s*.

EXERCISE 74

For this use the rhyme,

> Seesaw, Margery Daw,
> Up and down we go

to give the rhythm.

This is especially appropriate here because it helps by the suggested imagery to give the right slant.   The *s* is so frequently written incorrectly that it is important to get this slant right from the first.   It may be too nearly vertical or too nearly horizontal. In the first case call attention to the danger of teetering on such a board.   "What would happen to the one at the top?"   In the second case suggest that it would n't be any fun to play "Seesaw" on a board that could n't go any higher than that.   Show the desirable slant with the rhyme that suggests the image.

After the children have played "Seesaw" with Exercise 74, for a time, suggest that you will show them another way to do it. Then give Exercise 75, *s*, still using the rhyme.

EXERCISE 75

On the down-stroke throw the arm out noticeably to make the rounded line.   It is well to exaggerate this in the beginning to prevent the ugly flat *s* which is so undesirable.

Review Exercise 72, *my*, if a change seems best because of the children's interest.

Never keep at one exercise until the interest flags. Do not try to teach any letter completely the first time. The difficulty of the tip of the *s* will be more easily met if the swing is kept. Call attention to it. The reason for presenting this type of letter so late is just this difficulty.

LESSON 5.

Review Exercises 71, 72, 73, 74, 75.

FOURTH WEEK. LESSON 1

Review Exercises 74, 75, with rhyme. Then give each with metronome at 56. Give Exercise 76, *see*.

EXERCISE 76

Be very careful that the right slant for *s* is kept. Have the children compare the up-stroke of the *s* and the up-stroke of the *e*. If they are parallel, the work is likely to be right. If there is trouble, go back to Exercises 74, 75, for practice.

LESSON 2

Review Exercise 75, *s*. Give Exercise 77, *is*, *us*. Make the up-strokes parallel. Be sure that the children notice that the tip of

EXERCISE 77

the *s* is above the *i* and the *u*, but not so tall as the dot of the *i*. Review Exercise 76, *see*.

LESSON 3

Review Exercises 75, 61, "Now notice how I will put these together." Give Exercise 78, *she*. "How many can make this right? Look again." Count with the metronome as you write.

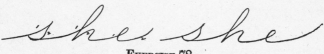

EXERCISE 78

"Now you may write. Ready. Write." Do not neglect this little formality in starting. The precision helps to keep in mind the need for regularity.

LESSON 4

Review the writing of numbers, first the digits — one row of each, then in succession up to 10. Next write in column formation 0–9, 20–29, 30–39, etc., to 99, writing with the metronome and keeping the columns straight. Write only one set as 20–29, at a time, stopping to criticize and pick out the best of the work.

Lesson 5

"Take clean paper. Write name." Give Exercises 75, 76, 77, 78. Then let the children write the numbers in columns as far as there is time to do it carefully.

Fifth Month.   First Week

The year is nearly half gone. The class has had all of the small letters except *r*, *k*, *v*, *x*, *z*, and has had the capitals *A*, *E*, *C*, *O*. Possibly some other letters have been used by the class incidentally. We shall not present *z* nor the capitals *Q*, *X*, or *Z*, in the first year because of the slight probability that the children will need them. We shall finish giving practice drill on the other letters within the next six weeks in preparation for drills for automatization of rhythm, movement, and form, to occupy the rest of the year.

Lesson 1

For four weeks the metronome has been used at 56. Now begin to use it at 60 except where giving an exercise for the first time. Review Exercise 75. Give Exercise 79, *r*.

Exercise 79

Call attention to the likeness to the *s*. These two are the only letters having the tip coming above the one-space letters. Be very careful of the count here. The correct form is much more easily gained if the rhythm is right.

Review Exercise 51, *an*. Then give Exercise 80, *ran*. Notice that in the *r* the down-stroke is a straight slanting stroke, not a curve. Try to see that the children get this.

Exercise 80   Exercise 81

Lesson 2

Review Exercises 79, 80. "Our new exercise to-day is much like this. Notice it."

Give Exercise 81, *run*. Be sure that all the down-strokes have the same slant. Draw lines through them once in a while to see if they could be used for car-tracks. Alternate in practice. Exercises 80 and 81.

Lesson 3

Write in columns digits *0–9*. Leave a wide space and write the numbers *20–29*, in column.   "When we count, what do we say after *9* before we reach *20?*   Now let us write these numbers in the space between the two columns."   Give what help is needed.   If the children have had these numbers before this in arithmetic, little help will be needed and the practice will be in making good figures and in good columns.   If the children are just learning to write them, they may not be able to take them all in one day.

The reason this group of tens is left to teach after the others are learned is because children often become confused in writing the "teens," and if they have had experience with all the others, so that they will recognize *31* as *thirty-one*, they are not so likely to use this order of the digits when writing *thirteen*.

Lesson 4

"We have not had a capital letter for some time.   Would you not like to learn another?   We will take this one."

Give Exercise 82, *B, Ben, Boys.*

Exercise 82

Practice the *B* alone counting by voice and metronome.   The two words are suggestive only.   If a child in the class has a name beginning with *B*, practice that instead.

Lesson 5

"Take clean paper.   Write name."   Give Exercise 79, *r,* for the swing.   Then give Exercises 80, 81, 82.

If there is extra time let the children find their own best example of each exercise and mark it.   Use extra time on individual practice of names, each writing his own.   Try to see how much improvement can be made in these before the next test is written.

Second Week.   Lesson 1

Review Exercises 1, 2, 74, at the beginning of each lesson this week, to get free swing and rapid movement.   Exercises 1, 2, should be given in the half-line swing.   Spend only a few minutes on this.

Review Exercise 9, *l,* and Exercise 60, *h.*   "We are going to make an exercise that is somewhat like both of these, but is different.   Notice it carefully."

Give Exercise 83, *k.*   "There are two things we must remember about this letter; the cross comes just opposite the top of the low part; the round part must be tiny and leave a little gateway opening into the *garden*." Notice that the two down-strokes of the *k* are parallel. Call attention to this.

EXERCISE 83

For the remainder of the period write the numbers in column in serial order. The teacher should write the copy for all these before the class, as the aim here is not so much to teach what to write as how to write it. Continue to write the copy, showing the children how, until relatively good results are obtained with some ease.

LESSON 2

Review the swinging exercises once each. Review Exercise 83, *k*.

Give Exercise 84, *look*. Call attention to the two bridge connections here. See that the *oo*'s have a good slant.

EXERCISE 84

LESSON 3

"We are going to have a new exercise to-day. It is another capital letter. It does not begin as any other has. We move backward instead of forward in beginning it." Show carefully, Exercise 85, *I*.

EXERCISE 85   EXERCISE 86

Begin at the base line. Go up, and down toward the left, then turn so that the down-stroke slants as the other letters do. This is a hard letter. Stop after a few moments' practice and give Exercises 1, 2, 74.

After practicing again stop and write names of children the initials of which have been learned.

Use *I* only as the word *I* unless there is a child whose initial it is, or unless some other work requires its use at the beginning of a word.

LESSON 4

Review Exercise 85, *I*.   "To-day we are going to have another letter much like this one.   It is different because it has a stem below the line."   Give Exercise 86, *J*.

Note that the two up-strokes cross the down-stroke at the same place, almost at the base line and that the down-stroke is straight. The children will like to lay their pencils along this line to see if they really have made it straight.   It will be necessary to emphasize the fact that both curves are on the same side of the straight stroke.   If the children have trouble, let them construct the letter a few times by drawing the straight down-stroke, putting on the two curves and then tracing it as the letter *J*.

LESSON 5

"Take clean paper.   Write name."   Give Exercises 83, 84, 85, 86, and have the numbers *1–29* written.

For review use the name exercises used this week.

THIRD WEEK.   LESSON 1

There are certain fundamental principles which it is assumed that the teacher will attend to continually even though they are mentioned only from time to time.   These are: position — allowing no habitual deviation in any one way; rhythmic movement — governed for the time being by an arbitrary, imposed rhythm; and definite evaluation and self-criticism — mostly by the selection of the best each has done as the standard of comparison for future work.

Review Exercise 15, *b*, and Exercise 46, *n*.   Give Exercise 87, *v, ve*.

EXERCISE 87

The first part of this is like the *n*, the last part like the *b*.   Make the combination so that the children can see that it is so.   Let them also make it.   Practice the *v*, writing several lines.   Have the children stop frequently long enough to select their best work and try to repeat it.

Review Exercise 17, *be*, before giving *ve*.   Call attention to the connecting line.   "We have the same kind of connecting stroke when we write *v e*.   Notice as we write it."

Let several put it on the board in time with the metronome. "Now you may write it.   Ready.   Write."

LESSON 2

Review Exercise 87.   Give Exercise 88, *have*.   "To-day we can

EXERCISE 88

use *ve* in a word that you know. Look at the first letter. Remember how straight we make its back."

See that the time is kept here.

Review Exercises 79, *r*, 80, *ran*, 81, *run*.

LESSON 3

Use Exercises 1, 2, once for free swing. Review Exercises 85, 88, 81. Then write the sentence, *I have run.*

Call attention to the sentence with capital and period. Try to have rhythm used in this continuous writing.

LESSON 4

"To-day we shall have a new capital. Watch carefully as I write it." Give Exercise 89, *M*. "How many hills are there? Do you think they look like steps? Let us make them so." "Have we written any word we can use this capital with? Yes, *my*. I will write it." Call attention to the time. Then let the class write it. "Here is another letter that is almost the same. I wonder if you can find the difference."

EXERCISE 89   EXERCISE 90

Give Exercise 90, *N*. "Now you can make this one, can you not? Ready. Write."

Give *no*, using the capital. If there are any children whose names begin with *M* or *N*, the names should be used.

LESSON 5

"Take clean paper. Write name." Give Exercises 88, 89, 90, and words beginning with these capitals which were practiced.

Review similar capitals as *A*, *E*, *C*, *O*; *I*, *J*; as time permits.

FOURTH WEEK. LESSON 1

"To-day we are going to have a queer letter. It looks somewhat like a sawhorse." Give Exercise 91, *x*.

If it helps, tell the class that this is the snake that came to get Raggylug and we will cut it right in two so that it cannot hurt him.

Review Exercise 75, *s*. Give Exercise 92, *six*.

EXERCISE 91   EXERCISE 92

LESSON 2

Review Exercise 82, *B*. Give Exercise 93, *P*, *Paul*.

EXERCISE 93

Let the children see that this is very much like the capital B. Give and practice the letter alone and then give the name. If the name of some pupil begins with *P*, use it instead of *Paul*.

Review the writing of numbers in columns, being sure that they are always straight, units under units, etc.

LESSON 3

Review Exercise 89, *M*. "We have to-day another letter a good deal like this, but it has a sharp point in the middle. Notice it carefully." Give Exercise 94, *W*, *Will*.

EXERCISE 94

The middle stroke is taller than the first stroke and the last stroke is shorter than either of the others. Be careful of the slant here. Practice the letter before giving the name, *Will*. Use any name of a child which begins with *W*.

LESSON 4

Review Exercise 94, *W*. "Let us make the first stroke of this letter. Now I shall finish it so as to make another letter."

Give Exercise 95, *Y*, *You*. "Notice the last part is just like a tall *j*." Practice the letter.

EXERCISE 95

Review Exercise 73, *you*. "Now we will write this with a capital." Call attention again to the joining of *o* and *u*.   Be sure it is right.

Review the numbers *10–19*, writing them in columns several times if there is time.

Give Exercise 96, *U*.   This is just like capital *Y* except the loop. The children will have little use for this capital, but it is well for them to see it.   Let them write it several times.

Lesson 5

"Take clean paper.   Write name."   Give Exercises 92, 93, 94, 95.

Spend extra time writing names with the metronome.   This should be accompanied by self-criticism, each finding where he is making some improvement.

EXERCISE 96   EXERCISE 97

Sixth Month.   First Week
Lesson 1

Review Exercises 82, *B*, 93, *P*.   Give Exercise 97, *R, Run*.   This is very similar to the exercises reviewed and the children will be helped by noticing this.   The upper curve in each extends nearly halfway down.   After the letter has been practiced, review Exercise 81, *run*, and then give it with the capital.

Lesson 2

Review Exercise 97.   Give Exercise 98, *Run to me*.   "Now we will take a new letter."   Give Exercise 99, *L, Let*.

EXERCISE 99

Make it a number of times with voice count so that the children will see how it is done.   Let them practice it freely at the board with voice count before they practice it with the metronome. Then use the metronome at 66.   This will probably be as fast as is desirable the first year for most classes.

Review exercises may be written at this speed, but new exercises should continue to be written slower.   The speed should never be such as to disorganize the writing movement.   The main aim here is not form, but habit of work.

Review Exercise 10, *let*. Then give it with capital. Give the name of any child which begins with *L*.

Lesson 3

The new capital to-day is somewhat like the *L* in the movement required to make it, but the relative size of the loops is quite different.

Give Exercise 100, *S*, *See*. Before giving *See*, review it with the small letter. Give Exercise 101, *See the dog run*. If necessary review the words separately before writing the sentence.

Exercise 100

It is important to make the first stroke of the *S* with such a slant that the finished letter slants at an angle of about thirty degrees instead of being nearly vertical. Too broad a curve at the top will produce this difficulty, and so should be avoided.

Lesson 4

The capital to-day is very much like the *S*, but it makes another turn before reaching the base line. It is well not to relate these two letters in the minds of the children because they are frequently confused.

Exercise 102

Give Exercise 102, *G*, *Go*. Show it on the board emphasizing the place where each count comes. Then let the children make it slowly at first, just the first part with count. Then show it all with voice count, then with the metronome. Let the children write it with voice count and then with metronome.

Lesson 5

"Take a clean paper. Write name." Give Exercises 98, 99, 101, 102.

Write numbers *9–19* in column. In extra time write the names of children.

Second Week. Lesson 1

Review Exercise 89, *M*. "What other letters have the first

stroke like the first stroke of the *M?*" (*N*, *W*, *Y*.) "To-day I will give you another letter which has the same first stroke."

Give Exercise 103, *H*, *He*, *He can see me.*

EXERCISE 103

The two down-strokes are parallel "like car-tracks." The cross touches the first down-stroke at about the middle and returning crosses itself at the point where it left the second down-stroke. Show this to the children and help them to get it by attention to count. Give the sentence when the children have practiced *He.*

LESSON 2

"Our capital to-day has its first stroke just like the *H*. The second stroke, instead of coming down to the base line and having a third stroke to join it to the first stroke, curves so as to join the first stroke before it touches the base line." Tell the class this as you write Exercise 104, *K*, *Kate.*

EXERCISE 104

"Where does the second stroke touch the first?" (Halfway.) Practice on this with care to have movement free and rhythmic. If a child's name begins with *K*, use that. If not, review Exercise 103, *He can see me.*

LESSON 3

"The letter to-day is like one letter we have had before. Look at it as I write it and tell me what letter it is." (L.)

Give Exercise 105, *D*, *Do.*

EXERCISE 105

The curve that leaves the base line, going up a short way and returning to it, is the common point and will need much practice. Let the children first practice the straight line with the curve returning to the base line. Then practice the complete letter and give *Do*, which they have had before with the small *d*.

LESSON 4

"To-day we will take two letters which are just alike except for one mark. This is the first one."

Give Exercise 106, *F*, *T*. Practice on *F*.

EXERCISE 106

Notice that the down-stroke curves and before the turn is made is farther to the left than the first stroke. Failure to note this results in a common fault in making this letter.

After this has been practiced, show *T*, saying that they know how to make this now and let them show what stroke to leave off. Give the names of any children which have these initials.

LESSON 5

"Take clean paper. Write name." Give Exercises 103, 104, 105, 106.

In the extra time have the children write two columns of numbers *1–50*, and any names which have been practiced.

THIRD WEEK

A regular method of grading will be followed for the rest of the year. This is based on the *Chart for Diagnosing Faults in Handwriting*, and where it is possible the teacher should make use of this.

The teacher should study this Chart this week for the purpose of beginning the grading next week. During the week that each category is being emphasized, that category alone should be graded; e.g., when *letter formation* is being emphasized, it will be graded in terms of the Chart and will be rated 2, 6, 10, or the intermediate points 4, 8.

For further information regarding the use of the Chart, refer to *The Teaching of Handwriting*, by Frank N. Freeman (Houghton Mifflin Company), pp. 123–42.

The children should understand that the marking is in "points," not in per cent as in other grades. When the marking is begun, the teacher should grade, in the special category for the week, the work done on the first day and on the last day. The child should be encouraged to study his work, not so much for the value of his estimate as to lead to a critical attitude toward his work.

Only one or two specimens will be given each week, with suggestions as to possible preliminary work before writing the selection as a whole. If the teacher thinks best, the verses may be used for a book of poetry which should be made of the last copy of each specimen written. It has not seemed necessary to give written copies for all these exercises. If there is any question as to form of letters, refer to previous copies.

Two types of work should be used from now on: (1) exercises such as are given here to increase facility in writing the letters, and the words which have been given, and (2) any work for which the class has a motive that will lead the children to see the value of writing. This might be the making of a booklet in which the child wishes to put some writing, or a note of invitation.

Do not increase the speed. Attempt to perfect the work at the speed now used, 66, for review and less than that for new exercises.

Copy for the Week

Work correlating with the other subjects may be substituted for these exercises if they give the same drill value. Some such work should be given.

Exercise 107, *Do you see Mary?*

Practice each word separately. Practice each exercise first with and then without the metronome. This sentence may be varied from day to day by substituting the names of other children.

FOURTH WEEK

This week the grading discussed in the general directions will begin. The category graded this week will be *letter formation*. Keep the work on the fifth lesson this week to compare with the work of the eighth month, first week.

Grade the work done on the first day on *letter formation* only. Compare this with the grade given on the last day on the same category.

Exercise 108:

Copy for the Week

1 2 3 4 5
I caught a hare alive;
6 7 8 9 10
I let him go again.

Here the capital *I*, the *g*, *h*, *a*, and *v*, give good practice. Use them in words or alone as seems best. Continue practicing each exercise with the metronome and without.

Say the verse to the children. Suggest that they may like to write it. "Can we write *caught?*" Show it and have the children practice it. Then in a similar way give *hare, alive, again.* "We have written *I, a, let, him, go*. Suppose we review them to be sure we can do well."

After three days of such work have the rhyme as a whole written on the other two days. Try to have the letters formed right.

Seventh Month. First Week

The category to be emphasized this week is *spacing*. Grade on this alone, but continue to call attention to *letter formation*.

Copy for the Week

> The friendly cow all red and white
> I love with all my heart;
> She gives me cream with all her might,
> To eat with apple tart.

This poem of Stevenson's may be recited to the children. Then it may be used as the source of sentences unless there is reason for writing it all.

These sentences may be used.

Exercise 109, *The cow is red and white.*

Practice *The* with the capital, *cow, red, white.* The joining of *wh* may need a good deal of practice. Call attention to this point.

Give Exercise 110, *She gives me cream to eat.*

Review *have*, then *ve*, then show and have the children write, *gives*. Give practice also on *She* with the capital, *me, to, eat, which*, which are all old words. Then show *cream* and give practice on it.

This work in some classes may take more than one week. If so, use only the first sentence. Have the work written both with and without the metronome. See that *all* writing that is done is done in the right manner.

Second Week

Emphasize *alinement* this week and grade on it. Examine the nearness of the letters to the base line and the relative height of the letters. Try to have no loss in *letter formation* and *spacing*, but do this incidentally, not as the main aim. If an advance in speed seems desirable, the tempo may be increased a little. Probably most classes will not need any advance.

Copy for the Week

Exercise 111, *Let the dog run to me.*

The capital *L* will be the point of emphasis here as the words are all review. The names of different children should be substituted for *me* part of the time.

Last week's work may be carried into this week if more work is desired. Distributed repetition is best in gaining skill, so it is better to do a little each day, not tiring the child, until he can write the whole verse. Do not hesitate to go back and review work if there is a little extra time.

THIRD WEEK

The emphasis this week should be on *quality of line*. This consists of two things: regularity of line as opposed to wavering, and pressure that gives a clear, not too black line. This can best be gained by right position, which prevents a cramped pressure, care in sharpening pencils, and keeping the metronome time, which leads to regularity. If a slight increase in speed does not disorganize the work, it may be made. Do not consider it necessary.

Copy for the Week

Thank you, pretty cow, that made
Pleasant milk to soak my bread.
Every day, and every night,
Warm, and fresh, and sweet, and white.

Give this verse as another verse about the cow and what she does for us.

Give Exercise 112, *The cow gives me cream to eat.*

This gives only what was practiced in the first week, but gives it in slightly different form.

Have the children practice *pretty, milk, Every, day.* Then give Exercise 113, *Every day the pretty cow gives me milk.*

While emphasizing and grading on *quality of line*, do not forget *letter formation*, and *alinement*.

FOURTH WEEK

Special attention should be given to *uniformity of slant* this week. Because this is largely controlled by position and rhythm, it should be good by this time. Therefore while it is the category to be graded, attention may also be given to the other four categories.

Exercise 114:

Copy for the Week

THE LITTLE PLANT

In the heart of a seed,
Buried deep, so deep!
A dear little plant
Lay fast asleep!

This verse with those of the next two weeks makes a complete poem.

This poem is one which may well be learned by the first grade at this time of year, and it is suggested that it be written to be included in a *Work Book, Spring Book*, or something of that kind, related to reading, literature, nature study, art, and constructive work.

If this is to be done, the new words to be practiced are *heart*, *seed*, *Buried*, *deep*, *dear*, *little*, *plant*, *Lay*, *fast*, *asleep*. Call attention to as many familiar points as possible. For example, give *see*, then *seed*. Follow this by *deep*, *sleep*, *asleep*. Give *lay*, *Lay*; *heart*, *hear*, *dear*; *it*, *lit*, *little*; *an*, *plant*; *as*, *fast*. *Buried* has no relation which will help much.

The teacher's attention to position and right type of movement should not flag, but it should be a helpful, kindly attention, not a nagging criticism.

EIGHTH MONTH. FIRST WEEK

For special emphasis this week we will again study *letter formation*. Grade on this. Tell the children that now we have covered all the points of good writing. We can do better and at the end of the week can compare our writing with what we did the first week we practiced on *letter formation*. (Sixth Month, Fourth Week.)

Use the metronome only part of the time this week, letting the children try to write without it part of the time.

Exercise 115:

Copy for the Week

"Wake!" said the sunshine,
"And creep to the light!"
"Wake!" said the voice
Of the raindrops bright.

Follow the general directions for last week. The new words are *Wake*, *said*, *sunshine*, *creep*, *light*, *voice*, *raindrops*, *bright*. Relate these to what is known as suggested in last week's work. Select the parts which prove most difficult for special practice.

SECOND WEEK

Give special attention to *spacing*, as the importance of this is more easily seen in writing poetry. Emphasize *letter formation*, too, as, "We want the whole poem to look well." As before, grade on the first and the last work. Try to have the children critical of their own work during the week. In their criticism train them to look for the best and note that.

Exercise 116:

The little plant heard
And it rose to see
What the wonderful
Outside world might be!

The new words are *heard*, *rose*, *What*, *wonderful*, *Outside*, *world*, *might*. Associate these with known words; as, *heart*, *heard*, *light*, *bright*, *might*.

If the class has learned this poem by heart in writing it, it may now be written as a whole, or each stanza may have been writ.en in its final form when practiced and each new one added.

THIRD WEEK

This week we will emphasize *slant* and compare our work with the work of the week when we first specialized on *slant*.

Copy for the Week

Exercise 117, *Grace has her new doll.   Tom has his new ball.*

The new words in these sentences are *Grace, has, her, new, Tom, his.*   Associate these with known words and use other names of children in writing part of the time.   Try from now on to arouse considerable pride in writing one's own name well.   One's own name is written so often that it should be well done.   Spend part of the spare time practicing names.

Try to have the children get the time by listening to the metronome and then follow it without using the metronome.   Practice either words or sentences, as seems best.

FOURTH WEEK

Emphasize *alinement* this week and see how much has been gained since we began to do this.   Also notice *quality of line.*   This should be satisfactory now as a result of free movement and good tools.

Experiment this week to determine the metronome time at which your class does the best work and record this.

Exercise 118:

Copy for the Week

Sing a song of sixpence,
A pocket full of rye;
Four and twenty blackbirds
Baked in a pie.

Probably each teacher will have now some work which the children wish to write well.   If so, it should be substituted for this verse.   If not, recite this to the children and let them work on parts of it, though they may not write the whole verse.

NINTH MONTH

During this month there may be need for writing invitations for a spring party, entertainment, or festival, or for books to be carried home.   If this is so, all the subject-matter for writing this month may be drawn from other subjects.   If this is done, the manner of writing should be held to standards established and a sufficient amount of practice for the work should be given.

Exercises will be given for the month to be used in part or wholly as is desirable.

Exercise 119:

FIRST WEEK

Copy for the Week

> Here blows the warm, red clover,
> There peeps the violet blue;
> O happy little children,
> God made them all for you.

The capital letters, *H, T, O, G*, should receive careful practice. The new words are *Here, blows, warm, clover, There, peeps, violet, blue, happy, children, God, made, them, for*. These should be related to words previously learned, as, *her, here, there;* then introduce them with the capitals.

It may not be necessary to spend a long time in practicing each word alone. It is worth while to have the children as soon as possible learn to write by phrases, but the teacher should appreciate all the new situations and be prepared to give help wherever needed. The verse may or may not be written as a whole finally, but it should be the motive for the writing, and if there is a reason for it, it may be written as a whole.

SECOND WEEK

It is assumed that the teacher has by this time so got the spirit of the course as to give sympathetic guidance, not nagging criticism, and so to motivate the work as to call forth the child's best efforts.

Exercise 120:

Copy for the Week

> I know, blue modest violets,
> Gleaming with dew at morn,
> I know the place you come from,
> And the way that you were born.

Capitals *I, G, A*, should receive more drill. The new words are *know, modest, Gleaming, dew, morn, place, come, from, way, that, were, born*. Helpful review words are *for, born, morn, her, were, now, know, lay, way*.

Lead the children to be critical with regard to all five categories now and to decide in what their writing is good and where it needs improvement. Where practice is needed, let each settle on what he will work for. If any child adopts an individual rhythm and actually keeps to it, do not force him to change to the imposed rhythm.

THIRD WEEK

Begin this week by a comparison of last Friday's work with that which was done one month ago — the writing of the poem, "The Little Plant." Discuss special improvement on any of the categories. Lead the children to find their own improvement. Then secure from the children, perhaps by questions, the statement that "We can do better yet"; and go on with that ideal this week. Always look for the best and get the children to try to imitate that.

Exercise 121:

Copy for the Week

When God cuts holes in Heaven,
The holes the stars look through,
He lets the scraps fall down to earth,
The little scraps are you.

Have the capitals *W, T, H*, practiced. The new words are *When, cuts, holes, Heaven, stars, through, scraps, fall, down, earth.*

Work on this in the same way as on the other stanzas, taking pains to see that the children enjoy the work, also that they understand it and are developing no bad habits.

A two-minute test should be given at the end of this week to compare with the first test given this year. Use the directions on page 8 for this and give the same verse that has been written for this test before.

FOURTH WEEK

This week the children may perfect their writing of the three stanzas and write them as an entire poem.

Final practice may be given on names and on numbers.

Determine and record the speed at which the class prefers to write. Let the children express preference, but see that they actually use the time that they say they prefer.

CHAPTER VI

EXERCISES FOR GRADE TWO

OBJECTIVES

Content. At the end of the second year the child should be able to write independently all small and capital letters and the digits sufficiently well for his recognized needs. He may still require frequent assistance on the more difficult combinations of letters; as, *wi, br, vo, oi, oe.* He should be able to write independently such words as the following:

let	little	ball	eat	bad
told	ice	if	of	came
made	one	found	glad	good
long	that	thing	help	open
they	baby	saw	stand	best
sick	take	kind	thank	book
five	gave	have	seven	box
six	blue	table	behind	light
white	plant	anything	house	last
school	spell	afternoon	around	brother

He should be able to write several commonly used names of persons, some of the days of the week, all the numbers to *200*, using correct column placing from copy or dictation. He should learn to observe right and left margins in writing. The margins may be indicated by rulings in this grade.

Movement. At the end of the second year the child should have developed a motor control characterized as follows: A fluency of thirty letters a minute; freedom of movement with arm resting on desk resulting in continuous and coördinated lateral movement; a position which is closer to the standard than in Grade 1, the factors most emphasized being healthful body position, paper at an angle of thirty degrees to the edge of the desk, loose grasp of the pencil with no serious, continuous deviation from the standard position.

MATERIALS AND METHODS

Materials. An unglazed paper of better quality than that used in Grade 1 and having five eighths spacing ruled. Any ordinary-sized medium soft pencil may be used. The size of the writing may be about one fourth inch for small letters.

Methods. *A. Position.* It is well here to have the children use the blackboard for new exercises and frequently for supplementary work. For the writing on paper the position should be the same as in Grade 1, except that the arms may rest lightly on the desk. The arm may move in making the letters and in so doing may slide on the desk.

B. Types of exercises. 1. Drills for developing free rhythmic movement, and for training in letter formation, with the letters separate and combined in words. These should be given first with voice count and later with metronome. In applying the count to letter forms, it is important that the count should conform to the natural unit of form of the letters and should allow the same time for similar strokes in different combinations. This is provided for in the class exercises given in this Manual. Beginning in this grade the motivation should come largely from the child's feeling of need for writing in other subjects, but he may also get pleasure from rhythmic activity.

2. In addition to the exercises in the Manual, the child should practice with material drawn from other class work, using words and sentences for which he has need.

C. Standards and criticism. The development of a critical attitude should begin by leading the child to compare different parts of his own work and to pick out the best examples of particular words and letters. This is in harmony with the educational principle that attention should be on the products which represent successful effort more than on those which represent comparative failure. The teacher may here introduce the terms *uniform slant* and *uniform alinement*, and call attention to *quality of line* by noticing good quality and suggesting a method of improving writing of poor quality. The standard in form for this grade is 11 on the Freeman Scale, and 35 on the Ayres Scale, and the standard in speed is thirty letters a minute.

EXERCISES

Note to teacher. If a first-grade class does most or all of the handwriting on the blackboard and so has not finished the exercises for Grade 1, the class may begin the second-grade work at the beginning of the second year, provided it has gone far enough to have written all the letters that are given in Grade 1. The letters are all introduced by the second week of the sixth month.

FIRST MONTH. FIRST WEEK

A test will be given on the first Friday. The teacher should look ahead and prepare for this by teaching, this week, the verse to be written.

Lesson 1

(A short talk something like this will be a good way to begin the course. It should be suited to the class.)

"We all want to learn to write well so that when we write letters or stories our friends can read them. We can write well and make hard work of it or we can write easily and well. I am going to try to show you how to write so that it will be easy to write and then you will be glad to do it. First, we must sit straight, hips back in seat, feet on the floor." See that all are doing so. "Put paper in place, at an angle of thirty degrees to the desk line. Put both arms on the desk and let them rest there easily. Make runners of your two little fingers. Let them carry the whole hand sliding back and forth on the paper" (no pencil in hand). "Go all the way across the paper. Do it as I count. One-two, one-two, one-two, one-two. Again, One-two," etc. "Can you keep just with my count? Are you sliding on your runners? Is your wrist raised just a little so as to form a bridge? Now, again, one-two," etc. (four times). "Take pencil, hold it so."

Show the correct position. Be sure that the index finger is on top of the pencil, not at the left side, and that the thumb is higher on the pencil — farther from the point — than the index finger. See that every child's position is correct this time and every time. It will take less time on the whole if insisted on the first and every time. *Place* each pencil right where it is necessary. Above all things do not get impatient with the child who does not get the position right. They all want to.

"Now you may use your runners with the pencil. Try it as I count. All the way across the paper, but do not write yet. Ready. Slide. One-two," etc. "Now I will show you something to write." Say as you write it on the board:

> To and fro, sway the trees,
> Bending in the passing breeze.

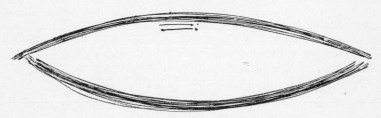

Exercises 1 and 2

Give Exercise 1. "Now you may do it as I did." Repeat the verse as they write. "You may say it as you write. Again."

This is sufficient for the first lesson. If there is more time, vary the one exercise by letting part do it at the board while the rest do it at their seats. These first two exercises are for the purpose of accustoming the pupils from the beginning to correct position of body, arms, hand, and paper, and to correct pencil-holding, and to begin the formation of the habit of sliding the hand along the line while the letters are being formed. Attention should be directed particularly on these phases of the writing activity until they are habitual.

Lesson 2

"Sit straight, hips back, feet on floor. Arms on desk. Can you place your paper right? Good." Do not neglect commendation when possible to give it. "Without pencils use your runners, 'way across the paper. Ready. Slide. One-two," etc. (four times). "Now pencils. Is your position like this?" Be sure that it is. "Now slide, but do not write. Ready. Slide. One-two," etc. "Look."

On the board write Exercise 1, saying the verse. "You may write it. Ready. Write. 'To and fro,'" etc. "Did you keep the time? Once more. 'To and fro,'" etc. "Now we have made the tree-tops. Do you like to swing clear up to the tree-tops among the leaves? Look; I am going to swing up."

Give Exercise 2. While making the curve say:

> How do you like to go up in a swing,
> Up in the air so blue?

"Now you may swing up into your tree-tops. Ready. Write. 'How do you like to go up in a swing,'" etc. "Make the tree-tops again. Are your runners ready? Is your pencil right? Are you holding it loosely?" Test a few by pulling the pencil from the fingers. "Ready. Write. 'To and fro,'" etc. "Let's swing to the tree-tops! 'How do you,'" etc. "Now we will slide another way. I will show you." Give Exercise 3, i.

Exercise 3

"Make long slides so that you can put only three on a line. Try again. See how I count." Put it on the board again with count. Notice that the count is on the forward stroke. "Ready. Write. One-two, one-two." Repeat several times to your count by voice, and watch hands for position, looseness of grasp and sliding on runners. Commend as much as possible. Quietly change the positions that are wrong.

Here the element of letter formation in very simple form is combined with the forward movement. The form may be very crude at first if the forward movement is not hampered. The form should be gradually improved as the forward movement is established. The count is given on the forward stroke so as to emphasize the forward movement.

Lesson 3

Give specific directions as to position as in the last lesson. Use Exercises 1, 2, 3, *i*, with voice count, and be particular to see that the position is kept. Where the course is introduced for the first time, there will probably be rather more difficulty in starting than where the class has done the work for first grade. In any case we go slowly in the beginning to give the children a chance to recover from the long vacation.

Give Exercise 4, *u*. "Let us make two of the down slants together. Yes, it makes a *u*. Make long slides so that you can put only three on a line."

Exercise 4

This exercise requires still greater control and finer coördination of the forward movement and the letter formation, but much crudity in form is still to be expected. By this time if there really is freedom of movement, you will be inclined to be disturbed by disregard for base line and proper height of letters. Let it go for the present. Work *only* for position, freedom of movement, and correct time. "Now, look. Make this once more." (Exercise 3, *i*.) "Now I will make it taller." Give Exercise 5, *t*.

Exercise 5

"You may try it. Watch the count. Have you the right position?" See that they have, but quickly. "Now. Ready. Write. One-two," etc. Use the count for all writing. It will not be given in the discussion from now on, but the teacher should use it as given in the exercises at all times.

Lesson 4

"Take position. Show me how your runners slide. Pencils." Review, with rhymes, Exercises 1, 2, putting them on the board first. Review Exercises 3, 4, 5, with count.

Each review exercise should be written once or twice. Don't make drudgery of it by too long repetition of an exercise. Don't expect perfection at first. Go back to each exercise often.

"Look, I am going to put two exercises together." Give Exercise 6, *it*. Write it two or three times on the board. "Now you may write it. Ready. Write. Again. You may dot the *i*'s and cross the *t*'s. Once more. Ready. Write."

EXERCISE 6

The variation in height of strokes here requires still greater control. In counting, emphasis should be put on the second count, on which the taller stroke is made. Otherwise there will be a tendency to make this stroke short. The teacher should practice this exercise and every exercise in her preparation of the lesson so that she can demonstrate it to the class.

LESSON 5

During this week the children have been adjusting themselves to school régime again after the vacation. It seems wise to delay the first test of the year until now so that normal classroom conditions will prevail. The test verse for Grades 1–3 should have been taught during the week without reference to writing. For the manner of giving the test see the directions on page 8, and follow these exactly. Save these papers for comparison during the year to show progress. There are two purposes in this comparison, the children will be encouraged by evidence of progress, and their spontaneous comparison of the work will be the first step in the development of critical judgment.

SECOND WEEK. LESSON 1

"Take correct position. Show me how you hold your pencil. Hand on runners. Let us make the tree-tops. Ready. Write. 'To and fro,'" etc. "Now the swing. Ready. Write. 'How do you like,'" etc. "I want to show you a new exercise." Give Exercise 7, *e*. Make it a second time.

EXERCISE 7

The back of this letter should be nearly or quite straight. Call attention to this and have the children attempt to make it so, but do not emphasize a matter of form at this time to such an extent that it will lessen freedom of movement.

"Now you may write. Ready. Write." "How many swing 'way across the paper? Let's try it again. Ready. Write." "Did you keep the time better then?"

Review Exercises 3, 4, 5. Then write Exercise 7, *e*, again three times. The teacher should put all the work on the board first.

Lesson 2

"Position." Be sure it is good. Review Exercises 1, 2, 3, *i*, 4, *u*, 6, *it*. Show Exercise 7, *e*, again. "Ready. Write. Again. Ready. Write. We will put three of our exercises together. Look."

Give Exercise 8, *tie*. Make the crosses and dots on count also. "Ready. Write. Now cross the *t* and dot the *i*. Did you get the right time? Are your runners in place? Without writing, slide once. Ready. Slide. Now again, write this exercise." Give Exercise 8, *tie*. "Ready. Write."

EXERCISE 8

Here we have shortened the swing, though there is still more than is used in writing the word naturally. The gradual shortening of the swing is for the purpose of developing muscular control. Care should be taken to see that the movement is still free and does not become cramped in grasp of pencil or in ease of movement. The purpose of introducing the slide movement in the midst of the lesson is to emphasize to the children the need of free movement and so help to establish the habit.

Lesson 3

Give attention to position and to free swinging movement. Review Exercises 1, 2, 3, 4, 6, 7, 8.

The early ones are kept up for the sake of automatizing the free swinging forward movement. If done to count and attentively, one repetition of each exercise is enough when they have been in use for a week. Write Exercises 6 and 8 three or four times each.

"Look carefully. See if you can tell how what I put on the board is different from this" (Exercise 7, *e*). Give Exercise 9, *l*, *let*. "Yes, it is taller and its back is very straight."

EXERCISE 9

If it seems too difficult when the pupils try it first with a single count, the letter may be written first with a count for each downstroke as well as for the up-strokes. This helps to make the downstroke straight, but if the children get it right from the first, the other way is better. When the *l* has been practiced several times, have the children write the two letters *le* and then separate the groups and write *let*. Use voice count with all this work.

LESSON 4

Have Exercises 1, 2, written once each. Review Exercises 3, 7, 9, each two or three times. Now review Exercises 6 and 8.

"Next we will write this —" Put on the board with count Exercise 10, *little*, *tell*.

EXERCISE 10

Both of these words will be known to this grade. They should be given one at a time and some classes may use only one. If so, use the first, as it gives practice on more letters.

The reason for providing more than one word in an exercise which gives drill on the same letters and connections is to prevent a feeling of drudgery due to the frequent repetition of the same form. Fewer repetitions also promote sharp attention and hence rapid improvement. Be sure that the class keeps the swing and that the words are spaced wider than is natural so as to emphasize this.

LESSON 5

"Take clean paper. Position. Without writing, slide on your runners. Ready. Slide. One-two," etc. "Now, holding your pencil right and keeping on your runners, write your name, grade, and the date on the top line."

Use Exercises 1, 2, 3, 6, 7, 8, 9, 10. Exercises 8, 9, 10, should be written twice each. After these papers have been collected to keep for comparison, give practice on the exercises which are not so well automatized.

THIRD WEEK. LESSON 1

Review Exercises 1, 2, with rhymes.
Introduce the digits, Exercise 11, *1*, *2*.

EXERCISE 11   EXERCISE 12   EXERCISE 13

Second-grade children have had some experience in writing numbers so that the purpose here will be to correct figure forms and to confirm the habit of writing them correctly.

The figure *2* frequently gives trouble to children. Show how it is made, calling attention to the fact that practice is necessary to make it right. Make it several times with voice count and call for volunteers to make it on the board. Then have all write it.

Following this have the children write the two figures to count several times. Emphasize the need of care. Let each pick out his best, then try again. If time allows, review Exercise 9, 10.

LESSON 2

"What figures did we practice yesterday? Who can make the *2* well to-day? How many tried to make it well in the number work to-day?" Let several put it on the board and let others tell why it is good or how to do it better. "To-day we will study the *3* and see how much better we can make that." Give Exercise 12, *3*, *4*.

The *3* when well made makes parts of two circles. Show this to the children and let them complete the circles to test the correctness of their figures.

When this has been practiced carefully with the count several times, give the *4*. The difficulty children have here is to know where to begin. Call attention to the fact that first we make the two lines that make a corner, then cross the lower one with the one straight line. After practice, review the digits *1*, *2*, *3*, *4*, with count.

LESSON 3

Give Exercise 13, *5*. This figure presents special difficulty to children and is seldom made well without much practice. See that the vertical line is made first and that it is followed by a good curve, not by a flat back or a curve stopping at the base line. Then see that the horizontal line is added joining the vertical line. After practice have the children write the digits *1* to *5*.

Review Exercise 8, *tie*.

LESSON 4

As a review of Exercises 11, 12, 13, digits, write, to count, the following numbers in column:

$$2 \quad 4$$
$$5 \quad 3$$
$$3 \quad 1$$
$$1 \quad 5$$
$$4 \quad 3$$
$$2 \quad 5$$

When numbers are to be written in columns, it is very important that the children should be shown how to do it correctly and that they be required to do it so thereafter in all such work.

When writing numbers in a column, each number should be separated from the number above it by a distance equal to one half the height of the figures. The columns corresponding to the different orders — units, tens, hundreds — should be separated by a space equal to the width of the figures.

The importance of attention to this from the beginning and all the time lies in the fact that correct column placing of figures has been found to increase the accuracy of computation.

Review Exercises 9, 10, 6, 8.

Lesson 5

"Take clean paper." Have the preliminary swing for limbering up before writing the name, grade, and date.

For this week's sheet write Exercises 6, 8, 9, 10.

Write, in columns four deep, combinations of any two of the five digits practiced this week, placing them on the page like addition examples.

Fourth Week.   Lesson 1

Review Exercise 9, *l.* "To-day we shall have another letter much like this, but ending differently."

Give Exercise 14, *b.*

EXERCISE 14

This exercise introduces a new element in the final stroke. In the count there is a pause at the turn just before the final stroke. See that the children get this point in listening to the count and then that they write it so in their practice. Alternate the *l* and the *b* in practice, after the beginning, to emphasize the difference. Use practice on digits *1* to *5* to break the practice on the letters so that it will not become thoughtless.

Lesson 2

Write Exercises 1, 2, swinging only half the way across the page instead of across the whole page.

Write Exercises 3, 4, 7, 9, lessening the swing so as to make two or three groups to the line according to the width of the paper. Be very sure that the swing is not lost in shortening it and that the hand really slides on the runners. This is far more important now than emphasis on correct form.

Review Exercise 14, *b.*   Give Exercise 15, *be.*

The connection between these letters needs attention. The connecting line must drop low enough so that the top of the *e* is not above the beginning of the connecting stroke. This combination

EXERCISE 15

is one which often presents much trouble to children. Call attention to the *right* way when first showing it, but do not mention the form that is not desired. This is a most important principle to follow at all times — emphasize what you wish done, disregard as much as possible what you wish left undone, only calling attention to it when it is necessary to break up bad habits.

LESSON 3

Give Exercise 16, *6, 7.* Neither of these digits presents special difficulty, the only common fault being a certain slovenliness in making them. The use of the count in writing them will help to give exactness to them and attention to the work should do the rest.

EXERCISE 16   EXERCISE 17

LESSON 4

Write Exercises 1, 2, with half-line swing.

Give Exercise 17, *8, 9.* The figure *8* is often found to be difficult for children. They "do not know where to begin" or they persistently turn the wrong way at the bottom. This necessitates careful explanation and attentive practice. See that the children begin first at the top and make first the curve to the left and down, returning with the straight slanting stroke.

The figure *9* commonly gives little trouble, but it is important to see that a well-formed figure is obtained.

Combine any two digits now in writing numbers in columns four deep. Be sure that the columns are correctly placed — units directly under units and tens under tens. Now is the time to form this habit that will be helpful later on.

LESSON 5

"Take clean paper." Note position and give preliminary swing. "Write name, grade, and date." Have written with short swing Exercises 1, 2, 3, 4, 7, 9, 10, 15.

Write four groups of numbers, tens and units, each group four deep. In this work see that all the digits are used and give more practice to the ones which are the most difficult.

SECOND MONTH. FIRST WEEK

Introduce the metronome. Sixty beats is suggested for the beginning. Determine the rate the class can follow easily and record it.

The introduction of the metronome to give the rate has two different purposes. It sets the teacher free to inspect and give suggestions to individual children. It gives an absolutely regular beat for a continuous period such as is not possible with the teacher's voice. Also it makes possible the definite determination of the rate to be used at a given time and the increase of the speed in a systematic way.

If a metronome cannot be obtained for use, the voice count should be regulated so as to follow the rates in the lessons as accurately as possible.

LESSON 1

Review with long swing Exercises 3, 4, 7, 9. Then give each with short swing. Begin each new exercise this week with voice count and rather slowly. After the first day give it with the metronome.

EXERCISE 18

Give Exercise 18, *a*. Notice particularly that the stroke does not turn down at the top. Call attention to this and see that it is kept level in this swinging exercise. It is better to let it go up a little than down at all. A good swing will help to accomplish this.

Review Exercises 6, 8, 10. Mix in more practice on Exercise 18, so as not to use it continuously enough to encourage carelessness. Call attention to the fact that this is a word by itself. Give Exercise 19, *a tie* (combining Exercises 8 and 18).

EXERCISE 19

LESSON 2

Use the metronome as set in Lesson 1 all the week. Remember that position is all-important.

Review Exercises 1, 2.   Then Exercises 18, 19.
Give Exercise 20, *at*, *eat*, *all*, *ball*.

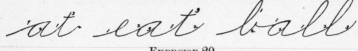

EXERCISE 20

Not all these words need be used, but after *at* is written, it is comparatively easy to write *eat*, and after *all* is written, a review of Exercise 14, *b*, should precede the writing of *ball*.   Write several lines keeping exactly to count.   If there is trouble in doing this, write the exercise on the board several times while the class listens to the metronome as they watch.   They will soon get the idea.

LESSON 3

Practice on the numbers *10* to *19*, giving drill on any digit that occasions trouble.

Review Exercises 10, 15.   Review Exercise 20, writing *eat* and *ball* at least three times each.   Review Exercise 19.

Give Exercise 21, *d*.   "Notice how much like *a* this is.   What is the difference?"   (The extension of the second up-stroke.)   Notice

EXERCISE 21

that this is made in the same time as the corresponding stroke of the *a*, but that it is made faster.

LESSON 4

Write Exercises 1, 2, half-line swing.   Review Exercises 21, 18. Alternate these two, joining them.   Review Exercise 14, *b*.

Give Exercise 22, *bad*, *did*.   Call attention to the swing between *b* and *a* that does not touch the line.   Write several lines.   Give

EXERCISE 22

close attention to the metronome.   Review Exercise 20, using the parts not used last time.   If there is more time, practice the numbers *10* to *19* in column formation.

LESSON 5

Be sure that the writing is with the metronome. "Take clean paper. Practice the slide without writing. Write name, grade, date." Have the numbers *10* to *19* written at the left of the paper in column. Give Exercises 18, 19, 20, 21, 22, one or two lines as paper permits.

After these papers are collected, review Exercises 20, 21, 22, or give the time to the practice of names.

SECOND WEEK

Be sure to keep the time. Note the holding of the pencil and see that it is right.

LESSON 1

Review Exercises 3, 4, long swing, twice each. Review Exercises 6, 9, 14, 18. Give Exercise 23, *o*.

EXERCISE 23

Here is another letter that has the bridge connection. Do not forget to pause at the turn before making the finishing stroke as in the *b*. Do this in your own writing and see that the children do so. Practice these exercises, changing from one to another to prevent fatigue, or carelessness, and direct the children's attention to the improvement that they make in the practice.

LESSON 2

Review Exercises 21, 23, 9. Give Exercise 24, *do, to, old, told*. Emphasize the straightness of the down-stroke of the *l*. The con-

EXERCISE 24

nection of the *o* and the *l* is somewhat difficult. It should be nearly a straight line as the cross on the *l* should be opposite the top of the *o*. These two letters may need practice together. Be sure the children understand the count and keep with the metronome.

LESSON 3

Review Exercise 24, *old, told*, with good swing and position. Let the children try to see where their work is better to-day than yesterday. Self-criticism which takes the form of searching for the best is very important. If the children give attention to their best production and try hard, they are bound to improve.

Review Exercises 3, 4. Give Exercise 25, *w.* "See how much this exercise is like the two we have just practiced. Where is it different? Yes, in the last stroke. What kind of a stroke is it?"

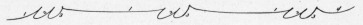

EXERCISE 25

(A bridge connection.) "What other letters have this stroke?" (*b, o.*) Make each of these a few times so that they will have in mind the pause on the sharp turn. "Now let us make the *w.* Everybody ready. Ready. Write."

After practice give Exercise 26, *we.* This is difficult because the connecting stroke must be dropped so that the top of the *e* will not be higher than the top of the *w.* It is a common mistake with children to make the *e* too high. Review Exercise 15, *be,* and call attention to this. Then practice *be, we,* for the remainder of the period with special attention to the connecting stroke.

EXERCISE 26   EXERCISE 27

LESSON 4

Write Exercises 1, 2, half-line swing. Review Exercise 26. Write it three or four times with the metronome. Give Exercise 27, *will.* Here we have again the same type of connection, but not quite so difficult because there is no loop necessitating the dropping of the line. Review Exercises 6, 24. Then write Exercise 28, *we will do it.*

EXERCISE 28

LESSON 5

"Take clean paper. Use free swing before writing. Let us try to write our names better than ever before. Write name, grade, and date." Give Exercises 24, 26, 27, 28. Let the children mark by underscoring what they think the best production of each exercise.

THIRD WEEK

Retain the metronome at 60 this week.

LESSON 1

Review Exercises 3, 4, long swing, twice each. Review Exercises 10, 18, 20, then write them together, *a little ball.*

Such phrase work in writing is preliminary to sentence writing. It is given for the purpose of having the children become accustomed to writing in context and so begin to get a feeling for sentence structure. It is believed that the carrying out of this plan will be a help to written composition in giving training in the mechanics of writing separate from the development of thought content.

Review Exercise 18. "To-day we shall take a new letter much like this. See if you can tell me what is different about it." Give Exercise 29, *c*. "Yes, the top of this letter *does* turn down. Notice

EXERCISE 29

the count carefully and see how many can make it right the first time."

Give practice on the two exercises, comparing them carefully so that the children will make the top of the *c* turn down. The *c* may be made either with the rounded top or the loop. The latter seems to make it a little easier to get the count.

LESSON 2

Review Exercises 18, 19, 24, *old*. Give Exercise 30, *cold*. Insist that the connecting line between the *o* and *l* be made right. It will be necessary to watch this. Review Exercise 22, *bad*, *did*.

EXERCISE 30　　　　　　　EXERCISE 31

LESSON 3

See that the hand is in good position. Review Exercise 18. Call attention to the top which keeps the upward movement. Review Exercises 29, 30. Give Exercise 31, *ice*. Write Exercise 32, *a cold ice ball*.

EXERCISE 32

LESSON 4

Review Exercise 20, *all*, *ball*. Review Exercise 29, *c*. Give Exercise 33, *call*. Review Exercise 28. Write Exercise 34, *we will*

EXERCISE 33

eat a little ice. It may be necessary to review some of these words alone before combining them.

we will eat a

little ice we

EXERCISE 34

Notice that frequent reviews of the old exercises are given, but in combinations such that a new interest is added. It is not expected that perfection will be reached with the first practice. Indeed, too long continued practice at one time may result in establishing a bad habit when frequently recurring short periods of practice will result in improvement. This agrees with the known principle that there is a tendency to variation in performance in acts of skill, and that the elements stressed and approved in successive periods of practice will tend to become fixed in time, in contrast to the faults which occur from time to time, but are disregarded.

LESSON 5

"Take clean paper. Give free limbering swing without writing, pencil held loosely. Write name, grade, date." By this time a good position should be maintained in writing these. Write Exercises 28, 30, 31, 32, 33, 34, writing the phrases in succession along the lines instead of in the old-style "copy-book" form. Write all phrases and sentences in this arrangement.

FOURTH WEEK. LESSON 1

Take time to-day to compare the papers written the first Friday with those written last Friday. Let each child see his two papers together and notice the improvement himself. The improvement may be in lightness of line, or in regularity of line, in regularity of slant, in keeping to the base line. The children may also make note of their success in making all *a*'s and *d*'s stay up at the top even though these letters did not appear in the first sheet. Ask the class to see how often they have kept the letters on the base line. Suggest that this week they try to do that especially. If there is more time, clinch this by practice. Review Exercises 28, 32. See if all the bridge connections are made right. Then increase the metronome to 63 and review Exercises 10, 15, 20, in part or whole as seems best.

LESSON 2

Review Exercise 9, *l.* "Our new exercise to-day is like this, but has something added. I will make it here." Give Exercise 35, *f, of.* "What is added?" (The loop below the base line.) Always

EXERCISE 35

write the exercise on the board enough times to make sure that there is no trouble about the time. "Let us make six *l*'s. Ready. Write." Make the count right. "Now see how I change these *l*'s into *f*'s." Add the loop. "You may do so with your six *l*'s. What kind of a line is the long down-stroke?" (Straight.) "On which side are the two curves?" (Right side.) "Where is the cross? Where does the closing come?" Questioning in such a way as to require the children to discover these points is more likely to result in success than telling them how the letter is made.

Review Exercise 24, *old.* "Notice the connection between *o* and *l.* We must make it just the same between *o* and *f.* Look as I write it." Give Exercise 35, *of.* "Now you may write it. Ready. Write." Keep up the preciseness of command in starting as it tends to encourage regularity and attention to the work.

LESSON 3

Review Exercise 20, *all, ball,* and Exercise 33, *call.* Give Exercise 36, *fall, if.* After practice give Exercise 37, *a bad fall,* and Exercise 38, *a little ball of ice.*

EXERCISE 36

EXERCISE 37

Write these in continuous arrangement. Whenever difficulty in rhythm is found, give practice on the word alone. Pay attention only to the most noticeable points of letter formation — the straight backs, the top of the *a* and the *d* kept up, the curved top of *c*, the connecting stroke of *b*, *o*, and *w*. We must first get relatively good position and freedom of movement.

LESSON 4

"Show me your position." Review Exercises 18, *a*, 35, *f*.
"I will show you a new exercise that is like parts of these." Give Exercise 39, *q*. Discuss as heretofore the likenesses and

EXERCISE 39

differences and allow the children to construct the letter from each of the others by the addition of the necessary parts and erasing what is not needed. Then have the children write *q* with the metronome.

EXERCISE 40

Give Exercise 40, *quiet*. After a little practice on this, take single words from Exercises 22, 24, 38, and write them with the metronome at 66.

This is the first attempt to increase the speed of familiar exercises much beyond that at which the new exercises are written. It is the beginning of *speed drills* which will be given from time to time, but which must never be taken at a rate sufficient to disorganize the rhythmic movement.

LESSON 5

"Take clean papers." Preliminary swing. "Let's try to keep exactly on the line, exactly with the metronome, and in perfect position to-day. Write name, grade, and date." Give Exercises 35, 36, 37, 38, 39, 40, writing Exercises 37, 38, twice each.

Give Exercise 41, *we will be quiet*.

THIRD MONTH. FIRST WEEK

During the first two months we have studied twelve of the small letters. Most of the emphasis has been placed on the forward swing and on rhythm. The class should begin now to show some effects of this in freedom of movement.

We shall try now to gain some degree of control that will lead to better alinement, but this must be acquired so gradually as not to interfere with freedom of movement. We shall study more of the small letters and begin with some of the capitals. Please remember that position, freedom of movement and rhythm are the important things.

Lesson 1

Review Exercises 1, 2, half-line swing with rhyme. Be sure the work is done with a free swing and suggest that the arm be allowed to touch the desk instead of being carried in the air. In Grade 1 the whole arm movement is allowed. In this grade, if the children still use it, little should be said about it while they are getting started, but by this time it is worth while to encourage the children to keep the arm resting on the desk. For this free swing the metronome may be set at 72. For other work the metronome should be set at 66, except that, as always, a slower rate is used when giving a new exercise.

Review Exercise 18. "We will take another exercise like this. See." Give Exercise 42, *A*. "What is different about this?"

EXERCISE 42

(The size.) "Yes, it is twice as high and here we count on the down-stroke." Show it again. After writing it yourself send several to the board to write it while the class counts. "Now you may try it. Ready. Write."

"Let us write this." Give Exercise 43, *A ball of ice*. Notice that here and in some of the following exercises, the count is on the down-stroke on some of the letters. In general when the first count is on the down-stroke, a half count is lost between the capital and the first small letter.

Lesson 2

Give Exercise 44, *m*. Call attention to the three curves and the fact that all the down-strokes are parallel. Have it written several

EXERCISE 44

times with the metronome. Then give Exercise 45, *me, come*. Call attention to the joining of *o* and *m* and to the fact that *m* has

three down-strokes. "Now we will write some of our old exercises,
but will begin them with capitals."

Review Exercise 42, *A*. Give Exercise 46, *Am, At, All*.

me come me

EXERCISE 45

Am At All

EXERCISE 46

LESSON 3

Review Exercise 44, *m*, making the swing so that two groups can
be written on one line; metronome at 72. Give Exercise 47, *n*.

n n n

EXERCISE 47

Call attention to the difference here, there being only two curves.
Give Exercise 48, *an, and, can, in, man*. These need not all be
given unless needed for variety. Write *an* with a capital *A*.

and can in

an man

EXERCISE 48

LESSON 4

Review Exercise 45. Give Exercise 49, *came, mile*. Call attention to the likeness of *come* and *came*. Give Exercise 50, *men, nice,*

came mile

EXERCISE 49

men nice

noon not an

EXERCISE 50

no, noon, not, on. All these words need not be used, but in the course of the review of this exercise all the words should be given. Take pains with the connecting strokes, and see that the children distinguish clearly the difference between *n* and *m*.

Lesson 5

"Take clean paper. Free swing without writing. Write name, grade, and date." Use the metronome at 66 for all work to-day. Write Exercises 43, 45, 46, 48, 49, 50, selecting words from each exercise.

Second Week. Lesson 1

Review Exercise 42, *A.* Give the names of children beginning with this letter as in Exercise 51, *Anna, Agnes, Alden.* Review Exercise 50. Use a good swing, metronome at 72.

Exercise 51

If more work is wanted, give words not previously used from review exercises.

Lesson 2

"To-day we are going to have a letter that begins like the *n*, but is different from any letter we have had yet. Look carefully as I write it." Give Exercise 52, *z*, being careful to write with the metronome.

Exercise 52   Exercise 53

Use the metronome at 66. Let the children notice this letter carefully and then write it and compare with the copy. Practice two lines, and then let each find the best he has made.

Give Exercise 53, *buzz.* Call attention to the *b.* See that the lower part is not closed.

Lesson 3

Give four groups of numbers in columns four deep, as for addition, using numbers from *20* to *50.* If the children can add these numbers, allow them to do so and be sure that they place the *hundreds* in a separate column. Do not spend too much time on this. They may add with you at the board and copy the answer.

Review Exercise 18, *a*, and Exercise 52, *z*. Give Exercise 54, *g*. "How is this like *a?* How like *z?* Where shall we cross the line in the stem? Let us see if we can write it correctly. Are you sure you know the count?"

EXERCISE 54

If any one is not sure of the count, give it again before it is written by the class, then give the signal for all to write.

LESSON 4

Review Exercise 54, *g*. Give Exercise 55, *go, gold, good.* Give one at a time, then use them interchangeably to avoid monotony. If more work is wanted, review the other exercises containing the letters *o l d* — *old, cold, fold,* and add *bold*.

EXERCISE 55

LESSON 5

"Take clean paper. Write name, grade, and date." Give Exercises 51, 52, 53, 54, 55.

After papers are collected have the pupils write numbers in columns, *1* to *50*, with the metronome, spacing carefully between groups and between the numbers in each group.

THIRD WEEK. LESSON 1

Set the metronome at 66 this week. If there is time to review older exercises than those mentioned below, use the metronome for them at 72. Review Exercises 54, 55, one line of each. Give Exercise 56, *big, get, glad, long.*

EXERCISE 56

The bridge connection here should cause no difficulty now. Be sure the *b* is correctly made and that the first strokes of the *g*, *a*, and *d* tend upward.

Lesson 2

"To-day we will study another capital letter. Perhaps you will know some name which begins with it. Notice it carefully." Give Exercise 57, *E*. Call attention to the resemblance of this letter to two circles interlocked. Let the pupils make the letter slowly without paying any attention to the time and finish the circles to see if it is correct. Then show them the rhythm by writing it with the metronome several times. Let them write half a dozen *E*'s with the metronome and then stop and see if they can complete the circles. Write the name of any child beginning with *E*.

EXERCISE 57   EXERCISE 58

Lesson 3

Review Exercises 9, *l*, 47, *n*. "Our new exercise is like these two." Give Exercise 58, *h*, *he*. Show that it combines the other two, and see that the loop is crossed just halfway up and the lower part makes a sharp angle with the stem, but does not retrace far.

To help the children they may construct the letter from both the *l* and the *n* by erasing the part not needed and adding in each case the part of the other that makes the letter *h*. When this is clear and they have practiced it, give the word *he*.

Lesson 4

Review Exercise 58, *h*. Give Exercise 59, *hand, hat, home*. Give particular care to the making of the *h*. Write names of the children in class beginning with the capitals studied, *A, E*.

EXERCISE 59

Lesson 5

To-day compare the work done last Friday with the work done on the first Friday of the second month; that is, after the first comparison. Lead the children to see improvements. Do not emphasize what should not be. Is the slant more regular? Is the line more even? Find letters that look better than before. If there is an inclination on the part of the children to try over some of their work to do it better, encourage them to do so.

FOURTH WEEK

Set the metronome at 66 for the beginning. Then try 72. The work this week should be in the nature of a review without the children's being conscious of it. We shall have all new exercises, but no new elements. Are you watching position carefully all the time? Keep the work exactly with the metronome. Try to have it on the base line.

LESSON 1

Give Exercise 60, *how*, *the*, and Exercise 61, *go get the little ball*.

EXERCISE 60

LESSON 2

Give Exercise 62, *what*, *with*, and Exercise 63, *what did he do?*

EXERCISE 62

LESSON 3

Give Exercise 64, *come with me*, and Exercise 65, *Eat a little ice with me.*

LESSON 4

Give Exercise 66, *hand me the little ball*, and Exercise 67, *how can he do it?*

LESSON 5

The work done to-day is to be graded. Put on the sheet first the heading: Full Name, Age, Grade, Date. Then give the two-minute test as directed on page 8, using the same verse as before. Be sure to follow the directions for this. Do *not* use the metronome for this two-minute test.

Then either below this or on the other side of the paper write with the metronome at 72, Exercises 63, 64, 65.

Fourth Month. First Week

It is desirable all the year in this grade to give much work on new exercises on the board. It is important that, as the class becomes used to the method and writes with some speed with the metronome, they do not neglect proper position. The children have sometimes been told in this grade that the little finger is the drum-major and must lead the procession. Any device to help them remember is allowable.

Lesson 1

Set the metronome at 72. Review Exercise 42, *A*. Give Exercise 68, *C*. Have the children notice how much alike these letters

Exercise 68   Exercise 69

are. After practice give Exercise 69, *O*, which is very much the same. Then practice any names which begin with these letters.

Lesson 2

Review Exercises 59, 42, 68, 69. Give Exercise 70, *p*. The *p* may be made either open or closed, but the teacher should decide which form to use, as in this grade all should be made alike.

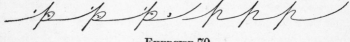

Exercise 70

Give Exercise 71, *help*, *open*. The joining of the *o* and *p* is the only point which may give trouble.

Exercise 71

Lesson 3

Review Exercises 42, 57, 68, 69, using any names which have been practiced. Call attention to the peculiarities of each capital. Some second grades may do better to omit part of the work. The teacher should use her judgment here. The aim is to give enough variety so that there will not be repetition enough to make the work irksome.

There should be constant vigilance on the part of the teacher to see that an easy position is maintained and a free rhythmic movement used.

Lesson 4

Give Exercise 72, B, Ben. This is especially difficult. See that the children have a right idea of the form and that they criticize their own work. The writing of the name may help to give interest.

EXERCISE 72

Lesson 5

"Take clean paper. Write name, grade, and date." Use the metronome for this. Give Exercises 68, 69, 71, 72.

After these papers are collected, allow each child to write his own name with the metronome. Show those whose names begin with capitals not yet practiced how to write their names with the metronome. Arouse much pride in writing their names as well as possible.

SECOND WEEK. Lesson 1

Set the metronome at 72. Review Exercise 72, B. Write names of any children which begin with B.

Give Exercise 73, y, day. Here we combine the last part of the n and the stem of the g. Let the children recognize such likenesses wherever they can, as it helps to fix ideas of form. Give the word day after practice of the letter.

EXERCISE 73

Lesson 2

Review Exercise 73. Give Exercise 74, away, boy, my, may. If there is time to practice all of these, give them in connected sequence, my boy may go away.

EXERCISE 74

Lesson 3

"Our new exercise will be different from any we have had. I will write it here." Give Exercise 75, *I*. Let the children tell where it begins and in what direction it goes. Then write it again showing the time carefully. Give Exercise 76, *I will tell the boy to come.*

EXERCISE 75   EXERCISE 77

Lesson 4

"To-day we shall write a letter very much like the one we wrote yesterday." Review Exercise 75, *I*. Give Exercise 77, *J*. Notice that both curved lines cross the straight line at the same place, that the back is perfectly straight, and that the curves are on the same side of the straight line. See that the children get these points and practice carefully. Write any name beginning with *J*.

Lesson 5

Have the children take clean papers and write name, grade, and date, with the metronome at 72. Give Exercises 72, 75, 77, with some names.

After papers are collected, dictate sentences having some interest for the children and using material practiced. Names may be used beginning sentences, or words which have been practiced may be begun with capitals where they have been studied.

Third Week.   Lesson 1

Review Exercises 70, *p*, 73, *y*, *day*. Use the metronome at 80 for this.

Give Exercise 78, *happy*, *play*, *to-day*. Be sure the slant is right. Give Exercise 79, *I will play and be happy to-day*. If there is more time review Exercise 76.

happy play

EXERCISE 78

Lesson 2

Give Exercise 80, *s* swing. This is given in Grade 1 with the rhyme,

Seesaw, Margery Daw,
Up and down we go.

If it seems desirable, it may be given so first here instead of with the metronome. The advantage of this exercise is to give with the free swinging movement the right slant to the *s*. The letter has too

EXERCISE 80   **EXERCISE 81**

often an ugly appearance due to standing too nearly upright or too nearly horizontal. The same imagery suggested in Grade 1 may be used here if it seems to help.

Give Exercise 81, *s*, using the same time as for Exercise 80 whether the rhyme is used or not. See that the children get a definite swinging motion into the down-stroke.

LESSON 3

Review Exercises 80, 81. Give Exercise 82, *as*, *has*, *is*, *his*, *say*, *see*, *side*, *sit*, *some*, *song*, *she*, *this*, *was*, *yes*. It is not expected that

EXERCISE 82

all these words will be given at this time. The words given are those which occur in Courtis's 100 per cent spelling list [1] for Grade 2B, in which *s* is used with such other letters as have been previously practiced.

EXERCISE 83

LESSON 4

Review Exercise 81. Give Exercise 83, *r*. Call special attention to the time and to the likeness to the *s*. The point extending above

[1] S. A. Courtis: *Teaching Spelling by Plays and Games.*

the first space is likely to give trouble. These two letters are the only one-space letters which have a point above the first space. There is a perceptible pause at the top of the letter. The second stroke in this letter is the one particular difficulty. See that it is not merely a part of the down-stroke.

Give Exercise 84, *after, are, bring, dear, door, for, her, mother, near, or, our, poor, ran, read, red, ride, ring, run, sister, spring, story, three, train, tree, yard, tour.* The source of the words is the same as

EXERCISE 84

in Exercise 82. The idea is that the teacher shall select from these words for practice and in reviewing this exercise give other words for variety.

Give Exercise 85, *A dear little boy ran after my sister.*

Lesson 5

"Take clean paper. Write name, grade, and date." Give Exercises 78, 81, part of 82 that has been practiced, and 85.

If there is more time, give other words from Exercises 82, 84.

Fourth Week. Lesson 1

Set the metronome at 72. Give Exercise 86, *M*.

Call attention by question to the number of curves and to the fact that each is not quite so tall as the one before it. Then give

EXERCISE 86   EXERCISE 87

the signal for writing. Keep the formal signal for beginning and catch the metronome time in giving it. This week the metronome will be at 72 for all work.

Write the names of any children beginning with *M*.   Write *May* with the capital.

Give Exercise 87, *N*, letting the children see the slight difference and compare the two.   Give any names beginning with this also.

LESSON 2

Review Exercise 72, *B*.   Give Exercise 88, *P*, *Paul*.   Let the children make three *B*'s and erase the lower curve.   This gives

EXERCISE 88

the *P*.   Give the word *Paul*.   Give Exercise 89, *Paul can see his little red ball.*

The use of these sentences is especially to give practice in context writing, and proper spacing instead of putting the words in columns or squeezing more than is desirable on a line.

Give part of Exercise 84 not yet practiced.

LESSON 3

Review Exercises 86, *M*, 87, *N*.   Give Exercise 90, *W*, *Will*. This is different from the two reviewed because after the first stroke all the turns are sharp instead of round, and the second stroke comes above the first, but the last stroke is lower than any other and is slightly curved.

Have numbers written in good column form from copy and from dictation, using any of the numbers *1* to *99*.

EXERCISE 90   EXERCISE 91

LESSON 4

Review Exercises 9, *l*, 58, *h*.   "We are going to take a letter somewhat like both of these, but different.   Notice it carefully."

Give Exercise 91, *k*.   "There are two things we must remember about this letter; the cross comes just opposite the top of the low part; the round part must be tiny and leave a gateway opening into the *garden.*"

Notice that the two down-strokes of the *k* are parallel.   Call attention to this.   Give Exercise 92, *kind, book, look, thank, think.* These will probably not all be used the first day.   After practicing a word it will be well to go back to the practice of the letter *k* alone, writing it three or four times, then trying the word again and comparing to see if it is improved.

kind book look

thank think

EXERCISE 92

LESSON 5

"Take clean paper. Write name, grade, and date." Give Exercises 86, 87, 88, 89, 90, and parts of Exercise 92 that have been practiced.

When papers have been collected, give parts of Exercises 82, 84, not yet practiced and give Exercise 93, *Bring my ring to our mother*.

See that proper form for context writing is preserved.

FIFTH MONTH.   FIRST WEEK

The year is nearly half gone. The class has had all the small letters except *j*, *v*, and *x*, and twelve of the capitals. Possibly some of the others have been used by the class incidentally. We shall finish the introduction of the letters this month in preparation for drills for automatization of rhythm, movement, and form, to occupy the rest of the year.

LESSON 1

For four weeks the metronome has been used at 72. Begin now to use it at 80. Review Exercises 87, *N*, 90, *W*. "Our new exercise begins just like these, but is different after the first stroke."

Give Exercise 94, *Z*. "The last part is just like the small *z*. Let us practice that." (Exercise 52.) Then let them write the capital *Z*, being sure that they keep the time. If they have trouble with the form, let them make the first stroke half a dozen times and then add the rest of the letter. If this is done, they should then trace these to get the feeling of the continuous movement in making the letter. If any child's name begins with this letter, write it.

EXERCISE 94   **EXERCISE 95**

LESSON 2

Review Exercise 73, *y*. Have several of these made on the board and then suggest that the first up-stroke and the first down-stroke be erased. "Does any one know what letter we have now? Yes, *j*." Give Exercise 95, *j*, and have them write it. Then give Exercise 96, *jump*.

jump jump

EXERCISE 96

LESSON 3

Show Exercise 86, *M*. Have the class write it. "Who can write another letter that begins like this?" Have it put on the board, letting several do it until you get *M, N, W, Z*, on the board. "Let us write each of these six times seeing how well we can make them and keeping in exact time." "There is another letter which begins just like these. Look." Give Exercise 97, *Q*. "You may all try it now. Ready. Write." Be sure they understand the time. Review Exercise 40, *quiet*. Then give it with the capital *Q*.

EXERCISE 97   **EXERCISE 98**

LESSON 4

"To-day we have still another letter that begins as the *M* does." Give Exercise 98, *Y*. "What does the last part look like?" (A tall *j*.) "Watch again while I write it. Can you write it now? Ready. Write."

Give Exercise 99, *You, You may go*. Give the word alone first, then the sentence.

Y You may go

EXERCISE 99

LESSON 5

"Take clean paper. Write name, grade, date." Give all the exercises practiced this week. If these do not fill the sheet, use some of the names which have been practiced.   Use extra time for individual practice on names, each writing his own with the metronome.   Try to see how much improvement can be made on these before the next test is given.

Second Week.   Lesson 1

Begin each lesson this week with a free swing to emphasize its use in writing.

Review Exercises 72, *B*, and 88, *P*.   Then give Exercise 100, *R*, *Ruth*.   Let the children make it just like the *P* and then add the

EXERCISE 100

last stroke.   If some child's name begins with *R*, use it instead of *Ruth*.   Give Exercise 101, *Ruth, come to see me.*

Lesson 2

Give free swing.   Give four groups of numbers in columns four deep keeping correct form and good spacing.

Give Exercise 102, *L*.   Here is a letter different from any we have practiced and nearly all curves.   It will be hard for the children to get.   If the down-stroke is nearly or quite straight, it need not be criticized, though it will tend to take a little curve if it is practiced to count. Give it several times; compare, each finding his best; have it written again.

Give Exercise 103, *Let Ruth go with you.*

EXERCISE 102   EXERCISE 104

Lesson 3

Review Exercises 47, *n*, and 14, *b*.   The new letter to-day combines parts of these.   Give Exercise 104, *v*.

Practice carefully calling attention to the pause before the connecting stroke.   "What other letters are like this?"   (*b, o, w*.) "Let us write one line of each and see if we can make the pause every time."   Give Exercise 105, *brown vine*, which includes them all.

EXERCISE 105

LESSON 4

Review Exercise 104. Give Exercise 106, *five, give, gave, have, seven.* Here we have enough different letters to discover on what

five give gave have seven five

the children need drill. If the needs differ, different children may work on their own problems until they feel that they have improved. Do not make it drudgery.

LESSON 5

"Take clean paper. Write names, grade, date." Give Exercises 100, 101, 103, 105, 106.

For further review give any name exercises or write numbers.

THIRD WEEK. LESSON 1

Continue the metronome this week at 80. Review exercises may be written at 92, if the teacher finds it is best. Call attention to the time and to the slant. "To-day we are going to have a queer letter. It looks like a sawhorse."

Give Exercise 107, *x.* The first part is like the last part of the *n.* The cross should cut the down-stroke in the middle.

EXERCISE 107   EXERCISE 108

Give Exercise 108, *box, six.* Give Exercise 109, *Ben gave his sister six balls in a box.*

LESSON 2

Review Exercise 81, *s,* giving a good swing. Give Exercise 110,

EXERCISE 110

Show how much like the small *s* it is by erasing the top.　This will be nearly as hard as the *L*, but it is not best to connect these in the child's mind as they are not enough alike to help and he may become confused.

Unless *S* is used in the name of some child, give the words *See*, *She*, already written, beginning them with capitals.

Give Exercise 111, *She will give Jane a little ice.*　Use a name which needs practice.

LESSON 3

Give Exercise 112, *G, Go.*　The count on this is very important as it marks the units of the letter so definitely.　Keep the count

EXERCISE 112

exactly and let the class count it as you write.　Then have them practice, criticize, and practice again.

Give Exercise 113, *Go get Pearl a little red ball.*

LESSON 4

Review Exercises 110, 112.　"Our new capital to-day is easier than these.　It is somewhat like some others we have written."

Give Exercise 114, *H.*　"Notice the way I tie the two lines together."　Let the children tell what other letters begin this way.

EXERCISE 114

Write it again.　After the children have practiced so as to have a little facility, give Exercise 115, *How, How do you do?*　Give the word alone first, then the sentence.

EXERCISE 115

LESSON 5

"Take clean paper.　Write name, grade, date."　Write Exercises 107, 109, 110, 111, 113, 115.　Review similar capitals, as *A, O, C; M, N, W, Z, Q;* as time permits.

FOURTH WEEK.   LESSON 1

Review Exercise 114, *H*.   Give Exercise 116, *K*.   Let the children see how much alike these two letters are.   This letter is likely to give trouble and the teacher may be satisfied with crude results at first if the work is done right.   Call attention to the fact that the

K.   *Keep the ball*

EXERCISE 116   **EXERCISE 117**

second stroke touches the first at about the middle.   Have the children try to get this.   Improvement will come with ease of writing through keeping the time.   Give the name of any child or other name the children need to write that begins with a *K*.

Give Exercise 117, *Keep, Keep the ball I gave you.*

LESSON 2

Give four groups of numbers four deep from the numbers *100* to *200*.   See that they are written correctly in columns.

Give Exercise 118, *D*.   Relate this letter to the *L*, as it has the

D   D   D   D   D

EXERCISE 118

same loop at the base line.   See that this curve is correct.   The letter will require considerable practice.   Use the capital for names.

Give Exercise 119, *Did, Did you see David?*

Did you see David?

EXERCISE 119

LESSON 3

Give to-day Exercise 120, *F, T*.   These are not like any other letters, but can be learned together, as they are so much alike.   The

F F F F F F

EXERCISE 120

first stroke must not be too long and the down-stroke on its curve extends farther to the left than the first stroke.   Let the children practice the two and then practice any names which come from the class.

Give Exercise 121, *The, Fred, The boy saw Fred come this way.*

The Fred The

boy saw Fred

come this way

EXERCISE 121

LESSON 4

Give Exercise 122, *U.* "What other letters begin like this?" Have them named, but not written now. "Notice it is like the *Y*

U U Union

EXERCISE 122

because its second stroke is shorter than the first." Give Exercise 123, *Union.*

"Here is another letter that begins in the same way and is much like the *U.*" Give Exercise 124, *V.*

V V V V V

EXERCISE 124

If this is approximately right without the compound curves, be satisfied.

Give Exercise 125, *Very, Very many boys play here.*

Very Very many

boys play here

EXERCISE 125

Lesson 5

"Take clean paper. Write name, grade, date." Give Exercises 114, 116, 118, 119, 120, 121, 122, 123, 124, 125.

The letters are given separately because it seems desirable to have the children practice them before combining them in words. It calls attention to them more definitely.

Sixth Month

For the first two weeks of this month we shall review some of the letters, introducing words which come in the grade list for the second half of the year. We shall follow here the same order of introducing the words as was followed at first in presentation of the letter exercises.

First Week. Lesson 1

Review Exercises 14, *b*, 18, *a*, 21, *d*. Give Exercise 126, *blue, but, table*, Exercise 127, *late, bed*, and Exercise 128, *I go to bed late.*

Give the words one at a time and have the children practice them several times with the metronome. A little practice with careful attention is better than much heedless practice. A child cannot attend to the same thing long. Therefore change the exercise and return to it later on. Set the metronome at 92.

Lesson 2

Review Exercises 23, *o*, 25, *w*, 29, *c*, 35, *f*. Give Exercise 129, *blow, two, face, foot, full, time*, using these letters. Remember all belong to the 100 per cent spelling list for Grade 2A.

The chief need for spelling is in writing, therefore these writing exercises should help to habituate the correct spelling of the words. It is not necessary to call the children's attention to the fact that these are spelling words, but the teacher should take account of it and use all the advantage that comes from it.

Give Exercise 130, *Blow two times on Ned's horn.*

Lesson 3

Review Exercise 47, *n*. Give Exercise 131, *an, cent, clean, down, end, fine, mine, name, new, ten, went.* It is not expected that all of these will be practiced in one period. Select those containing letters on which the children need more practice; for example, *fine*, for the *f*. When the exercise is reviewed, use words not written before until all have been used.

Lesson 4

Review some of this week's work which has given difficulty or write parts of exercises not yet used. Then give the sentence, Exercise 132, *Little John has a ten cent foot-ball to play with.*

LESSON 5

"Take clean papers. Write name, grade, date." Give all sentence exercises written this week.

Then pass out the papers written a month ago. Let the children make comparisons, always discovering where they have made improvement. If they find this hard to do, point out to them some improvement. Then suggest that each one find something on his old paper that he can write better now and let him prove it by writing a line or two.

SECOND WEEK. LESSON 1

Some one has said, "Success is too valuable a tonic for us to invite failure by fault-finding." This is very true with the children's work. Always call attention to the good. If necessary to point out a mistake, do it in immediate contrast to the right form and with the emphasis on that.

Review Exercise 54, *g*. Give Exercise 133, *coming, game, got.* Give Exercise 134, *Arthur is coming to play a game of ball with you.*

Do not allow the writing to be cramped in order to put more than is desirable on a line. The column form of writing looks neater, but does not give the training in the form which ordinary business and social usage requires.

LESSON 2

Review Exercise 58, *h*. Give Exercise 135, *behind, fight, head, light, much, night, nine, to-night, when, white.* As before select from these and return later to practice others.

Give Exercise 136, *Frank will clean the head-licht to-night.*

LESSON 3

Continue the work on Exercise 135. Review Exercises 134, 136.

LESSON 4

Review Exercise 70, *p*. Give Exercise 137, *deep, plant, top, up.* Give Exercise 138, *Plant the tree deep. Keep the top up.*

Give practice on the words with capitals first. Then encourage the pupils to write freely keeping the metronome at 92.

LESSON 5

"Take clean paper. Write name, grade, date." Call attention before the children do this to the fact that we write our names very often so we should do it very well.

Give Exercises 134, 136, 138.

Devote the rest of the period to writing examples in addition and subtraction in correct form.

THIRD WEEK

A regular method of grading will be followed for the rest of the year. This is based on the *Chart for the Diagnosis of Faults in Handwriting*, and where possible the teacher should make use of this.

The teacher should study the Chart this week and prepare to use it next week. During the week that each category is being emphasized that category alone should be graded; for example, when *letter formation* is emphasized, it will be graded in terms of the Chart and may be rated 2, 6, 10, or the intermediate points 4, 8. Further information regarding the use of the Chart can be obtained from *The Teaching of Handwriting*, by Frank N. Freeman (Houghton Mifflin Company), pp. 123–42.

The children should understand that the marking is in points, not in per cents as in other subjects. When the marking is begun, the teacher should grade, in the special category for the week, the work done on the first day and on the last day.

The child should study his own work every day, not so much for the value of his estimate as to lead to a critical attitude toward his work.

Only one or two specimens will be given for each week, with suggestions as to possible preliminary work before writing the selection as a whole. If the teacher thinks best, the verses given may be used for a book of poetry which should be made of the last copy of each selection written. It has not seemed necessary to give written copies of all these exercises. If there is any question as to the form of letters, refer to previous copies.

Two types of work should be used from now on — first, exercises such as are given here to increase facility in writing the letters; and, second, any work for which the child has a motive that will lead him to see the value of writing — perhaps the making of a booklet in which the child wishes to put some of his work, or a note of invitation.

Do not increase the speed. Attempt to perfect the work at the speed now used — 92.

Copy for the Week

Any teacher desiring to do so may substitute for the copies given work which will correlate with other subjects.

Exercise 139:

> March winds and April showers
> Bring forth May flowers.

Give practice on *March*, *April*, *May*, and *Bring*. It will probably be necessary to do so with *showers*, *forth*, *flowers*. Practice each exercise first with, and then without, the metronome. No more than three days should be spent in preliminary exercises. The other two days should be spent in practicing the verse as a whole, with and without the metronome. We shall continue the use of words from the spelling list, but shall not entirely confine ourselves to them.

Fourth Week

This week the grading discussed in the general directions for the third week will begin. The category graded this week will be *letter formation*.

Keep the last work of this week to compare with the eighth month, first week. Grade the writing done on the first day on *letter formation* only. Compare this with the grade given on the last day on the same category.

Copy for the Week

Review Exercises 73, *y*, 81, *s*. Give Exercise 140, *any, anything, by, city, pay, way;* and Exercise 141, *class, easy, house, inside, its, last, lesson, lost, same, school, send, sent, show, shut, so, soft, sold, spell, stamp, stay, stone, us.*

In these words will be found most of the letters of the alphabet so that the practice of letter formation may be given much variety.

Seventh Month. First Week

The category to be graded this week is *spacing*. Grade on this alone, but call attention to *letter formation* also.

Review Exercise 85, *r*. The spelling list coming in here is Exercise 142, *afternoon, around, brother, burn, car, care, farther, first, forget, from, here, horse, hurt, large, letter, more, paper, part, party, race, rain, rest, right, room, short, try, warm, winter.* Any of them may be practiced with a capital letter if used at the beginning of a sentence. Two or three sentences should be organized using some of these words with others which have been practiced. The sentences should relate if possible to some immediate interest of the children's.

Second Week

Emphasize *alinement* this week and grade on it. Consider the base line and the relative height of the letters. Try to have no loss in quality of *letter formation* and in *spacing*, but do this incidentally, not as the main aim. If any advance in speed seems desirable, the time may be increased a little, perhaps to 96. Probably most classes will not do so.

Copy for the Week

Exercise 143:

> The friendly cow all red and white
> I love with all my heart;
> She gives me cream with all her might,
> To eat with apple tart.

Suggested for practice — capitals, *T, I, S, friendly, heart, might.* Some classes may find it too much to write the whole verse. If so, let them write only the first two lines, using the rest next week. Be sure that what is done is done with care. Let the children say the whole verse, and if they are making Work Books they may cut a cow free-hand and put it in with the verse or cut out a picture to paste in and then paste the written verse below it. Write both with and without the metronome.

THIRD WEEK

This week the emphasis should be on *quality of line.* This has two elements: regularity of line as opposed to wavering, and pressure that gives a clear, not too black, line. This can best be gained by right position, which prevents cramped pressure, care in sharpening pencils, and keeping the metronome time, which leads to regularity.

The verse begun last week may be finished, or, if this has been done, the two verses given may be reviewed. Distributed repetition is best in gaining skill, so that it is better to return once in a while to an exercise which has been partly learned. In this way the child will gain facility without tiring of the work. Also this week review Exercises 91, *k,* 104, *v,* and give Exercise 144, *ask, black, cork, keep, like, make, week, work; live, love, river.* These may be placed in sentences as seems best to the teacher.

FOURTH WEEK

Special attention should be given to *uniformity of slant* this week. Because this is largely controlled by position and rhythm, it should be good by this time. Therefore, while it is the category for grading this week, attention may also be given to the other four categories.

Copy for the Week

Exercise 145:

> If all were rain and never sun,
> No bow could span the hill;
> If all were sun and never rain,
> There'd be no rainbow still.[1]

---

[1] From Christina G. Rossetti's *Poems,* by permission of The Macmillan Company.

The capitals and the words *never, could, span, rainbow,* may be used for practice. Use the metronome only about half the time now.

Eighth Month. First Week

For this week we will combine the study of *letter formation, spacing,* and *alinement.* Grade on each, summing the points for the score for the week. Let the children hear the metronome and then try to write in the correct time without hearing it. Start it again later on so that they may see if they are keeping the right time. Do this, repeating a single word, and later with a line or the whole verse.

Copy for the Week

Exercise 146:

> Thank you, pretty cow, that made
> Pleasant milk to soak my bread.
> Every day and every night
> Warm, and fresh, and sweet, and white.

Practice the capitals and the words *Thank, pretty, Pleasant, Every,* and any others where there are combinations which have caused trouble. Two or three days may be spent on such work and then the entire verse may be written.

Second Week

Review this week Exercise 86, *M*, 110, *S*, 120, *F*. Give Exercise 147, *Monday, Friday, Sunday.*

These are given before the other names of the days because they are much easier to spell than the rest. The children should recognize that they have already written *day,* so these words are not really hard. Give the rest of this week to practice in correct writing of numbers for the four fundamental processes and to the practice of the names of the children or other names which they have occasion to use; as, city, school, state, street, etc.

Third Week

Use the metronome only part of the time, in the beginning and intermittently throughout the period. It is important here to make sure that, when allowed to write independently of an imposed rhythm, the children maintain good position and an easy, free movement with a tendency to a rhythm which may or may not conform to the imposed rhythm. There will naturally be some variation in rhythm with the different letters.

The work for the next three weeks is a short poem. One verse should be used each week. If desired, when the whole poem is practiced, it may be written as a whole for use in a Spring booklet.

Copy for the Week

Exercise 148:

THE LITTLE PLANT

In the heart of a seed,
Buried deep, so deep!
A dear little plant
Lay fast asleep!

Suggested for practice: the title, *heart, Buried, asleep.* For a class that is doing this work for the first time, the suggestions for Grade 1, seventh month, fourth week, will be helpful. If the poem has been written at that time, recall it to the class and suggest that "we see how much better we can write it." A certain amount of familiar material is a pleasure as well as being good review practice.

FOURTH WEEK
Copy for the Week

Exercise 149:

"Wake!" said the sunshine,
"And creep to the light!"
"Wake!" said the voice
Of the raindrops bright.

The added difficulty of the quotation marks and the exclamation points in this verse will give variety to the practice. If the pupils only approximate the correct forms here, they will do well. Give practice on any words that are likely to present difficulties to the class.

NINTH MONTH. FIRST WEEK
Copy for the Week

Exercise 150:

The little plant heard
And rose to see
What the wonderful
Outside world might be!

This week grade on all the categories and sum the points for the score. Let each child decide how he has improved and where he needs more improvement. To do this it will be well to spend one period talking about the Chart and letting the children compare their latest writing with that written a month ago — the first week of the eighth month. Try to have the children get the time by listening to the metronome and then follow it without using the metronome.

Second Week

It is possible that during this last month there will be material in other subjects which requires writing and may need all the time given for practice. A teacher should feel free to substitute other material for which the child feels a need for the material given for this week and the next two, provided, first, that the work substituted *is* of real value, second, that the writing is done in the position and manner of writing required by the established standards.

Copy for the Three Weeks

Exercise 151:

DAISIES

At evening when I go to bed
I see the stars shine overhead.
They are the little daisies white
That dot the meadow of the night.

And sometimes when I'm dreaming so,
Across the sky the moon will go.
She is a lady sweet and fair
Who's come to gather daisies there.

But in the morning when I rise
There's not a star left in the skies.
She's picked them all and dropped them down
Into the meadows of the town.

Frank Dempster Sherman.

Third and Fourth Weeks

Whatever the material that is used during this time, the teacher should maintain the standards of the grade. Keep the pride in well-written names and encourage the children to watch their position and not to tighten the grasp. It is well to do writing that is related to other subjects in the writing period as much as possible in this grade so that it will be directly under supervision and the right habits more firmly fixed. During this year the metronome will not for most classes go higher than 92. While increase in speed is desirable, it should only advance with the quality, as too much speed is likely to disorganize the writing movement. A two-minute test should be given at the end of the third week to grade and compare with the first graded test of the year.

Optional Material

The material given under this heading is to provide for classes that need more material or to allow substitutions if the teacher wishes in these last weeks.

Little Bo-Peep has lost her sheep,
And can't tell where to find them;
Leave them alone and they'll come home,
And bring their tails behind them.

Humpty Dumpty sat on a wall;
Humpty Dumpty had a great fall;
All the king's horses and all the king's men
Cannot put Humpty Dumpty together again.

One misty moisty morning,
When cloudy was the weather,
I chanced to meet an old man
Clothed all in leather.

Mary had a little lamb,
Its fleece was white as snow;
And everywhere that Mary went,
The lamb was sure to go.

Twinkle, twinkle, little star;
How I wonder what you are!
Up above the world so high
Like a diamond in the sky!

THE WIND [1]

Who has seen the wind?
    Neither I nor you:
But when the leaves hang trembling,
The wind is passing through.

Who has seen the wind?
    Neither you nor I:
But when the trees bow down their heads
The wind is passing by.

---

[1] From Christina G. Rossetti's *Poems*, by permission of The Macmillan Company.

CHAPTER VII

EXERCISES FOR GRADE THREE

OBJECTIVES

Content. By the end of the third year the child should be reasonably independent in writing any combinations of letters in words for which he has use. His writing vocabulary should include, besides the words used in previous grades, such words as the following:

about	every	low	fell	meet
land	boat	now	began	ago
then	mine	child	catch	high
camp	half	south	year	pass
where	why	war	talk	just
ever	across	over	next	build
done	near	mountain	again	belong
once	teach	people	many	because
bought	country	block	know	ticket
church	leave			

In this grade a good habit of arrangement of material on the page and of spacing should be started. The following items should be considered: margin, indentation, distance from the top, distance between lines and between words. A simple correspondence form should be introduced where need for its use is recognized. The child should be able to write some of the names of the months and should add to his list of commonly used names, as, his own address and the given names of his own friends, and all capitals used in beginning sentences. The child should be able to write numbers to *1000* in any order and in columns either from copy or dictation. Correct forms should be used for work in addition and subtraction, in multiplication with one multiplier, and in short division.

Movement. At the end of this year the child should write with about the same quality as in Grade 2 and with a fluency of forty letters a minute. The introduction of pen and ink in this grade presents to the child a difficulty of such proportions that he does well to reach by the end of the year the same coördination of movement with the new medium which he had acquired with the pencil. Habitually free, rhythmic movement should be quite well established in this grade.

MATERIALS AND METHODS

Materials. For the first part of the year, rough-surfaced paper with one half inch ruling and pencils; for the latter part of the year, paper that will take ink well and with one half inch ruling. Penholder medium size and with cork or rubber tip. Pen with rounded point.

Methods. *A. Position.* A reasonably correct position should be maintained now from habit.

B. Types of exercises. 1. It is no unusual experience to have the introduction of pen and ink result in the breaking down of a formerly satisfactory coördination. In view of this, exercises to encourage free rhythmic movement are especially desirable in this grade. These exercises should always be presented by the teacher on the blackboard and analyzed as to count. The motivation in this drill should be the result of the child's desire to do well the writing for which he feels a need in other subjects, as in spelling or in written composition.

2. Much of the practice in the writing period should be on words which are derived from necessary written work in other subjects.

3. The speed of the writing should be increased from time to time by increasing the speed of the metronome. In the last three months of the year *speed drills* may be introduced in which the class for a short time writes familiar exercises at a speed greater than that usually used. This should never be carried so far as to interfere with coördination.

4. Pupils should be encouraged consciously to "carry over" the habits of the writing to writing done in other subjects.

C. Standards and criticism. Continue the development of a critical attitude in each child by comparing specimens of his own work, by discussion of good points in the work of others and by analysis of the difficulties in the copy as given by the teacher. These comparisons of his own work may be made immediately after the work is written and the comparison may be repeated after an interval has elapsed. The discussion of the good points in the work of others may be brought about by the display of work and the same type of criticism which has been carried on with one's own work; that is, picking out the best and stating why it is good. By this means the attention is focussed on what should be repeated instead of what should be discarded. Introduce the terms *letter formation* and *spacing* and make a special study of the elements, adding them to the three elements, *uniformity of slant*, *uniformity of alinement*, and *quality of line* which were introduced in Grade 2.

The standard in quality for this grade is 14 on the Freeman Scale, 45 on the Ayres Scale, and in speed forty letters a minute.

FIRST MONTH.   FIRST WEEK

A test is to be given on the first Friday.   The teacher should prepare for this by looking ahead and teaching the verse assigned this week.

A short talk somewhat like this will be a good way to begin the course.   It should be suited to the class.

"We all want to learn to write well so that when we write letters or stories our friends can read them.   We can write well and make hard work of it or we can write easily and well.   I am going to try to show you how to write so that it will be easy to write and then you will be glad to do it.   First we must sit right.   Sit straight, hips back in seat, feet on the floor."   See that all are doing so.   "Put paper in place at an angle of about thirty degrees to the desk line." Illustrate with a diagram on the board.   "Put both arms on the desk and let them rest there easily.   Make 'runners' of your two little fingers."   Let the children carry the whole hand sliding back and forth on the desk in this way without the pencil.   "Go all the way across the paper.   Do it as I count — One-two, one-two, one-two, one-two.   Again, one-two," etc.   "Can you keep just with my count?   Are you sliding on your runners?   Is your wrist raised just a little so as to make a bridge?   Now, again, one-two," etc. "Take pencil, hold it so."   Show correct position, be sure index finger is on top of the pencil, not on the left side, and that the thumb is higher on the pencil — farther from the point — than the index finger.   See that every child's position is right the first time and every time.   It will take less time in the long run if insisted on the first and every time.   *Place* each pencil right where it is necessary. Above all things do not get impatient with the child who does not get the position right.   They all want to.

"Now can you use your runners with the pencil?   Try as I count.   'Way across the paper, but do not write yet.   Ready. Slide.   One-two," etc.   "Now I will show you something to write." Give Exercise 1, saying as you write it on the board:

> To and fro sway the trees,
> Bending in the passing breeze.

"Now you may do it as I did."   Repeat the verse as the children write.   "You may say it as you write.   Again.   Now we have made the tree-tops.   Do you like to swing 'way up in the tree-tops among the leaves?   Look.   I am going to swing up."   Give Exercise 2, saying as it is written:

> How do you like to go up in a swing,
> Up in the air so blue?

EXERCISES 1 AND 2

"Make the tree-tops again. Are your runners ready? Is your pencil right? Are you holding it loosely?" Test a few by pulling them out from the fingers. "Ready. Write. 'To and fro,'" etc. "Let's swing up to the tree-tops, 'How do you like,'" etc.

LESSON 2

"Sit straight, hips back, feet on the floor. Arms on desk. Can you place your paper right? Good." Do not neglect commendation when it is possible to give it. "Without pencils use your runners — 'way across the paper. Ready. Slide. One-two," etc. (Four times.) "Now pencils. Is your position like this?" Be sure that it is. "Now slide, but do not write. Ready. Slide. One-two," etc. "Look." Write on the board Exercise 1, saying the verse. "You may write it. Ready. Write. 'To and fro,'" etc. "Did you keep the time? Once more. 'To and fro,'" etc. "Now we will swing to the tree-tops. Ready. Write. 'How do you like,'" etc.

Examine the work quickly to see that it is being done freely and in good position. Repeat this, asking beforehand, "Are you holding the pencil loosely? Are your runners ready?" "Now we will swing another way. I will show you."

Give Exercise 3, *i*. "Make long slides so that you can put only three on a line. Try again. See how I count." Put it on the board again. Notice the count is on the forward stroke. "Ready.

EXERCISE 3

Write. One-two, one-two." Repeat several times to your count by voice and watch hands for position, looseness of grasp, and sliding on runners. Commend as much as possible. Quietly change the positions that are wrong.

"Now let us change this a little making two strokes close together, then a long swing before two more close together. Put three groups of two each on a line." Show Exercise 4, *u*.

Alternate the practice of these two exercises. Try to have the down-stroke slant nearly if not quite to the base line instead of

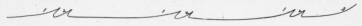

EXERCISE 4

curving off to the right; but keep the movement, even if there is a slight curve.

LESSON 3

Give specific directions as to position as in the last lesson. Use Exercises 1, 2, 3, 4, with voice count, and be particular to see that position is kept. By this time if there is really freedom of movement, you will be inclined to be disturbed by disregard of base line and proper height of work. Let it go for the present. Work *only* for position, freedom of movement and correct time.

Give Exercise 5, *t*. "Now look. Make this once more." (Exercise 3.) "Now I will make it taller. You may try it. Watch

EXERCISE 5

the count. Have you the right position?" See that they have, but quickly. "Now. Ready. Write." Give the count for every exercise as shown in the written exercises.

"Now we will combine some of the exercises we have had." Give Exercise 6, *it*.

EXERCISE 6

We will use the connecting stroke between words for a time with this exercise to emphasize the long free swing. When words are written separately it is entirely possible to raise the arm each time for a new word instead of using the lateral swing which accompanies an easy, rhythmic writing movement.

LESSON 4

"Take position. Show me how your runners slide. Pencils." Review with rhymes, Exercises 1, 2, putting them on the board first.

Review Exercises 3, 4, 5, 6, with count. Each review exercise should be written once or twice. Don't make drudgery of it by too long repetition of an exercise. Don't expect perfection at first. Go back to the same exercise often.

"Look. I am going to put two exercises together." Give
Exercise 7, *tut*. Write it two or three times on the board. Prob-

tut   tut   tut

ably only two groups should be on a line. "Now you may write
it. Ready. Write. Again. Again. You may cross the *t*'s."
Do this and the dotting of *i*'s to count.

"Here is a new exercise. Notice just how I make it. See, the
back is nearly straight." Give Exercise 8, *e*.

e   e   e

Be sure the pupils make it with a free swing. In this grade and
those above, where the pupils have had some experience in writing,
the danger of establishing wrong habits is greater than where the
children have no confidence in their ability and are writing entirely
or almost entirely under supervision. For this reason short attentive periods of practice with frequent review is most desirable.

LESSON 5

To-day the first test of the year should be given. Use the verse
for Grades 1 to 3 and follow exactly the directions given on page
8. The children should have learned the verse this week without
reference to writing. To-day they may write the verse twice before
beginning the two-minute test, so as to feel free in the writing.

SECOND WEEK. LESSON 1

"Take correct position. Show me how to hold your pencil, hand
on runners. Let us make the tree-tops. Ready. Write. 'To and
fro,'" etc. "Now the swing. Ready. Write. 'How do you
like,'" etc.

Review Exercises 3, 5, 8. "Now we will combine these." Give
Exercise 9, *tie*.

tie   tie   tie

Make the spacing within the words rather greater than natural
and put three words on a line. "Notice the count. Now are you
ready? Ready. Write. How many swing 'way across the paper?

Let's try it again. Ready. Write. Did you keep the time better then?"

Review Exercises 6, 7. Then give Exercise 9 again three times. The teacher should put all work on the board for the class.

LESSON 2

"Position." Be sure it is good. Review Exercises 1, 2, 3, 4. Then show Exercise 9, *tie*, again. "Ready. Write. Again. Ready. Write."

Review Exercise 8, *e*. "We will make one much like this." Give Exercise 10, *l*.

EXERCISE 10

Call attention to the back. It is very straight. If necessary in order to get this, count on the down-stroke as well as on the up-stroke for a time, but lead the children as soon as possible to use the same count as for the *e* by making the stroke quicker. "You may write this. Ready. Write. Did you get the right time? Are your runners in place? Without writing, slide once. Ready. Slide. One-two," etc. (Four times.) Now again write this exercise. (Exercise 10.)

The introduction of the sliding exercise in the midst of the lesson tends to emphasize the desirability of the free movement.

LESSON 3

Call attention to position and freedom and rhythm of movement. Review Exercises 1, 2, 3, 4, 6, 7, 8.

The early ones are kept up for the sake of automatizing the swinging forward movement. If done to count and attentively, one repetition of each is enough when they have been in use for a week.

Write Exercises 9, 10, three or four times each. "We will make a word with some of these exercises." Give Exercise 11, *let, tell*.

EXERCISE 11

Keep a wider spacing than normal and put two or three words on a line. As the two words give drill on the same letters and combinations, probably both can be used in this grade without difficulty.

Lesson 4

Review Exercises 1, 2. Review Exercises 8, *e*, 10, *l*, each two or three times. "Next we will write this." Give Exercise 12, *b*, counting as it is written. "How is this different from the *l*?" (Last stroke.) "Watch carefully as I write. Can you tell me where I stop in the writing?" Do this three or four times and see

EXERCISE 12   EXERCISE 13

if the children can discover the pause at the sharp turn before the last stroke. If not, call their attention to it and write once more.

After several lines of practice review Exercise 11, *tell*, and give Exercise 13, *bell*.

This use of a word with only one new letter makes the work easier than using an entirely new word. Be sure the children understand the count. "You may write. Ready. Write. Did you pause at the right place? Could you keep the time? Again. Ready. Write."

If time permits, review Exercises 6, 8, each once. Be sure that the class keeps the swing and that the spacing is quite wide.

Lesson 5

"Take clean paper. Position. Without writing slide on your runners. Ready. Slide. One-two, one-two, one-two, one-two. Now, holding your pencil right and keeping on your runners, write your name, grade, and the date on the top line."

Give Exercises 1, 2, 6, 9, 8, 10, 11, 13. Exercises 6, 9, 11, 13, should be written twice each.

After these papers have been collected to keep for comparison, give practice on the exercises that are not so well automatized as some others.

Third Week. Lesson 1

By this time it is probable that the work in arithmetic has demonstrated the need for drill on making figures and correct placing. Call attention to this and say, "We will take part of our writing time to study the figures and learn how to make them right. Then it will be easier to make them well when we use them in arithmetic work."

Give Exercise 14, digits, *1, 2, 3*. The only need for attention to

EXERCISE 14

the figure *1* is that it should be made with some regularity as to slant and not in a slovenly manner. Practice a line of these with the count and test them as to regularity of slant. Then show the *2* with count and practice it. Follow this by the *3*, and when they are understood as to form and time write them serially.

LESSON 2

Continue the work with digits to-day, studying Exercise 15, digits, *4*, *5*, *6*. Except for the *5* the chief reason for study of these

EXERCISE 15

digits is to overcome careless work and to develop a nicety in the making of figures which will improve the appearance and the legibility of the written work in arithmetic.

LESSON 3

Give Exercise 16, digits, *7*, *8*, *9*. There is a general tendency to make these digits poorly, which may be due to carelessness or to

EXERCISE 16

lack of a clear idea of how the figure should be made. Demonstrate each figure with count and drill on them until the children understand. Then repeat the exercise from time to time until the correct form has become established.

The study of digits is made early in the year so that the effect of this study may be felt throughout the year in the writing of numbers. Neither the teacher nor the children should feel that this study ends the matter, but there should be continued emphasis on the right form in all work requiring the writing of numbers.

LESSON 4

Review Exercises 1, 2, 8, *e*, 10, *l*. These are reviewed for the purpose of definitely recalling the lateral swing, which is little used in writing detached figures.

Give Exercise 17, *a*. Give this with a good swing. Call atten-

EXERCISE 17

tion to the upward tendency of the top and see that the children do not make a hook at the top of this letter.

Give Exercise 18, *eat, late, table*. The special emphasis here is on the *a*. But in *table* care should be taken with the *b* and *l*.

EXERCISE 18

LESSON 5

"Take clean paper." Give the preliminary swing for limbering up before writing name, grade, and date.

Give Exercises 14, 15, 16, digits, in vertical column at the left of the paper. Then give Exercises 13, 17, 18.

When this is finished, give drill on numbers *1* to *200* — that is, using any of the digits for numbers, either units, tens, or hundreds, and placing them properly.

When numbers are to be written in columns it is very important that the children should be shown how to do it correctly and that they be required to do it so thereafter in all such work.

When writing numbers in a column each number should be separated from the number above it by a distance equal to one half the height of the figures. The columns corresponding to the orders — units, tens, hundreds — should be separated by a space equal to the width of the figures.

The importance of attention to this from the beginning and all the time lies in the fact that correct column placing of figures has been found to increase materially the accuracy of computation.

FOURTH WEEK. LESSON 1

Review Exercises 1, 2, 17, 18. "To-day we shall write an exercise very much like the *a*." Give Exercise 19, *d, led*.

EXERCISE 19

Have the *d* practiced first. Call attention to the difference between *a* and *d* — the stem is the lengthening of the up-stroke of the *a* and is written in the same time. The end of the first stroke should tend upward as in the *a*.

LESSON 2

Review Exercises 1, 2, swinging only half the line instead of the whole line. Give Exercises 3, 4, 8, 10, lessening the swing somewhat. Be very sure that the swing is not lost in shortening it, and that the hand really slides on the runners. This is far more important just now than emphasis on form. The only form yet noted is the top of the *a* and the *d*, attention to which may be called when any exercise containing either is given. But it is the swing that will bring it right. Keep the swing from dropping down.

Give Exercises 17, 19, using the long swing. Then practice the words in Exercises 18, 19.

LESSON 3

The time to-day should be given to the discussion of margins in written work, for the purpose of leading the children to develop a standard for this work. A suggestion as to procedure follows.

Show two written sheets to the class where the writing is of the same quality and the evident difference is in the arrangement of the paper with regard to pleasing spacing. (The teacher may prepare the sheets so as to have the writing the same.) Ask for a choice as to the most pleasing. Then ask for reasons for the choice. "Why do you like this better?" When the children have discovered, as a result of questioning if necessary, that the regular margins make the work more pleasing, let them take the last sheet of their own writing and examine it with reference to margins. "How wide margins should we use? Should they all be the same?" Have some samples showing different margins, with either written or printed material. Finally show the children one which is generally accepted and suggest that they try to-morrow to write a sheet using this marginal arrangement and see how they like it.

LESSON 4

Decide on margins and make light dots to indicate the limits of the writing.

Give Exercises 1, 2, half-line swing within these limits.

Give Exercises 6, 9, 11, 13, 18, 19, *led*.

LESSON 5

"Take clean paper. Mark the paper for margins and try to keep within them." Note position and give preliminary swing. "Write name, grade, and date."

Give with short swing Exercises 1, 2, 3, 4, 8, 10, and the words in Exercises 9, 11, 13, 18, 19.

SECOND MONTH. FIRST WEEK

Introduce the metronome.[1] Set it at 84. This is lower than the

---

[1] If a metronome cannot be obtained for use, the voice count should be regulated so as to follow the rates indicated in the lessons as accurately as possible.

rate at the close of the second year, as it is well to give the children a chance to recover gradually the place they reached before the vacation and the attention to rhythm is likely to be better if it does not cause too much strain.

The introduction of the metronome to give the rate has two different purposes. It sets the teacher free to inspect and give suggestions to individual children. It gives an absolutely regular beat for a continuous period such as is not possible with the teacher's voice. Also it makes possible the definite determination of the rate to be used at a particular time and the increase of speed in a systematic way.

Call attention to the margins and, if necessary, rule a line lightly at each side throughout this month.

Lesson 1

Review with long swing Exercises 3, 4, 8, 10. Then give each with short swing. Give each new exercise this week with voice count first and rather slowly. After the first day it may be given with the metronome.

Give Exercise 20, *o*, *lot*, *boat*, *about*. Show the letter *o*, calling attention to the pause before the connecting stroke. "What other

Exercise 20

letter have we studied which is like this?" (*b*.) "Let us write the *b* a few times, thinking especially of the pause."

Then write the *o* again on the board and have the class write that. Give the signal, "Ready. Write," in time to the count which is to be used. Give the word *lot* first because it has only one "bridge" connection, and the joining with the *t* is quite easy. Then call attention to the *bo* in the other words and see that the children get the time and the form right. In these words in every case the connecting stroke dips only a little and is almost horizontal.

Lesson 2

Remember that position is all-important. The metronome is to be used all this month at 84.

Review Exercises 1, 2, 20, *o*. Then give Exercise 21, *w*.

"Here is another letter which has the same connecting stroke as the *b* and the *o*." After some practice with the free exercise let the children combine the three letters in a long swing as shown in Exercise 22, *b o w*. Then have them shorten the swing so as to get the word *bow*.

EXERCISE 21   EXERCISE 22

Have them write several lines keeping exactly to count. If there is trouble in the rhythm, write it on the board two or three times and have the children listen to the metronome as they watch. They will soon get the idea.

Review the words in Exercises 19, 20.

LESSON 3

Write three columns of numbers, four deep, as for addition. Include all digits and the cipher and give large and small numbers in the same group. Use any numbers *1* to *500*. Lead the children to be critical of the figures. Review Exercise 21. Give Exercise 23, *low, law, well*.

EXERCISE 23

LESSON 4

Give Exercises 1, 2, half-line swing. Review the letters in Exercises 17, 19, 10, 21.

Write Exercise 17, *a*, without swing, as a word. Give Exercise 24, *A*. "Notice that the capital *A* is like a small *a* made larger. Let us make it several times."

EXERCISE 24

If there are children in the class whose names begin with *A*, use their names. If not, give Exercise 25, *Ada, At, Abbie*.

EXERCISE 25

In our exercises we do not introduce letters which have not been studied. Wherever the child has a reason for writing, the fact that the letters needed have not been studied should not prevent their being written.

LESSON 5

"Take clean paper. Are you sure your margins are right?" Be sure that the writing is with the metronome. Practice the slide without writing. "Write name, grade, date."

Give Exercises 19, 20, one line of each word. Call attention to the tops of *a* and *d*, to the connecting strokes of *b* and *o*, and see that the *b* is not closed.

SECOND WEEK

Metronome 84. Be sure to keep the time. Note the holding of the pencil and be sure that it is right. Looseness of grasp is important.

LESSON 1

Review Exercises 3, 4, with long swing, twice each. Review Exercise 17, *a*.

Give Exercise 26, *c, cut*. Notice that the *c does* turn down at the

EXERCISE 26

top in distinction from the *a* which does not. Call attention to this and see that it is accomplished in this first swinging exercise. If it seems easier for the children, use the *c* with the under-curve initial stroke.

Give Exercise 17 and Exercise 26 interchangeably so as not to use the new exercise continuously enough to encourage carelessness. Give the word *cut*. For variety after some practice give Exercise 27, *cat, cab*, which contain only letters that have been studied, and combine the *a* and *c* in one word.

EXERCISE 27

LESSON 2

Give six examples placed properly for subtraction, using numbers *1* to *500*. Place three on a line and give attention to the spacing.

Review Exercise 25, writing any names which begin with the capital *A* that have been practiced. Give each alone three or four times. Keep the writing with the metronome.

Lesson 3

"To-day we shall study another capital which is hard to make. Notice it carefully. See if you can find out anything about it that will make it easier to write."

Give Exercise 28, *E, Ed, Ella, Etta.* Make it on the board so

Exercise 28

that the two ovals are strongly suggested. The children will probably call them circles. We have allowed that before because we do not expect accurateness of image at the beginning. Suggest now that they are nearly round, but are not circles as they are a little flattened and give the name *oval*.

"If we can make these so that we can finish the oval every time, the letter will be right. Let us make one slowly first without counting at all."

This is simply a study of form and should be carefully distinguished in the mind of the teacher from writing. "Now notice how I count so that you can write it just so." Use names of any members of the class that have the initial *E* instead of the names given above.

Lesson 4

Give Exercise 1, 2, half-line swing. Review Exercise 24, 25, 28. Review Exercise 10, *l.* Give Exercise 29, *f, fell, fill, fall, full.*

Exercise 29

"Notice that this letter has the same long straight line as the *l*, but it is still longer. It comes a space below the base line." Call attention to the point of closing and the point of crossing. "Are they the same?" The crossing is at one space height and the closing at the base line. "See if we can make it so." This group of words nearly alike has variety enough to hold attention.

LESSON 5

"Take clean paper." Give Exercises 1, 2, without writing. "Write name, grade, date."

Give three examples for addition, four deep. Then give Exercises 23, 26, 27, 29, 28. Collect papers.

Review the words in Exercises 18, 20, 23.

THIRD WEEK

Metronome 84.

LESSON 1

Review Exercises 3, 4, long swing, twice each. Review Exercises 11, 13, 18.

Review Exercises 29, *f*, 17, *a*. "Our new letter to-day puts parts of these together." Give Exercise 30, *q*, *quiet*. Let the children tell how it is like each of the other exercises.

EXERCISE 30

Call attention to the need for closing on the base line. The direct association of the *q* with the *f* is likely to prevent the fault of confusing it with the *g* and so making the loop wrong.

LESSON 2

"Look at the work you did yesterday. Are the margins good? How could they be made better? Watch that to-day as you write."

Review Exercises 24, 28. "We shall write another exercise much like these." Give Exercise 31, *C*, *Call*, *Coat*. Use any names of pupils that are appropriate.

EXERCISE 31

LESSON 3

See that the hand is in good position. Give Exercise 17, and Exercise 30, with a good swing. Then shorten the swing. Call attention to the top of the first part that keeps an upward movement.

Give Exercise 32, *m*, *meet*. Call attention to the three curves here and see that they *are* curves, not sharp turns. For variety give simple combinations of letters already studied.　Exercise 33, *me, met, mat, mate, time.*　Any or all of these may be used as seems best.

m m m meet

EXERCISE 32

me met mate

mate time

EXERCISE 33

LESSON 4

Review Exercise 32.　Give Exercise 34, *n, into, land, mine, now.*

n n n nnn into

land mines now

EXERCISE 34

Give the letter *n* first.　Call attention to the difference between it and the *m*.

In combining these two letters with others where they are not initial letters, be particularly careful about the first stroke so that the first turn shall be a curve and not a sharp turn.

LESSON 5

"Take clean paper."　Give free limbering swing without writing, pencil held loosely.　"Write name, grade, date."　By this time a good position should be held in writing these headings, and this week the children may write them with the metronome.　Do not spend too much time on this as it will be given special practice later.

Give Exercises 30, 32, 33, 34, 31.

FOURTH WEEK.　LESSON 1

Metronome 84.　Take time to-day to compare the papers written the first Friday with those written last Friday.　Let each child see his two together and notice the improvement himself.　The improvement may be in lightness or regularity of line, in regularity of slant, in keeping to the base line.　The children may also note their success in making all *a*'s, *d*'s, and *q*'s stand up at the top even though these did not appear on the first sheet. Ask the class to see how often they have kept their letters just on the base line. Suggest that this week they try to do that especially. If there is more time, clinch this last by practicing.

Use Exercises 33, 34.

LESSON 2

Review Exercise 31, *C*. Give Exercise 35, *O, Out, On, Oct.*

O OO Out On Oct.

EXERCISE 35

Give the letter *O* first, comparing it with the *C* and getting a good oval. If the children get it better so, the oval may be retraced four times. Too long-continued practice tends to fatigue which leads to carelessness.

Give any proper names beginning with *O* which are suggested by the class; as, names of persons, city, state, school, street, river, etc. Let the children know that *Oct.* is the abbreviation for *October*, but do not have them write the whole name as we have not yet studied the *r*.

LESSON 3

Write one line each of the digits, making them in time with the metronome and each as nearly perfect as possible. Let each find and mark his best. Write numbers coming from *500* to *1000*, from copy and from dictation. For example:

7 5 9	6 9 4
3 9 6	2 8 7
2 8 0	5 0 3
4 0 1	1 8 0

LESSON 4

"Show me your position." Review Exercises 24, 25, 28, 31, 35. Give Exercise 36, *Ada told Etta about a boat.* The word *told* has not been given in this grade, but it is a second-grade word and may be reviewed before the sentence is written.

This is the first context writing which is given in this grade. There are two reasons for the use of context writing. It helps the child to see the use of practice in writing and it gives him training in the type of writing which is most used in ordinary out-of-school situations. The sentences are most of them purposely made too long to fill one line so that there may be definite drill on proper spacing as to margins and spacing within the words, and between words.

Lesson 5

"Take clean papers." Give the preliminary swing. "Let us try to keep exactly on the line, exactly with the metronome and in perfect position to-day. Write name, grade, date."

Give Exercises 31, 35, 36. Give three examples in subtraction across the page, with the answers, spacing well.

These examples may be worked together at the board and the answers copied. The aim is to secure right placing of the answer.

After collecting the papers, give practice on the names with the metronome.

Third Month. First Week

The metronome should be used this month at 88. If with a new exercise the class finds it difficult, the metronome may be dropped to the rate for last month. No further instruction will be given as to the use of the metronome this month.

Lesson 1

Review Exercise 34, *n*. Give Exercise 37, z, *fizz*, *buzz*.

Exercise 37

"The z begins just as the *n* does, but the last part is not quite like any letter we have had." It is much like the stem of the *g*, which has not yet been studied, but has the peculiar curve that is different from any other letter. If the children have trouble with the letter, let them experiment on it a few times without the metronome, drawing it carefully and then retracing it in time with the metronome. The word *buzz* was given in the second grade. It has the connecting stroke which needs attention. The word *fizz* is new and gives practice on the *f* as well as the *z*.

Lesson 2

Review Exercises 17, 19. Give Exercise 38, *g*, *good*.

Exercise 38

"Here is another letter which begins just as the *a* and the *d* do, but it has a loop stem. Notice how straight the down-stroke of the stem is.   Can you make it so?"   After practice give Exercise 39, *age, ago, began, gone.*

Exercise 39

The association of the *a* and *g* in these words should emphasize the common point — the upward direction of the top of the letter. There are two points of difficulty, first, the joining between the letters *b* and *e* where the connecting stroke must drop low enough so that there will be a good loop in the *e* without its being higher than the one space part of the *b;* second, the joining of the *o* and *n* where there should be a rounded turn at the top of the *n*.

Lesson 3

Be sure the position is good.   It would be fatal to good results to allow carelessness in this now.

Review Exercise 10, *l*, 34, *n*.   Give Exercise 40, *h*.   This letter

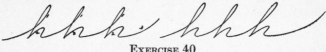

Exercise 40

combines the first part of the *l* and the last part of the *n*.   There should be very little retracing of the down-stroke in making the second up-stroke.

Let the children compare these letters and, if they care to do so, construct the *h* from the other two.   Spend most of the time writing with the metronome and then finding the best to use as a standard for future practice.

Give Exercise 41, *then, half, child, catch, had, high, them, watch.*

Exercise 41

All these words are in Courtis's [1] 100 per cent spelling list for the
[1] S. A. Courtis: *Teaching Spelling by Plays and Games.*

3B grade, and should all be written, but they need not all be written at this time. When an exercise is reviewed, use words not given before until all the words have been used.

Lesson 4

Review Exercise 25, any names which have been practiced.

Give Exercise 42, *Ada can catch the little child.* Any other name which has been practiced may be substituted for *Ada.* Let each child find his own difficulty and practice on that until he sees improvement. Then write the sentence again and compare it with the first writing.

Lesson 5

"Take clean papers. Write name, grade, date."

Write Exercises 37, 38, 39, 40, 41, 42.

When papers are collected, give some of the harder exercises which have been used.

Second Week

This week all of the new work given will be capitals, for the sake of furnishing drill on as many names as possible.

Lesson 1

Review Exercises 24, *A*, 28, *E*, 31, *C*, 35, *O*. Review names beginning with these letters. Give Exercises 36, 42.

Lesson 2

Review Exercise 42. Give Exercise 43, *B, Belle.* There should

EXERCISE 43

be two good curves of about equal size, the lower one being somewhat larger. Perhaps it will help the children to see that if the curves are cut away from the first two strokes, they make a rather good figure *3*.

Lesson 3

Review Exercise 43. "To-day our capital is different from other letters we have had." Give Exercise 44, *I, Ida, It, In.*

EXERCISE 44

"The first stroke goes to the left instead of to the right as in most of the letters. Then the down-stroke must have the same slant as the other letters have. Watch carefully as I write it two or three times. Do you see the count? Can you follow it? This is a word alone and one we are likely to write often, so we should learn to write it well." When the directions are understood, give the signal, "Ready. Write." Never spend much time talking when the children should be practicing for the development of skill. Give the words as soon as the children are ready for them.

Lesson 4

Review Exercise 44. Give Exercise 45, *J, John, Jane, June.*

Exercise 45

"See how much *J* is like the *I*. Notice that both loops come on the same side." If there is any trouble in writing the letter, have the children draw a straight slanting line, put two curves on the left side both crossing nearly at the base line and trace this in time to the metronome until the feeling of direction is fixed. It ought not to take long, but if a child is found making the lower loop the wrong way, set him to practicing again.

Lesson 5

"Take clean paper. Write name, grade, date." Write Exercises 43, 44, 45, using the letters and any names which have been practiced with them.

After papers are collected, practice writing any names in the class which begin with capitals practiced in former exercises.

Third Week. Lesson 1

Give Exercise 46, *p, camp, put.* The one-space part of the *p* may

Exercise 46

be written either open or closed, but the teacher should decide which way to use it and have all write alike, as in this grade uniformity facilitates practice. A common fault with the *p* is to make the first stroke only one space high. It should be as tall as the *t*.

See that it stands well above the one-space part of the letter.   The *c* in *camp* may require some practice.   Otherwise there is no difficulty in the exercise except the *p*.

LESSON 2

Review Exercise 46.   Give Exercise 47, *M, Mat, Millie*, and Exercise 48, *N, Nell, Ned*.

M M Mat Millie

EXERCISE 47

N N N Nell Ned

EXERCISE 48

Here are two letters which are very much alike.   The *M* has three curves, each a little shorter than the one just preceding. Sometimes the children see it as "a good hill to coast on."

As usual write any names of children that begin with these letters.

LESSON 3

Review Exercise 43, *B*.   Now write one *B* on the board and erase the lower curve.   Let several of the children do the same.   "What letter have we?"

Write Exercise 49, *P, Paul, Put*.   Write only the letter first.

P P Paul Put

EXERCISE 49

Have the class write it several times and then give one or both words.

LESSON 4

Review Exercise 43, 49.   Give Exercise 50, *Paul put the bell on the table*.

LESSON 5

"Take clean paper.   Write name, grade, date."
Give Exercises 46, 47, 48, 49, 50.

FOURTH WEEK

No new elements will be given this week, but those given before will be combined in new ways. The class will not know that the work is all review. This will help in automatizing the activity.

Lesson 1

Give Exercise 51, *Place the bag on the seat, Nell.* Practice all names with the metronome. Show those whose initials have not been studied how to write them with the metronome. Practice any words which need it separately.

Lesson 2

Give Exercise 52, *Come to the table now and eat.*
Review Exercise 51.

Lesson 3

See that the pencil is held right and that the hand moves easily.
Give Exercise 53, *A big dog led the blind man.* Review Exercise 52.

Lesson 4

Insist on having every one write with the metronome.
Give Exercise 54, *Belle and Ellen went down town to-day.* Review Exercises 52, 53.

Lesson 5

The work done to-day is to be graded. On a clean sheet of paper have the class write names, grade, age, and date. After the papers are prepared in this way, give a two-minute test, using the same material that was used in the first test, and follow the directions on page 8 exactly. Do not use the metronome for this writing.

On the same paper, on the other side if necessary, have written Exercises 52, 53, using the metronome at 88. This is to have a basis of comparison to determine whether there has been a "carrying over" of the effect of the writing with the metronome to the writing that is done without the metronome.

Fourth Month. First Week

Set the metronome for this month at 96. If it seems best, a lower rate may be used for new work.

Lesson 1

Review Exercise 47, *M.* "We will write another capital that has the same kind of beginning stroke as this."
Give Exercise 55, *W, William.* "Notice that here the middle

EXERCISE 55

stroke is taller than the first stroke and the last stroke shorter than any other. What kind of turns have we here?" (All sharp.)

Give Exercise 56, *William came to school on time.*

LESSON 2

Review Exercises 56, 37, z. "The capital Z is very much like the small z. I will write it." Give Exercise 57, *Z, Zella.*

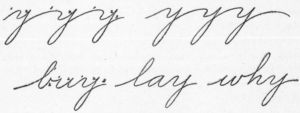

EXERCISE 57

The children who have been trained this year to study their writing will see that the difference is mainly one of size and the place of beginning which is above the base line in the capital. The children will seldom need this letter and if they remember that it is like the small z they will be likely to use it when need arises.

LESSON 3

Review Exercises 3, 17, 32, 40. Give Exercise 58, *y, buy, lay, why.*

EXERCISE 58

Give the letter *y*. "Who can tell what other letter is like this? Yes, the *n* and the *g*. If it is made right, it is also just like the *h*, only upside down." Have several lines written using a free swing. Find the best to use as a standard for future work. Give the words.

Review Exercise 56.

LESSON 4

"To-day we are to write a letter different from any we have

written.   We will first take a swinging exercise to give us the right
direction."   Give Exercise 59, swing, with count.

The children may be told that the smaller children play this is
a teeter and say, "Seesaw, Margery Daw, Up and down we go,"
with it.   It may help to give them the imagery.

EXERCISE 59   EXERCISE 60

Give Exercise 60, *s*, exaggerating the swing of the down-stroke
so as to make a good full letter.   The common fault with *s* is to
make it too flat and there is little danger of the continuance in
natural writing of too full a curve.   Review Exercise 58.

LESSON 5

"Take clean paper.   Write name, grade, date."   Give Exercises
55, 56, 57, 58, 59.

After the papers have been collected, review Exercises 38, 40,
using such parts of these as there is time for.

SECOND WEEK.   LESSON 1

Instead of writing to-day take Friday's work and compare it with
that done just after the comparison made in the second month,
fourth week, first lesson.   By self-criticism in the class during these
weeks the children should be able to find many points where they
have improved.   Do not look for mistakes.   They are easy to find.
Encourage each child to see where he has improved in writing.   Is
his slant more even?   Are the letters better formed?   Let each
find special instances of this for himself.   Is the spacing better
between words?   Between letters?   Neither too great nor too
small?   Is the alinement better?   Has he kept on the line?   Are
the letters made with the height in correct proportion?   Is the
quality of line better?   Neither too heavy nor too light, and smooth
instead of wavy?

"Is there some exercise you would like to try to write better?"
Perhaps a suggestion of where improvement can be made will
encourage all to try.   Allow the class to keep the papers until the
next lesson for this practice.

LESSON 2

Review Exercises 59, 60.   Then allow each to write the exercise
he has decided to improve.   This may be written three times
keeping strictly with the metronome and watching position.   Com-

mend as much as possible and encourage questions where the child is in doubt as to form or time, but do not allow waste of time.

Give Exercise 61, *these, small, soap, ship, soon, glass, south, miss, must, outside, stop, pass, sea, seen.*

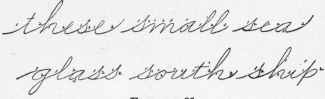

EXERCISE 61

LESSON 3

Review Exercises 59, 60. Give words from Exercise 61 that were not given yesterday. These words are those contained in the spelling list for Grade 3B which contain *s* and such other letters as have been studied in this grade. It is not expected that all of them will be written at any one period, but all of them should be practiced from time to time as the exercise is reviewed or when other work calls for them.

Give Exercise 62, *We must be still as we pass outside.*

LESSON 4

Review Exercises 59, 60, and part of 61. Give Exercise 63, *r.*

EXERCISE 63

Make a definite pause at the sharp turn. This is like the *s* in that the point comes above the first space. Call attention to this. See that the stroke following the point is a separate stroke, not just part of the down-stroke. Children are apt to make this too steep or else to make it a dipping curve with a sharp point at the end. It may help them to think of it as a hill for coasting — if too steep it would be dangerous, but it would be no fun to coast into a ravine.

Give Exercise 64, *year, round, where, across, far, firs, four, girl,*

EXERCISE 64

north, other, sport, street, war. The source of these words is the same as for the words in Exercise 61, and they are to be used in the same way.

Give Exercise 65, *A girl was seen across the street, building a fire.*

LESSON 5

"Take clean paper. Write name, grade, date." Are you holding to the definite signals for writing? (Ready. Write.)

Give Exercises 62, 65, parts of 61, 64.

After the papers are collected, practice some of the unused words in Exercises 61, 64.

THIRD WEEK. LESSON 1

Review Exercises 58, *y.* Give Exercise 66, *Y.* These are so

EXERCISE 66   EXERCISE 67

nearly alike except in height that the children will find little difficulty in making the *Y* well. Give Exercise 67, *You, Yes.*

LESSON 2

Review Exercise 40, *h.* "The letter we shall study to-day is much like this. It has the same straight back and the one-space part is joined to the loop in the same way." Give Exercise 68, *k, kill, lake, talk.*

EXERCISE 68

Be sure the two down-strokes are parallel. There is a general tendency to make the second down-stroke slant or curve to the right. See that the crossing of the loop is just opposite the top of the one-space part and that the curve at the top of this part is nearly but not quite closed. This is one of the hardest letters to make. Encourage the children to examine their own work, finding the best and making improvements in that. If the count is kept

exactly, it will be much easier to make the letter right.   Give the
words as soon as the children can handle them.   Let those who
need more practice on the letters use the same word longer.

LESSON 3

Review Exercise 58, *y*.

After practice write one *y* on the board and erase the first two
strokes.   "Does any one know what letter this will make now?
What must we do to make it a *j*?"   (Dot it.)   Let several write *y* on
the board and erase part of it.   If a good *y* is made, a good *j* can be
made from it.

Write on the board, then, Exercise 69, *j*, *just*, *jump*.   Practice

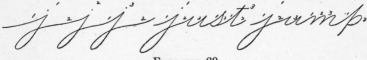

EXERCISE 69

the letter several times and then give the words.   Review Exercise
45, *J*, and give Exercise 70, *Jump just this way*.

LESSON 4

Review Exercise 43, *B*, and Exercise 49, *P*.   Give Exercise 71, *R*,
Rose, *Rob*.

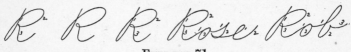

EXERCISE 71

Call attention to the similarity of these three letters.   It is only
necessary to add one line to the *P* to make the *R*.   The children will
probably be able to write it quite easily.   Whenever capitals are
given, continue to use the names of children for practice material
wherever possible.

Give Exercise 72, *Rob and Rose ran to the fire with Paul and Belle*.

LESSON 5

."Take clean paper.   Write name, grade, date."   Give Exercises
66, 67, 68, 69, 70, 71, 72.

After papers are collected, give Exercises 61, 64, parts that have
not been practiced or that need more practice.

FOURTH WEEK.   LESSON 1

Review Exercises 12, *b*, 34, *n*.   Give Exercise 73, *v*, *ever*, *never*,
over.

EXERCISE 73

The first part of the *v* is like the first part of the *n*, and the last part is like the last part of the *b*. The last up-stroke should have a slight in-curve, not the swinging final stroke as at the end of the *n*. Here we have the bridge connection again. It would be well, since the combination comes in every word given for practice, to give some special drill on the group *ver*.

Lesson 2

"Our new exercise is a very queer one. It looks much like a sawhorse." Show Exercise 74, *x, fix, next*.

EXERCISE 74

To make the *x* have the children write the letter *n* once, erase the first curve, and cross the down-stroke in the middle with a straight line. Let them make it in this way a few times before they make it to the metronome beat. They may test their work by putting on the first curve to see if it will make an *n*.

Give Exercise 75, *You may fix the box next.*

Lesson 3

Review parts of Exercises 73, 74. Give Exercise 76, *L, Laura*.

EXERCISE 76

It is important to have the right slant for this letter. There will also be some difficulty with the loop at the base line. This should rest on the base line and the final stroke should be either on the base line or extend a little below it. Use any names that are appropriate and within the experience of the children.

Lesson 4

Review Exercises 73, 74, 75, 76. Give Exercise 77, *Let Ida come with you.*

LESSON 5

"Take clean paper. Write name, grade, date." Give Exercises 73, 74, 75, 76, 77.

After the papers are collected, spend the time in practice on names.

FIFTH MONTH. FIRST WEEK

This month we shall begin writing without the metronome part of the time. Write each exercise using the metronome and then write it without, trying to keep approximately the same rhythm. Some allowance should be made for individual difference in rhythm. Use this method during the month unless definite instructions are given for a change of method. Set the metronome for this month at 104.

LESSON 1

Review Exercise 60, *s*. After writing three lines of the swinging exercise, write *s* separately several times. Have the children do this also. Then show the children that, by adding a good loop, at the top you make the capital *S*.

Then give Exercise 78, *S*, *Spring*, *Summer*. Show the further

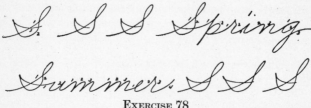

EXERCISE 78

difference from the small *s* in the sharp turn at the bottom followed by an additional stroke to the right. Give the letter *S* alone several times and then put on the board the remainder of the exercise one word at a time.

LESSON 2

Give Exercise 79, *G*, *Grace*, *George*. Call attention to the count.

EXERCISE 79

This is exceedingly important here because the count indicates the letter units. This letter is more closely related to the *S* than to any other letter, but it is not desirable to call the children's attention to this, as it is not a likeness which is apt to help in writing the letter. The joining of the *o* and the *r* in *George* is a particularly difficult point. Drill on this combination should precede the writing of the word. The connecting stroke should drop low enough so that the *r* is not too high and the cross-stroke of the *r* has its full value.

Lesson 3

Review the letters in Exercises 78, 79. Give Exercise 80, *Laura and Grace go to the lake in Summer*. Write alone any words which need special practice.

Lesson 4

Review Exercise 80. Give practice in writing numbers from dictation. Let each child find the figure on which he needs the most practice and work on that until it is much improved. Then place on the board three examples in multiplication with a single multiplier and have the children copy them with special attention to making good figures and to spacing. Then dictate to them Exercise 81, which gives practice on all the digits.

Exercise 81:

$$704 \qquad 358 \qquad 912 \qquad 587$$
$$\times 6 \qquad \times 7 \qquad \times 8 \qquad \times 9$$

Lesson 5

"Take clean paper. Write name, grade, date." Give Exercises 78, 79, 80, 81.

Spend any time which may remain in writing the names first with, and then without, the metronome.

Second Week. Lesson 1

The matter of arrangement on the page should receive attention at every lesson. See that the margins are good and that the work is well spaced within these.

Review Exercise 48, *N*. "Our new exercise has the first line just like the first line of the *N*. Let us make several of these lines quite far apart. Now see how I make the next stroke and join the two."

Give Exercise 82, *H, Harriet, Herbert*. The connecting stroke of

EXERCISE 82

the *H* should drop low enough so that the one-space letters are not too high.

Lesson 2

Review Exercise 82, *H*.   Give Exercise 83, *K, Kenneth.*

K K K Kenneth

EXERCISE 83

This is a much harder letter than the *H* to write.   The point of contact of the two parts should be at the middle of the first stroke. When made accurately, the last part of the *K* has two compound curves, but in this grade, if it is made with simple curves, it may be regarded as satisfactory.

Lesson 3

Review Exercises 82, 83.   Give Exercise 84, *Keep Harriet with you until I come.*

Lesson 4

By this time the class should have gained some facility in rhythmic writing without the metronome.   To-day we shall use all review work.   Start the metronome for each new exercise, but stop it as soon as the class is fairly started, perhaps after one or two words, and have them continue writing.   It will be well to start it at intervals and have all begin with the beat.   The same exercise should be written three times so as to get a regular swing and test it once or twice. Use Exercises 82, 83, 84.

Lesson 5

"Take clean paper.   Write name, grade, date."   Give Exercises 82, 83, 84.   If more work is wanted, select one exercise that has been given which has occasioned trouble and practice on that, using the metronome to test the rhythm as in Lesson 4.

THIRD WEEK.   LESSON 1

Give Exercise 85, *D, Dick, Dora.*   The *D* proves to be a difficult

D D D Dick Dora

EXERCISE 85

letter for many persons.   The compound curve in the second stroke presents the chief trouble.   This is like the *L*.   See that the *toe* and the *heel* of the *D* are both on the base line.   There is a general tendency to wrong alinement in this letter.   More practice is given here on the combination *or* in *Dora*.   If necessary, practice it alone again.

LESSON 2

Give Exercise 86, *F*, *T*, and Exercise 87, *Frances*, *Fred*, *Thomas*, *Thelma*.   If there are names more suited to the experience of the

EXERCISE 86

children, use them.   There is so little difference in these letters that they should be learned together before any word is written

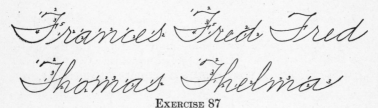

EXERCISE 87

with either.   Some cautions need to be given in the early part of the practice.   The horizontal stroke should not be made too long. The long downward stroke should have such a slant that the final stroke will extend farther to the left than the beginning of the letter. It is better not to join the *F* to other letters, as it has the cross at the end of the last stroke.   This is a definite point of distinction from the *T*, which may be joined to other letters.   If the *F* is joined to other letters, a cross must be made on the stem.

LESSON 3

The only letters not yet given are *U*, *V*, *X*, *Q*.   Review Exercise 48, *N*.

Give Exercise 88, *U*, *V*.   "The *U* and *V* have the same kind of first stroke as the *N*.   Then there is a curve instead of a sharp turn at the bottom.   In the *U* the up-stroke is straight and somewhat

EXERCISE 88   EXERCISE 89

shorter than the down-stroke.   In the *V* the up-stroke curves a little toward the down-stroke."   The last stroke of the *V* is the one which is most likely to cause difficulty. If it curves away from the first stroke, it presents a very ugly appearance. The words *Union* and *Up* may be used if desired.

After practice on these letters review Exercise 74, *x*, and show the class that the capital *X* (Exercise 89) is made in the same way except that it does not begin at the base line. Tell them if they ever need to write it they may remember that it is like the small *x*. Let them write it a few times and return to the practice of Exercise 88. We shall not give the *Q* in this grade, as the pupils are not likely to have any need for it.

Lesson 4

Review Exercises 86, 87, 88. Give Exercise 90, *Vines grow over our schoolhouse.* Practice the words alone and then the whole sentence.

Lesson 5

"Take clean paper. Write name, grade, date." Use the metronome intermittently as in the practice periods. Give Exercises 85, 86, 87, 89, 90. If there is more time, review Exercise 81.

Fourth Week

This week the work will all be review, but arranged in new sentences so that it will appeal to the children as new. For this reason the exercises will not be assigned to days. Select what is most needed by the class, and on Friday proceed as usual, using part or all of the exercises written during the week. Spend one day or half of each of two days on drill on writing figures. This time specialize on the short division form, putting four examples on a line; as Exercise 91:

$$5)\overline{7\,4\,3} \qquad 7)\overline{2\,6\,8} \qquad 8)\overline{5\,0\,3} \qquad 9)\overline{7\,3\,1}$$

Copies for the Week

Exercise 92: *We will play out-doors before work begins.*
Exercise 93:

> Jack and Jill went up the hill
> To fetch a pail of water.

Exercise 94, *Zinnias grow in my garden.*

Sixth Month

The children should begin to use pen and ink at about this time. In individual cases it may be a month earlier or a month later. It is best to give the children time at the beginning of the third year to establish somewhat firmly the habits that were introduced in the second year. On the other hand, it is important that they have sufficient practice during this year with the new medium so that it will not be unfamiliar to them at the beginning of the next year.

The first lesson with the new medium is very important. First see that all children are ready for it. Begin to talk about it as a pleasant anticipation two weeks before it is to be taken up and give directions as to exactly the kind of material to be used. Examine each penholder as it comes in. It should not be so large as to be clumsy, but should have a rubber or cork tip. It is best to have the pens supplied by the school, as it is exceedingly hard to get any uniformity otherwise. The cost is relatively small when pens are bought by the gross. A round pointed pen should be used.

While carelessness in the use of pens should not be encouraged, the children should not be stinted in their use, as by requiring them to use one pen for a week or two. If the children are to learn to use the pens, they must *use* them. This is another argument for the school's supplying the pens — the difficulty of keeping the child properly equipped if he must provide his own.

Second, when ready to begin the use of the pen, show the children *how* to use it. (Have several blotters at the teacher's desk, but do not allow the children to have any. If the pen is used correctly, they are not needed and a blotter can ruin a pen very quickly.)

The pen needs wetting first to remove the oil. Then have the children put the pen into the ink carefully, and in withdrawing it draw it over the edge of the ink-well. This takes off all the surplus ink which might make a blot. Another advantage of having little ink on the pen is that the quality of line will not suffer so much from the heavy pressure which the children exert.

Do not allow the pen to be dropped into the ink-well and then withdrawn, to ink the fingers, and do not allow the pen to rest in the ink-well when not in use. If the ink-container is not fastened to the desk, it is important to see that it stands every time in exactly the same position on each desk. The children will soon become used to this and it will avoid accident.

If these matters are presented to the children in a kindly way and the reasons explained, they will enjoy trying to do exactly right so as to have no accidents.

The first two weeks of this month will be spent in review of some of the letters using words which appear in the 100 per cent spelling list for Grade 3A, in addition to those which we have already practiced. Set the metronome at 112.

First Week. Lesson 1

Review Exercises 19, *d*, 32, *m*, 34, *n*. Give Exercise 95, *build, dead; meet; alone, band, done, line, mountain, once.*

Lesson 2

Review Exercises 38, *g*, 40, *h*.   Give Exercise 96, *again, begin, belong; bought, both, each, held, hold, might, nothing, teach.*   Review Exercise 28, *E.*   Give Exercise 97, *Each has done his work alone.*

Lesson 3

Review Exercises 46, *p*, 58, *y*.   Give Exercise 98, *paid, people; eye, many.*   Review Exercise 43, *B.*   Give Exercise 99, *Begin again and do your best.*

Lesson 4

Review Exercises 61, *s*, 63, *r*.   Give Exercise 100, *because, beside, cost, goes, most, push, said, sight, stole, west; army, before, better, children, church, country, dress, early, flower, grand, ground, morning, pretty, road, round, under, water, were, word.*

Return to this exercise for review until all the words have been practiced.   Give Exercise 101, *The children dress early in the morning.*

Lesson 5

Prepare the paper as usual.   Give Exercises 97, 99, 101.   Then write some of the words practiced this week.

When papers have been collected, have the class practice words from this week's exercises which have not yet been given.

Second Week.   Lesson 1

Continue work on Exercise 100 to-day, using words that have not been practiced.   Then give Exercise 102, *A pretty flower lies on the ground near the water.*

Lesson 2

Review Exercises 68, *k*, 73, *v*.   Give Exercise 103, *block, know, ticket, took; every, leave.*   Give Exercise 104, *I know where to leave every ticket.*

Lesson 3

Spend the time to-day in writing numbers from copy and dictation.   Use multiplication and short division examples and arrange for individual practice of any digits that are not well made. The children have practiced every digit properly, but frequent repetition is necessary to ensure that all the digits shall be habitually correctly made.

Lesson 4

Give Exercise 105:

> If every day we do our best
> Our best will better grow.

The two capitals will need practice. The words *every* and *better* have just appeared in exercises, so probably the word *our* is the only one that will need special practice.

LESSON 5

Prepare the papers as usual. Give four examples in multiplication with a one-place multiplier and four in short division. (If the class uses two-place multipliers in arithmetic, they should be given here.) Then give part or all of the sentence exercises given this week. Exercises 102, 104, 105.

THIRD WEEK

A regular method of grading will be followed for the rest of the year. This is based on the *Chart for the Diagnosis of Faults in Handwriting*, by Frank N. Freeman (Houghton Mifflin Company). Where possible the teacher should make use of this.

The teacher should familiarize herself with the Chart so as to be ready to use it at the beginning of next week. During the week that each category is being emphasized, that category alone will be graded; for example, when *letter formation* is being emphasized, it will be graded in terms of the Chart. The scores 2, 6, 10, or the intermediate scores 4, 8, may be used. Further information regarding the use of the Chart can be obtained from *The Teaching of Handwriting*, by Frank N. Freeman (Houghton Mifflin Company), pp. 123–42.

The children should understand that the marking is by points, not in per cents as in other subjects. When the marking is begun, the teacher should grade in the special category for the week the work done on the first day and that done on the last day.

The child should study his own work every day, not so much for the value of his estimate as to lead to a critical attitude toward his work.

Only one or two selections will be given for each week, with suggestions as to possible preliminary work before writing the selection as a whole. If the teacher thinks best, the verses may be used for a book of poetry which may be made of the last copy of each verse. It has not seemed necessary to give written copies for all these exercises. If there is any question as to form of letters, refer to previous copies.

Do not increase the speed for the regular writing above 112. Attempt to improve the writing at the speed used. Write each selection first with, and then without, the metronome. Use one or both selections for the week as seems better, but do not carry over the work from week to week. Select the most difficult parts of the work for preliminary practice.

With the writing of poetry there arises a new problem of arrangement. Talk this over with the children and decide on how the verse should be placed so as to give the best appearance. The arrangement of printed verses will give suggestions for this.

Copies for the Week

Exercise 106:

> I saw a ship a-sailing,
> A-sailing on the sea;
> And O! it was all laden
> With pretty things for thee.

Exercise 107:

> Crimson clover, I discover
> By the garden gate.

The capitals and any words that are likely to cause difficulty to the children should be studied before the verse is attempted as a whole. Divide the work into periods as seems best for the class.

FOURTH WEEK

This week we begin to give special attention to one category, grading writing as directed in the general directions for the third week. Be sure that the pupils understand that they are marked by points instead of per cent grades. The special category for this week is *letter formation*. Encourage each pupil to criticize the form of his own letters, to discover the best of his own work and to try to make the rest of his work as good. Direct attention to writing in other subjects and suggest that the children try to write as well and in about the same time as in the writing period.

Take a few minutes a day for *speed drill;* for example, select one or two easy words from the verse, and after having written them with the metronome at the regular speed, increase this a little at a time to see how fast the pupils can write and still keep good work. Do not continue when even a few do poorer work. Keep the first graded copy to compare with the last.

Copy for the Week

Exercise 108:

> Old King Cole
> Was a merry old soul
> And a merry old soul was he;
> He called for his pipe,
> And he called for his bowl,
> And he called for his fiddlers three.

There is an advantage in this rhyme, in that it furnishes so much repetition of the same words without seeming to be for that purpose.

There are also a number of capitals to practice.   Probably the one verse will give enough work for the week.

SEVENTH MONTH.   FIRST WEEK

Emphasize *spacing* this week.   Consider both spacing of letters and of words.   Experiment a little and determine what is best.   It should not be cramped nor yet scrawly.   Do not forget *letter formation*, but grade on *spacing*.   Give practice without the metronome after the time is given.   Return to the use of it every few days.

Copy for the Week

Passages selected from other subjects may be substituted for the copies in the following exercises.

Exercise 109:

A DEW DROP

Little drop of dew
Like a gem you are.
I believe that you
Must have been a star.

When the day is bright,
On the grass you lie.
Tell me then, at night
Are you in the sky?

Frank Dempster Sherman.

BEES

Bees don't care about the snow;
I can tell you why that's so;
Once I caught a little bee
Who was much too warm for me.

Frank Dempster Sherman.

SECOND WEEK

The category for grading and emphasis is *uniformity of alinement*. This includes position on the base line and the relative height of the letters.

By incidental suggestion keep both *letter formation* and *spacing* in mind.   Use the metronome only to set the time, and to test regularity, by starting it during the writing.   If there is any difficulty in keeping the time have the class write a few minutes with the metronome.   The speed drill may be given once or twice a week, and in this the metronome should always be used.

Copy for the Week

Exercise 111:

It is n't raining rain to me,
It's raining daffodils.
In every dimpled drop, I see
Wild flowers on the hills.

Exercise 112:

If all were rain and never sun
No bow would span the hill.
If all were sun and never rain [1]
There'd be no rainbow still.

Third Week

Emphasize this week *quality of line*. This refers to evenness in the thickness of the line and to smoothness as distinguished from waviness. The factors contributing to good quality are: good ink and pen; good position, which prevents cramping and undue pressure; and keeping the rhythm, which prevents wavy lines.

Copy for the Week

Exercise 113:

C was a cat
Who ran after a rat.

Exercise 114:

P was a pig
Who was not very big;
But his tail was too curly,
And that made him surly.
Cross little pig.

Edward Lear.

Fourth Week

This week emphasize *uniformity of slant*, and grade it. Lead the children to be critical of their own work. The slant should be quite good because it depends on good position and rhythm. Recall to attention *letter formation*, *spacing*, *alinement*, and *quality of line*. Give speed drill occasionally, increasing the metronome rate for this.

Copy for the Week

Exercise 115:

Violets, violets, sweet March violets,
Sure as March comes they'll come too,
Pretty violets!

---

[1] From Christina G. Rossetti's *Poems*, by permission of The Macmillan Company.

By and by there'll be so many,
We'll pick dozens and not miss any.
Sweet, sweet violets!

EIGHTH MONTH. FIRST WEEK

This week emphasize and grade on *letter formation, alinement,* and *spacing,* summing the scores in each for the total points. Start an exercise with the metronome and then have it written two or three times without. Spend one day this week in practicing numbers for addition and subtraction.

Copy for the Week

Exercise 116:

Good night! good night!
Far flies the light;
But still God's love
Shall flame above
Making all bright.
Good night! good night!

Special practice should be given to the capitals.

SECOND WEEK

Emphasize and grade on *letter formation, alinement,* and *quality of line.* As far as possible use the metronome only for starting an exercise and then write without. Give the speed drill for a brief time during three periods this week.

Copy for the Week

Exercise 117:

All things bright and beautiful,
All creatures great and small,
All things wise and wonderful,
The Lord God made them all.

He gave us eyes to see them,
And lips that we might tell,
How great is God Almighty,
Who hath made all things well.

Suggest that good writing be carried over into regular work.

THIRD WEEK

Grade on the five categories this week. Try to have the class listen to the metronome in starting and then write without it. The writing should have improved very much in the last two months. If necessary emphasize *letter formation.*

Copy for the Week

Exercise 118:

> Boats sail on the rivers,
> And ships sail on the seas;
> But clouds that sail across the sky
> Are prettier far than these.
>
> There are bridges on the rivers,
> As pretty as you please;
> But the bow that bridges heaven,
> And overtops the trees,
> And builds a road from earth to sky,
> Is prettier far than these. [1]

Fourth Week

This week one easier verse is given and the teacher may review or use some verse which has been omitted if more work is needed.

Copy for the Week

Exercise 119:

> F was a fish
> Who was caught in a net;
> But he got out again,
> And is quite alive yet.
> Lively young fish!
>
> *Edward Lear.*

Ninth Month

During the last month of school in this grade the work in other subjects is likely to provide enough material for all the writing periods. Work such as the following may be done: Spring booklet, containing story, poem, or report of some nature-study project; Mother's Day booklet; invitation to Spring festival or program; a letter, the need for which arises in carrying out plans made by the class. Any work motivated by the school activities which requires writing may fill the writing period. This work may be quite individual in character. Certain cautions are necessary, however, in carrying out the work in this way. First, all standards set up during the year, in position, manner of writing, quality, and speed should be maintained. Second, this freedom of choice as to subject-matter is not to be taken as a reason for omitting the regular writing period or for "filling in" with something which is not distinctly worth while. For those who have difficulty in finding worth-while material for this month the following selections are given. It is suggested that one of them be used the entire month, being prac-

[1] From Christina G. Rossetti's *Poems*, by permission of The Macmillan Company.

ticed a verse at a time and finally all written together and put in a booklet with a cover and illustrations prepared in the art or industrial period.

A two-minute test according to the directions on page 8 should be given the third week of this month, to compare with the graded test at the beginning of this year.

Copies for the Month

Exercise 120:

SHOWER AND FLOWER

Down the little drops patter,
Making a musical clatter,
    Out of the clouds they throng:
Freshness of heaven they scatter
    Little dark rootlets among.
"Coming to visit you, Posies!
Open your hearts to us, Roses!"
    That is the Raindrops' song.

Up the little seed rises:
Buds of all colors and sizes
    Clamber up out of the ground.
Gently the blue sky surprises
    The earth with that soft-rushing sound.
"Welcome!" the brown bees are humming:
"Come! for we wait for your coming!"
    Whisper the wild-flowers around.

"Shower, it is pleasant to hear you!" —
"Flower, it is sweet to be near you!" —
    This is the song everywhere.
Listen! The music will cheer you!
    Raindrops and blossom so fair
Gladly are meeting together
Out in the beautiful weather:
    Oh, the sweet song in the air!

Lucy Larcom.

Exercise 121:

TO A HONEY BEE

Busy-body, busy-body,
Always on the wing,
Wait a bit where you have lit,
And tell me why you sing.

Up, and in the air again,
Flap, flap, flap!
And now she stops and now she drops
Into the rose's lap.

Come, just a minute, come,
From your rose so red.
Hum, hum, hum, hum —
That was all she said.

Busy-body, busy-body,
Always light and gay,
It seems to me for all I see,
Your work is only play.

And now the day is sinking to
The goldenest of eves,
And she doth creep for quiet sleep
Among the lily leaves.

Come just a minute, come,
From your snowy bed.
Hum, hum, hum, hum —
That was all she said.

Alice Cary.

OPTIONAL MATERIAL

The following selections may be used if additional work is needed or if the teacher wishes to substitute them for some of the assigned exercises. If used they should be treated as the assigned exercises are treated.

Blow loud for the blossoms that live in the trees,
And blow low for the daisies and clover;
But as soft as I can for the violets shy,
Yes, softly — and over and over.

Mary Mapes Dodge.

DON'T GIVE UP

If you've tried and have not won,
Never stop for crying;
All that's great and good is done
Just by patient trying.

Phœbe Cary.

GOING TO LONDON

Up, down! Up, down!
All the way to London town —
See how fast we're going!
Feel the jar
Of the car?
Feel the wind a-blowing.

Mary Mapes Dodge.

D was a duck
With spots on his back
Who lived in the water
And always said, "Quack!"
Dear little duck!

Edward Lear.

K was a kite
Which flew out of sight,
Above houses so high,
Quite into the sky.
Fly away, Kite!

Edward Lear.

CHAPTER VIII

EXERCISES FOR GRADE FOUR

OBJECTIVES

Content. The range of words to be written should increase in proportion to the increased needs with the development of vocabulary in other subjects. The child should be able to write and spell correctly any word for which he has use. The purpose of the practice in this and the following years is to gain greater facility in the processes which the child has already learned. New words and sentences are introduced partly because they present difficulties he has not mastered before, due to their greater length, and also because they give variety to the drill, and, being drawn from subject-matter at the child's level of development, give him a greater sense of the importance of the practice. Such words as the following may be added to those already used.

able	built	date	life	few
could	would	should	mail	town
dozen	while	those	money	always
brought	charge	front	speak	leave
expect	became	woman	been	among
tenth	thought	young	finish	question
bridge	hour	price	there	wrote
yesterday	alike	broke	cover	even

The habit of using capitals in names, dates, beginning sentences, and beginning each line of poetry should be confirmed. New names used in other subject-matter, as states, cities, or noted persons, should be added to the writing vocabulary. Column writing of numbers to 1 000 000 from copy or dictation should be done with some degree of facility, and correct form should be maintained in all arithmetical operations already learned; also in multiplication where the multiplier is a number of two or three orders, in long division and in simple fraction examples. In composition correct form should become habitual in writing a paragraph, and simple correspondence forms should become familiar. The correspondence forms should include the writing of an informal friendly letter, an informal note of invitation, acceptance or thanks, and a simple business letter, as in asking for needed information, ordering supplies, buying garden seed, etc.

Movement. The child, having now become accustomed to the use of pen and ink, should improve his muscular coördination, gain a fluency of fifty letters a minute by development of rhythm, and should maintain in the writing required in all subjects a good arrangement of material on the paper.

MATERIALS AND METHODS

Materials. Paper of good quality with half-inch ruling. Penholder as in Grade 3. The pen may be somewhat finer if desired.

Methods. *A. Position.* Any departure from satisfactory position should be corrected in this grade and the aim should be to establish by the end of the year the habit of writing in standard position.

B. Types of exercises. 1. Drills for maintaining free rhythmic movement, with the aim of gradually developing an individual rhythm in place of the imposed rhythm of the metronome. The motivation arises from the child's feeling of need derived from his other work.

2. Practice on material from content subjects where the child recognizes a reason for the practice, as, in the satisfactory writing of compositions which have been previously prepared. This enables the child to meet the handwriting difficulty in isolation from the difficulties of composition when he should be just beginning to be free in self-expression in writing.

3. Speed drills should be used, taking care that quality is maintained so that the speed and quality will be developed coördinately. In the last three months the use of the metronome should be gradually discontinued.

C. Standards and criticism. Form should be developed along the line of *uniformity of slant and alinement, quality of line, letter formation,* and *spacing.* Systematic self-criticism should be introduced by reference to the *Freeman Chart for the Diagnosis of Faults in Handwriting.* The chief emphasis in this grade should be the development of a conscious attitude of self-criticism by reference to an established standard.

The standard in *speed* in this grade is fifty letters a minute. The standard in quality is 16 on the Freeman Scale and 50 on the Ayres Scale.

FIRST MONTH
FIRST WEEK. LESSON 1

A good way to begin the work this year is to use a talk somewhat like the following, adapted to the conditions of the class.

"We find good writing easier to read than poor writing, so we consider it a desirable thing. *Any one* can write well if he takes time enough and works hard enough. We shall try to learn to write so that we can do better writing with less effort.

"In order to do this, we pay attention to these points: first, we must hold the pen loosely, without cramping the fingers; second, we must let the hand rest on the third and fourth fingers instead of the side, so that it will be easier to move across the page; third, we must have the paper directly in front, slanted about as we want the writing to slant. The position of the body is important, too, because if we bear much weight on our arms we tire much sooner than if they can move freely. Sit in an easy position with feet resting on the floor, then place the arms on the desk without bearing weight on them. Take the pen and hold it loosely." Explain the position as much as is necessary. "Now slide across the paper and see how freely you can move. If your wrist is raised a little, it will be easier. Now I will show you something to write." Give Exercise 1, the over-swing, using voice count, "one-two, one-two, one-two, one-two." "Now you may do it just as I did. You may count as you do it. We shall take the under-swing in the same way."

EXERCISES 1 AND 2

Show Exercise 2, the under-swing. Give this with the same count as Exercise 1.

What we want here is to develop a freedom of swing which will carry over into the writing exercises later. Where the class has had three years' training in this type of writing, little effort on the part of the teacher should be necessary to secure free movement. However, there are always some children who, through lack of opportunity or otherwise, do not measure up to the class standard. Discover these children as soon as possible and give individual work, frequently on the blackboard, so that they may acquire facility in the correct type of movement.

Repeat Exercise 1, 2, three times, and then give Exercise 3, *i*. Be sure that this is given with the long free swing. Emphasize to the children the need of this freedom and say to them that we care more just now about the way the work is done than about the way it looks. There is not likely to be any great amount of disorganization of the movement after three years of training, but, because habits are slowly formed, it is probable that there has been some relapse during the summer that will need to be overcome.

LESSON 2

"Sit straight, hips back, feet on floor. Arms on desk. Can you place your paper right? Good." Do not neglect commendation wherever possible to give it. "Without pen slide on your two fingers — 'way across the paper. Ready. Slide. One-two, one-two, one-two, one-two. Now pens. Is your position like this?" Be sure that it is. "Now slide, but do not write. Ready. Slide. One-two," etc. (Four times.) "Look." Write on the board Exercise 1, counting. "You may write it. Ready. Write. One-two," etc. "Did you keep the time? Once more. One-two," etc. "Now we will make the lower swing." Show Exercise 2, and have the class write it. Make both swings again to gain free movement. Show Exercise 3, *i*. Have the class write it. "Are your fingers

EXERCISE 3

ready to slide? Is your pen right? Are you holding it loosely?" Test a few by pulling the pen from the fingers. "Make long slides so that you can put only three on a line. Try again. See how I count." Put it on the board again with count. Notice that the count is on the forward stroke. "Ready. Write. One-two, one-two." Give Exercise 4, *t*. "We will make the same stroke, but

EXERCISE 4

nearly twice as high. Swing 'way across the paper making three *t*'s." Do this twice. This long swing is not appropriate for many of the letters and so will be shortened somewhat, though a free swing will be used. Follow the copies in the length of swing for the different letters.

Give Exercise 5, *it*, *tit*. Give *it* first alone, giving a long swing

EXERCISE 5

between the words. Then give the combination *tit*, making a longer swing than natural, but writing the groups alone. This work introduces a definite problem in control, in the length of the swing which is likely to hold the attention of the children.

Give Exercise 6, *u*, making two short strokes together and a long

EXERCISE 6

swing between each two groups.　Follow this by Exercise 7, *tut*, which, because of its slight difference from Exercise 5, requires attention.　Alternate these two writing them with long swing.

tut　tut　tut

EXERCISE 7

EXERCISE 7

If a large part of the class has not had training of this type before, this work may be too hard or too much for the class.　If so, work more slowly, but give the new letters each day leaving out part of the word exercises.

LESSON 3

Give specific directions as to position as in the last lesson.　Use Exercises 1, 2, 3, 4, 6, with voice count, and be particular to see that position is kept.　If there is indication of disregard for base line and proper height of letters, due to the use of free movement, let it go for the present.　Work *only* for position, freedom of movement, and correct time.

Give Exercise 8, *e, tie*.　Here we have the loop swing.　The back

e　e　e　tie　tie

EXERCISE 8

should be nearly straight.　"Make long swings between the letters."　After practice of *e* for several lines, give the word *tie*.　Here we combine two types of letters, and it is very important that the children get the free swing in connection with this. ·

LESSON 4

"Take position.　Show me how your hands slide on the little fingers.　Pens."　Review, with count, Exercises 1, 2, putting them on the board first.　Review Exercises 3, 4, 5, 6, with count.　Each review exercise should be given once or twice.　Don't make it drudgery by too long repetition of an exercise.　Don't expect perfection at first.　Go back to the work often.

Review Exercise 8, *e*.　"Now we will make this tall as we did the *i*.　See how straight I make the down-stroke.　Can you make it so?"　Give Exercise 9, *l, till, tell, little*.　Give the letter first.

l　l　l　l　l　l

till　tell　little

EXERCISE 9

"Now you may write it. Ready. Write." Always give the count for the exercises as it is given on the written copies in the Manual. Repeat the practice of the *l* two or three times. See that a good straight down-stroke is kept in the writing. Give the words in Exercise 9. "How many kept the time exactly?"

LESSON 5

To-day give the preliminary test for the year. Follow exactly the directions on page 8 and use the material indicated for Grade 4. This test should be graded by the Standard Scale in use and kept for comparison from time to time through the year and with the work at the end of the year to show the year's progress.

SECOND WEEK. LESSON 1

"Take correct position. Show me how you hold your hand and pen. Let us make the over-curve. Ready. Write. One-two," etc. "Now the under-curve. Ready. Write. One-two," etc. Review Exercise 9, *l*. "I want to show you a new exercise." Give Exercise 10, *b*, *built*. Give the *b* alone. Make it again. "Notice

EXERCISE 10

the count. Be careful about the last stroke. Now you may write. Ready. Write. How many swing 'way across the paper? Let's try it again. Ready. Write. Did you keep the time better?" Call attention to the one-space stroke. It must curve toward the down-stroke, but must not close the gap. Review Exercises 3, *i*, 6, *u*, 8, *e*. Then write Exercise 10 again three times. The teacher should put all words on the board first. Now give the word, which has the horizontal connecting stroke and all the letters now studied except *e*.

LESSON 2

Study of the written work in arithmetic will probably result in the conclusion that there is need of practice in the forms of the figures and in arrangement. Pass out to-day a set of papers in arithmetic which has been saved for this purpose. Suggest the possibility of improving the looks of the work.

"Each find the figure which is made the best on your paper. Underline it. Is this figure made as well as this every time you have made it? Write on the board each of the digits and the cipher, counting as you write. Compare your best figure with the same figure on the board. Does it need any change? If so, write it as

nearly correct as possible.   Now write this figure as well as you can
six times.   Find the figure you think needs the most improvement.
Can you tell how to improve it?"

A little general analysis of each figure will help the children to
see the form so as to be able to write correctly.   Now let each
practice for the rest of the period individually on the figures where
he needs the most improvement.   State that you will check the
improvement on the written arithmetic papers which are handed
in, and then *do not forget to do it*.   Allow the asking of questions
with regard to form and time.

LESSON 3

Give attention to position and freedom and swing of movement.
Review Exercises 1, 2, 3, 6, 8, 9, 10.   The early ones are kept up for
the sake of automatizing the forward swinging movement.   If done
to count and attentively, one repetition of each is enough after the
first week.   Write Exercises 8, 9, 10, three or four times each.

"Look carefully."   Give Exercise 11, *a, able*.   "See that the top

EXERCISE 11

of the *a* has an upward tendency.   A good swing will help to make
this so.   Better let it go up a little than down at all.   Notice that
it is closed at the top."   Notice that the *a*, when written from now
on as an initial letter, is written without the preliminary up-stroke.
In order not to change the practice of counting on the forward
stroke, count *one* for an imaginary first stroke and count for the first
up-stroke of the letter.   After a time the preliminary count may be
dropped.   The instruction applies also to the letters *d, g, o,* and *q*.
"Look again."   Write it again with count.   "Class.   Ready.
Write."   After several repetitions give the word *able*.

LESSON 4

Give Exercises 1, 2, for free swing.   Review Exercises 3, 8, 9, 10.
Write a line of each of the words which have been studied, writing
to count always.   "Are your *a*'s all closed at the top?   Do the tops
all keep up?"   Be sure that the class keeps the swing and that the
spacing is wide.   Then dictate numbers for addition examples, four
columns wide and five numbers deep.   Give three or four examples
as will best fill the page.

When numbers are to be written in column formation, it is very
important that the children be shown how to do it correctly and
that they be required to do it so thereafter in all such work.

When writing numbers in a column, each number should be separated from the number above it by a distance equal to one half the height of the figures. The columns corresponding to the different orders — units, tens, hundreds — should be separated by a space equal to the width of the figures.

The importance of attention to this from the beginning and all the time lies in the fact that correct column placing of figures has been found to increase materially the accuracy of computation.

LESSON 5

"Take clean paper. Position. Without writing slide your hand on the little fingers. Ready. Slide. One-two, one-two, one-two, one-two. Now, holding your pen right and keeping the hand up, write your name, grade, and the date, on the top line." Give Exercises 1, 2, 3, 6, 8, 9, 10, 11. Exercises 8, 9, 10, 11, should be written twice each.

After these papers have been collected to keep for comparison, give practice on the exercises which are not so well automatized.

THIRD WEEK. LESSON 1

Review Exercises 1, 2, with count. "What figure do you find it hardest to make?" In giving these for different pupils you will probably give most of the digits. If any is omitted which has been made somewhat carelessly, this is a good chance to analyze the figure and show the need for improvement.

Dictate three examples in addition and three in subtraction stating that the papers will be collected for grading on the figures. Then allow the children to work the examples and write the answers. Place on the board several more examples for the children to copy when they have finished solving the dictated examples. The accurate copying of numbers is a matter of importance and needs practice. The digits and cipher are given for reference in Exercise 13.

LESSON 2

Review Exercises 6, *u*, 8, *e*, with a free swing. Show Exercise 11, *a*, and have the class write it two or three times. "Now we will write another exercise much like this." Give Exercise 12, *d*, *date*, *died*. Write it two or three times on the board if necessary for the class to get the swing.

ddd date died

EXERCISE 12

1 2 3 4 5 6 7 8 9 0

EXERCISE 13

Call attention to the fact that the first stroke of the *d* has the upward tendency just as the first stroke of the *a* has, and that the lengthened up-stroke is made in the same time as the *a* stroke. "Class ready. Write. Again." After practicing the swinging exercise, give the words one at a time for writing. If more work is needed, review the words used in previous grades — *bad, bed, did, dead, led.*

LESSON 3

Review Exercise 11, *a.* Give Exercise 14, *A.* Notice that these

A A A A A A

EXERCISE 14

letters are the same except for size. In the capital *A* it is better to have the count on the down-stroke, and if this is joined to the rest of the word a count may be lost on the connecting stroke so as to bring the count on the forward stroke. Write with *A* any names which have an interest for the children, and any words which have been given in the lower grades with this exercise.

Give Exercise 15, *A little doll, A little ball.* Give these phrases to

A little doll

EXERCISE 15

the class for the sake of giving drill on context writing. In this connection a discussion of proper page arrangement is apropos. The class may practice these phrases without suggestion as to arrangement near the close of the period. This work should be used in the next lesson as the basis of discussion.

LESSON 4

To-day the phrase work written yesterday should be used as the basis for a discussion on page arrangement. The teacher should write a page of these phrases so as to illustrate good arrangement. A discussion somewhat like the following may be carried on: "We have been trying to improve our writing by making it easy and free, and with good letter form. To-day I want you to think whether there is any way to improve the looks of our work besides improving the quality of the letters." If they do not make the suggestion, ask, "Does it make any difference where on the page we put our work? Yes, the lines must be straight."

Draw out by questions if the children do not suggest them the following points: The lines must not be too close together, the words must not be too close together, the letters in a word must not be too close together; on the other hand, too wide spacing injures the appearance of the page. "Does it make any difference about the appearance of the work, how close we write to the edge of the paper at the sides, top and bottom? Has any one filled the whole page? Let us see the paper. Has any one written so that some space is left at the edge of the paper?" Compare papers which by chance show some marginal spacing. Then show the sheet prepared with good marginal spacing. Compare this with several which have been shown. "Suppose we try in our writing to improve the appearance of our page in this way as well as by making the letters look well."

LESSON 5

Recall the discussion of arrangement. "Let us see how well we can arrange our papers to-day. Suppose we make dots to show where we shall begin and where we shall stop, both at the beginning and end of the line and at the top and bottom of the paper. Prepare the paper." Give preliminary swing for limbering up before writing. Give Exercise 15, requiring good context writing, well spaced.

FOURTH WEEK. LESSON 1

Review Exercises 1, 2, 11, 12. Write three times each the words in Exercises 8, 9, 10, 11, 12. Keep the margins in the swinging exercises as well as in context writing; that is, instead of swinging from edge to edge of the paper, swing from margin to margin as marked.

LESSON 2

Review Exercises 1, 2, swinging only halfway across the page instead of across the whole page. Write Exercises 3, 6, 8, 9, lessening the swing somewhat. Be very sure the swing is not lost in shortening it, and that the hand really slides on the third and fourth fingers. This is far more important still than emphasis on correct form. The only form yet noted is the top of the a and the d, attention to which may be called when any exercise containing it is given. But it is the swing that will bring it right. Keep the swing from dropping down. The element of control enters largely here in the changing length of the swing and the adherence to margins. Encourage this in all the writing so that it will be consciously aimed at until the habit is established. Give for extra word review any of the words practiced with the idea of good spacing.

LESSON 3

Review Exercises 11, *a*, 12, *d*, making two or three groups to the line. Give Exercise 16, *o, loud*. Call attention to the pause at the

EXERCISE 16

top of the *o* and practice it with a long swing until the idea is clear and the children accomplish it reasonably well. Even adult writers are often careless about the connecting stroke so that the *o* and the *a* are not easily distinguished.

For practice on this give Exercise 17, *a, o*, alternating the two

EXERCISE 17

groups and keeping the connecting strokes distinct, the *a* always touching the base line before going on, the *o* never touching the base line with its connecting stroke. Then give the word *loud*.

LESSON 4

Review Exercises 1, 2, half-line swing. Review Exercises 5, 7, 8. Review Exercises 3, 6, 8, on the short swing. Write the words from Exercises 11, 12, 16.

LESSON 5

"Take clean paper." If necessary mark the margins by dots. Note position and give preliminary swing. "Write name, grade, and date." Give with short swing Exercises 1, 2, 3, 6, 8, 9, 10, 11, 12, 16. Spend any extra time practicing any names which begin with capital *A*.

SECOND MONTH. FIRST WEEK

Introduce the metronome setting it at 104.[1] The introduction of the metronome to give the time has different purposes. It sets the teacher free to inspect and give suggestions to individual pupils. It gives an absolutely regular beat for a continuous period such as

---

[1] If a metronome cannot be obtained for use, the voice count should be regulated so as to follow the rates indicated in the lessons as accurately as possible.

is not possible with the teacher's voice. Also it makes possible the definite determination of the rate to be used at a given time and the increase in a systematic way.

LESSON 1

Review with long swing Exercises 3, 6, 8, 9. Then give each with shortened swing. Give each new exercise this week with voice count and rather slowly. After the first day give it with the metronome. Give Exercise 18, *w*, *would*. The *w* gives again the

EXERCISE 18

connecting stroke at one space height. See that this is made right. There is frequent confusion of *u* and *w* even among adult writers, due to the failure to make this distinction. After practice with the swinging exercise, give the word *would* which involves two of these connections. Then for variety give selections from Exer-

EXERCISE 19

cise 19, *we*, *web*, *wed*, *wad*, *wait*, *two*, *dew*, *low*, *blow*, *wall*. All these are simple words including only letters already studied.

LESSON 2

Remember position is all-important. Use the metronome the entire month at 104. Review Exercises 1, 2, 11, *a*. Then give Exercise 20, *c*, *could*. Notice particularly that the *c* does turn down

EXERCISE 20

at the top in distinction from the *a*. Call attention to this and see that it is accomplished in this swinging exercise. Mix these two exercises in practice so as not to encourage carelessness by the too long-continued use of one exercise. Write several lines keeping exactly to count. If there is trouble in this, write it on the board two or three times and have the class listen to the metronome as they watch. They will soon get the idea. Review Exercise 18, *would*. Then give *could*. These exercises, if varied as suggested, should fill the whole period.

LESSON 3

Give work in writing numbers for multiplication using numbers of four places in the multiplicand and one place in the multiplier. Place two or three examples on the line according to the space allowed. Review Exercise 15, as context writing.

LESSON 4

Take Exercises 1, 2, half-line swing. Give Exercise 21, E, *Eda, Ella, Etta.* This is a hard capital to write and needs careful study.

EXERCISE 21

Write the letter on the board several times and show the count. Show also that the letter has two curves which can be completed to form ovals if the letter is well made. If possible give all of the class practice on this letter on the board where they can write with the metronome, test their work by trying to complete the ovals and then try again. At any rate, let them do some of this work at their seats. Give any names of interest to the class beginning with the E. Review Exercise 13, *A*, with any words used. Give Exercise 22, *Ella told a little tale.*

LESSON 5

Prepare the papers as directed for writing. See that the children attend to the margins. Practice the slide without writing. Give one line each of the letters in Exercises 11, 12, 16, 18, using the short swing. Give the words in Exercises 16, 18, 20, 21, 22.

SECOND WEEK

Be sure to keep the time. Note the holding of the pen and be sure that it is right.

LESSON 1

Review Exercises 3, 8, with a long swing, twice each. Give drill in writing numbers for short division using the form given in Exercise 23.

$$7\overline{)4\ 8\ 3\ 2} \qquad 6\overline{)5\ 2\ 9\ 7} \qquad 8\overline{)7\ 9\ 0\ 6} \qquad 4\overline{)3\ 8\ 2\ 0}$$

Be sure that the answers are correctly placed. Use four orders and place three or four examples on the line as space permits. Give the work both by dictation and from copy, having the class perform the division and write the quotient. As this is for the sake of the form, the teacher may if she thinks best have the children perform the division together and place the partial quotient as found so that the whole quotient will be correctly placed. No insertion of remainder to be used in further division should be allowed.

LESSON 2

Review Exercise 9, *l*.   Give Exercise 24, *f*, *fill*, *life*, *felt*, *few*, *wife*.

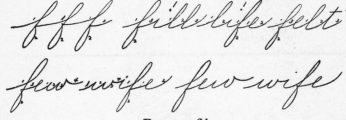

EXERCISE 24

Give the letter alone first. "Notice that this is like the *l* if I cover the lower loop. See how straight the down-stroke is." Do not allow this to become curved. Emphasize the straightness, even to excess at first. Call attention to the crossing halfway between the base line and the top of the letter and to the closing at the base line. If the letter is not made so, the *l* is not apparent in it. Practice to-day only the words containing both the *l* and the *f*. Keep the writing with the metronome.

LESSON 3

Review Exercise 24, *f*, with good swing and correct position. Review Exercise 18, *w*. Give the words *few*, *wife*, from Exercise 24. Review Exercise 22.

LESSON 4

Give Exercises 1, 2, half-line swing. Review Exercises 13, *A*, and 24, *f*. Give Exercise 25, *A little ball of ice*. Practice writing numbers in columns four to six deep and varying in size from units to thousands. The unit column should be kept straight as a guide for the whole. Dictate these.

LESSON 5

Prepare the papers as usual. Practice Exercises 1, 2, without writing. Write four short division examples, the dividend being of four places, performing the operation. Give Exercises 24, 25. After collecting the papers, review Exercises 18, 20, 21, 22.

THIRD WEEK.   LESSON 1

Review Exercises 3, 8, long swing, twice each.   Review the

letters in Exercises 9, 10, 11, 12.　Review Exercises 24, *f*, 11, *a*. Give Exercise 26, *q*, *quiet*, giving the *q* alone first.　"Show me what

q q q quiet quiet

EXERCISE 26

part of the letter is like the *a*.　What part is like the *f?*　Notice which way the loop turns.　We go forward in our writing — turning to the right."　Practice these three exercises keeping the attention on form — the top tending up, the loop closed at the line and the crossing at the top of the one-space letters.　Then give the word *quiet*.

LESSON 2

Review Exercises 11, *a*, 12, *d*.　Review Exercise 26, *q*.　Give Exercise 27, *m*, *mail*.　Emphasize the curved tops.　See that they

m m m mail

EXERCISE 27

are made so.　Give the word *mail*.　Give Exercise 28, *n*, *aunt*, *own*, *town*.　To emphasize the difference between the *m* and *n*, practice

n n n n n

aunt own town

EXERCISE 28

them several times in alternation, watching carefully the curves at the top.　Then give the words in Exercise 28.　It is especially necessary to watch the tops of the *m* and *n* in words where they are not initial letters because of the tendency to make a sharp turn at the first stroke.

LESSON 3

See that the hand is in good position.　Give Exercise 12, with a good swing.　Then with a shorter swing.　Call attention to the top which continues the upward movement.　Review Exercise 13, *A*.　Give Exercise 29, *Aunt Etta went to town*.　Give practice on column writing of numbers from one to four places.　Use ciphers in some of the numbers.

LESSON 4

Review Exercise 21, *E*. Give Exercise 30, *C*, *Come*, *Can*. This is much like the *E*, having only one oval instead of two. Practice

C C C Come Can

EXERCISE 30

the two letters and then give any names of interest to the class, and the words in Exercise 30. Give Exercise 31, *Can Edwin lift a table?*

LESSON 5

Prepare the papers as usual. Attend to the margins if necessary. Give free limbering swing, without writing, pen held loosely. By this time a good position should be maintained in writing the heading of the paper, and this week the children may write it with the metronome. Write the letters in Exercises 13, 21, 30. Then give names using these letters.

FOURTH WEEK. LESSON 1

Take time to-day to compare the papers written last Friday with the papers written the first Friday. Let each child see his own two together and notice the improvement himself. The improvement may be in lightness or regularity of line, in regularity of slant, in keeping to the base line, in making all *a*'s and *d*'s stand up at the top. This may be called an improvement even though these letters did not appear on the first sheet, as it is something the children have learned to do. Ask the class to see how often they have kept their letters just on the base line. Suggest that this week they try to do that especially. If there is more time, clinch this last suggestion by practicing. Use Exercises 29, 31, for this.

LESSON 2

Review Exercises 27, 28, 30. Give Exercise 32, *O*, *Otto*, *Out*.

O O O Otto Out Out

EXERCISE 32

Show the *O* alone first. Suggest the oval shape, and if the children care to do so let them retrace it four times. Practice it many times with the metronome. Then give the words. Use any names that are appropriate.

Lesson 3

Review Exercises 30, 32.   If necessary still continue to give new exercises at a slower rate.   Give Exercise 33, *Otto told Ella and Alice a new tale.*   After writing once, let each pick out the part on which he needs practice and work on that.   After having practiced for several lines with self-criticism, write the whole sentence again. Compare with the first writing, noting improvements especially. This is the time also for the teacher to discover where there are faults which the pupils are overlooking and which need improvement.   If the faults are individual, call attention to the correct way of making the letter, and if necessary, point out the difference between the child's letter and the correct one.

Lesson 4

Have written from copy numbers to add and to subtract as shown in Exercise 34:

6 4 2 8	5 4 0 8	7 5 0
3 0 2 4	2 6 0 0	4 9 0 6
8 6 0 5	5 0 8 3	3 0 0 7
4 8 3	7 6	5 2 1 8
2 9 6 0	2 0 9	3 0
7 4	4 3 6 0	9 0 4

6 5 2 8	5 9 8 3	6 0 7 0
−2 0 7 6	−2 8 9 4	−4 2 8 3

Practice on the digits that need attention.   The pupils that do not need this practice may write numbers serially beginning with *1000.*

Lesson 5

Prepare the papers as usual.   Preliminary swing.   "Let us try to keep exactly on the line, exactly with the metronome, and in perfect position to-day."   Give Exercises 31, 32, 33.   Then write from dictation numbers similar to those used yesterday.

Third Month

Set the metronome at 108 all of this month.

First Week.   Lesson 1

Review Exercise 28, *n.*   Give Exercise 35, *z, dozen.*   "The first stroke of this letter is like the *n* stroke.   The rest of the letter is

Exercise 35

rather strange. Notice it carefully as I write it." Write it two or three times on the board, keeping exactly with the metronome. Then give the signal for the children to write it. The little formality in beginning helps to keep the idea of regularity in writing before the children. Have practice on the *z* critically for a few minutes. Then give the words *dozen, buzz, fizz.* The last two have been used in lower grades and will give variety to the practice.

LESSON 2

Review Exercises 32, 33. Give Exercise 36, *B, Be, Belle.* Give

EXERCISE 36

any names from the class that are appropriate. Give Exercise 37, *Be on time.*

LESSON 3

Be sure the position is good. It would be fatal to good results to allow carelessness in this. Review Exercises 35, 37. Give Exercise 38, *I.* Give this as a word or as the initial of any word

EXERCISE 38

that may begin a sentence, but which contains only letters which have been studied. This capital is hard to make well. Children may have formed the habit of beginning it in the wrong place, which needs to be broken, or they may not get a good slant, which is very important in this letter. It is important to study the letter to see that the children understand just how to make it. The first stroke must turn to the left just far enough so that the down-stroke shall have the same slant as the other letters have. Give Exercise 39, *I am, I can, I will, I did.*

EXERCISE 39

Lesson 4

Review Exercise 38, *I*.   Give Exercise 40, *J, Jan., Janet, June.*

J Jan Janet June

EXERCISE 40

Here is another letter like the *I* except the stem is below the base line.   Notice that both curves are on the left of the straight downstroke and that they cross it at the same place on or near the base line. · Give the words.   The abbreviation for *January* is given, but not the entire word as the *r* has not yet been studied.

Lesson 5

Prepare the papers as directed.   Give Exercises 35, 36, 37, 38, 39, 40.

When papers are collected, give for practice some of the harder exercises which have been used. ·

Second Week

This week all the new exercises will be capitals, for the sake of furnishing drill on as many names as possible.

Lesson 1

Review Exercise 36, *B, Belle.*   Give Exercise 41, *M, Mamie,*

M Mamie Maude

EXERCISE 41

Maude.   The capital *M* is simple enough so that it should not give trouble to the children of this grade, but it is best to call attention to it so as to forestall any serious faults and encourage care in the work.   Give Exercise 42, *Maude and Belle can climb a mountain.* The word *climb* has not been given before and so should be practiced alone.   The word *mountain* was given in Grade 3, so is a review word.   It may be well to review it alone first.

Lesson 2

Review Exercise 41, *M.*   Give Exercise 43, *N, Nell, No.*   Relate

N N Nell No No

EXERCISE 43

this to the *M* and see that it is carefully made. Then write the words. Give Exercise 44, *No, Nell and Mamie could not come.*

LESSON 3

Review Exercise 36, *B.* Erase the lower loop and ask, "What letter have we now? Our next exercise is *O.* Look, and I will write it with the count." Give Exercise 45, *P, Plow, Put.* After practice

EXERCISE 45

write all names of children in the class, either given or family names, which begin with any of the capitals studied. These are, *A, E, C, O, B, I, J, M, N, P.*

LESSON 4

Review Exercises 41, *M,* 43, *N.* Give Exercise 46, *W, Wallace, Webb.* Call attention to the fact that the *W* is like the *M* and *N,*

EXERCISE 46

in the first stroke, but all the turns are sharp, and that the middle stroke is taller than the first, and the last stroke shorter than any other. Write it with a good swing and encourage the children to do so. Give Exercise 47, *Ben, tell Wallace to come to me.*

LESSON 5

Prepare the papers as directed. Give Exercises 41, 42, 43, 44, 45, 46, 47.

After papers are collected, practice any names in the class, beginning with capitals practiced in the exercises.

THIRD WEEK. LESSON 1

Review Exercise 11, *a.* Give Exercise 48, *g, along, gone, begun.*

EXERCISE 48

Call attention to the likeness to *a*.   The top must keep up.   Also call attention to the straight line of the stem.   See that this is made with great care.   "Which way does the curve of the stem turn?" Have several lines written of *g*'s, mixing in some *a*'s and *d*'s to avoid careless work.   Then give the words in Exercise 48.   If more work is wanted, review the easier words from lower grades; as, *go*, *get*, *bag*, *begin*.

LESSON 2

Review Exercises 9, *l*, 28, *n*.   Give Exercise 49, *h*, *while*, *them*, *those*, *who*.   This letter is one which is frequently made poorly.

EXERCISE 49

Even though it has been analyzed in previous grades, it is worth while to introduce the *h* by showing that it is like both the *l* and the *n*, and that the beginning of the one-space part retraces the lower part of the loop very little.   The one-space part is rounded at the top and the crossing of the loop is opposite the top of the one-space part.   See that there is a good free swing with the pen held easily and no cramping.   Give the words in Exercise 49.

LESSON 3

Review Exercises 45, *Put*, 35, *dozen*, 48, *g*, 49, *h*.   Give Exercise 50, *Put a dozen eggs on the table*.   Use this as context writing.   There is a tendency on the part of children and some teachers to write the words in columns "because they look better."   Avoid this.   The aim is to teach writing in the form in which it is to be used.

LESSON 4

Give Exercise 51, *p*, *hope*, *page*, *pound*, *upon*, *happen*.   A com-

EXERCISE 51

mon error in making the *p* is making the long stroke only one space above the base line. This stroke is not quite two spaces above the base line, but should be distinctly above the one-space part. The one-space part may be either open or closed as the teacher chooses. After the letter has been practiced, review Exercises 48, 49, before giving the words. If more work is desired, give Exercise 52, *Put a pound of coffee on the table.* This exercise need not be used unless the teacher wishes. If it is given, the word *coffee* should be practiced.

LESSON 5

Prepare the papers as usual. Give Exercises 48, 49, 50, 51, 52. Review Exercises 31, 42, after the papers are collected.

FOURTH WEEK. LESSON 1

Dictate ten numbers of five orders, including some containing ciphers. Give particular attention to the way the figures are made. Then dictate two rows of examples for multiplication using a multiplier of two orders as in Exercise 53.

$$7\ 3\ 9\ 4\ 8 \qquad 4\ 9\ 2\ 0\ 3 \qquad 5\ 2\ 7\ 0\ 9$$
$$\times 7\ 5 \qquad\quad \times 8\ 6 \qquad\quad \times 9\ 3$$

Have the class solve these and test the accuracy of placing the figures. Then have each pupil practice on his especial difficulty. Place on the board examples to be copied by those who are ready for more work.

LESSON 2

Review Exercises 41, 43, 46. "The new capital is very much like these in the first stroke." Give Exercise 54, *Z, Zoo.* Recall

EXERCISE 54

Exercise 35, *z.* "The stem of the capital *Z* is just like the stem of the small *z.* Let us write this several times. Now let us write the capital *Z.*"

"You will not find much use for this letter, but if you need it you can remember that it is like the small *z.*"

Give the word *Zoo.* Explain, if the children do not know it, that it is an abbreviation, but that we use it as a word. Give Exercise 55, *I will go to the Zoo with Nell.* Watch the letter formation carefully and practice any words which need it as exercises.

Make this largely as individuals or in groups having similar difficulties.

LESSON 3

Review Exercise 54, Z.   Give Exercise 56, Q, *Quiet, Quill.*   This

2 2 Quiet Quill

EXERCISE 56

is begun just like the Z, but the stroke goes a little farther to the left at the bottom.   Give either of the words which is desired.   The children may recognize the likeness of the Q to the figure 2.   It is much the same as a large *2*.   If more work is desired choose a review exercise which needs practice.

LESSON 4

Review Exercises 28, *n*, 48, *g*.   Give Exercise 57, *y*, *body*, *money*, *only*, *yet*.   Let the children analyze the *y* and how it is like both the

yyyy body money

only yet yyy

EXERCISE 57

n and the *g*.   See that the second up-stroke is so made that it will permit right connection with the stem stroke.   There should be very little retracing at this point.   Give the words.   Give Exercise 58, *John can get only a little money yet.*   The aim in giving sentences is to introduce review words so as to give opportunity for practice where needed.

LESSON 5

The work to be done to-day is to be graded.   On a clean sheet of paper the full name, age, grade, and date should be written.   After the papers have been prepared in this way, give a two-minute test. Follow the instructions given on page 8 exactly and use the material indicated for Grade 4.   Do not use the metronome for this writing.   On the same paper, on the other side if necessary, have written Exercises 55, 58, using the metronome.

Fourth Month. First Week

Set the metronome for this month at 112.   No new elements will be given this week, but those given before will be combined in new ways.   The class need not know that the work is all review.   This will help in automatizing the work.

Lesson 1

Review Exercise 57.   Give Exercise 59, *gay, pay, toy, boy, buy.*

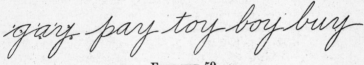

Exercise 59

The last two words are reviewed from other grades.   The others are simple combinations of letters recently practiced.   Give Exercise 60, *I will buy a gay toy.*

Lesson 2

Review Exercises 3, *A*, 48, *g*.   Give Exercise 61, *Aunt, May began to put lunch on the table.   Now we will eat.*   In connection with this, teach the indentation of the first word in the paragraph in context writing.

Lesson 3

Review Exercises 36, *B*, 26, *quiet*, 49, *while*.   Give Exercise 62, *Be quiet while we eat lunch.*

Lesson 4

Review Exercise 43, *N*.   Give Exercise 63, *Nancy*.   Review

Exercise 63

Exercise 51, *hope*.   Give Exercise 64, *Nancy hoped to go down town with you.*

Lesson 5

Prepare the paper as usual.   Give Exercises 60, 61, 62, 64.

Then review Exercises 57, 51, using such parts of the exercises as you have time for.

Second Week. Lesson 1

Instead of writing to-day, take Friday's work and compare it with that done just after the last comparison was made, in the second month, fourth week, first lesson. Because of the use of self-criticism in the class during these weeks, the children should be able to find many points where they have improved. Encourage the child to see where he has improved in writing. Is his slant more regular? Are the letters better formed? Let each find special instances of this for himself. Is the spacing better between letters? — between words? — neither too great nor too small? Are the margins good? Is the alinement better? Is the height even? Is the quality of the line better? — neither too heavy nor too light, and smooth instead of wavy? "Is there some exercise you would like to write better?" Perhaps a suggestion of places where improvement can be made will encourage all to try. Allow the class to keep the papers until the next lesson for this practice.

Lesson 2

Review Exercises 28, 35, 48. Then allow each child to write the exercise he decided to improve. This should be written three times, keeping strictly with the metronome and watching the position. If there is more time, write the names with the metronome.

Lesson 3

Give Exercise 65, s, *swing*, to get a free swing and right direction for the letter *s*. Give Exercise 66, s, *son, almost, always, east, lost,*

Exercise 65

Exercise 66

please, post, says, something, wish. Give the s with the long connecting swing. Call attention to the slant. It must be neither too nearly vertical nor too nearly horizontal. If there is trouble with the slant, make several of the swinging exercises, "just as you would like it for a teeter," and let the children make the letters over these so that the up-stroke comes on the swinging slant. Emphasize the swing in the down-stroke so as to get a good outward curve instead of a flat stroke. There is little danger of having too full a curve in natural writing even if it is exaggerated now. Give any of the words which can be used immediately in other work if there is a choice. All of these words should be used finally as they come from the 100 per cent spelling list for this grade.

LESSON 4

Review Exercises 65, 66. Give Exercise 67, *r, air, bear, born, brought, card, charge, from, free, front, great, heard, heart, herself, learn, picture, railroad, ready, rule, start, trip, true, world.* The *r* is

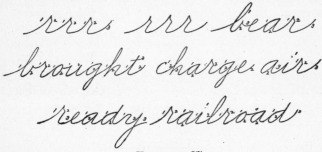

EXERCISE 67

in general like the *s.* These are the only letters which have the tip above the first space. Make this a definite point of study in both and make a definite pause here. See that the stroke following this in the *r* is a separate stroke instead of a part of the down-stroke. It is a straight slanting stroke, not a curve as it is frequently made. When the letter has been studied and practiced, give selected words from the exercise. All these words are to be included eventually as they are from the 100 per cent list.

LESSON 5

Prepare the paper as usual. Are you holding to the definite signals for writing? ("Ready. Write.") Give the words practiced from Exercises 66, 67, 51.

After the papers are collected, give Exercise 61.

THIRD WEEK. LESSON 1

Review Exercise 57, *y.* Give the capital *Y*, Exercise 68, *Y, Yellow, You.* Give Exercise 69, *You may go to the woods to-day.*

EXERCISE 68

LESSON 2

Give Exercise 49, *h*.   Give Exercise 70, *k*, *speak*, making the type

EXERCISE 70

of comparison with the *h* suggested heretofore.   Be sure the loop is a little open.   Have the crossing at the top of the first space.   For further practice give Exercise 71, *kill*, *lake*, *talk*, *sick*, *kind*, *take*, *back*, *book*, *look*, *thank*, *think*, which are words given in former grades.

EXERCISE 71

LESSON 3

Review Exercise 70, *k*, and part of 71.   Review Exercises 36, *B*, 45, *P*.   Give Exercise 72, *R*, *Ralph*, *Rachel*.

EXERCISE 72

LESSON 4

Review Exercise 57, *y*.   Show Exercise 73, *j*, *jelly*.   Let the

EXERCISE 73

children discover how these two exercises are alike.   Practice the *j* and give the words.   Then give Exercise 74, *Ralph and Rachel like to eat jelly with bread.*

LESSON 5

Prepare the papers as directed. Give Exercises 69, 70, 71, 74. After papers are collected, give words from Exercises 66, 67.

FOURTH WEEK

This week at the beginning of each lesson write numbers in five orders for addition, subtraction, multiplication, and short division on the respective days. Give one line of each.

LESSON 1

Review Exercises 28, *n*, 10, *b*. Give Exercise 75, *v*, *leave*. Com-

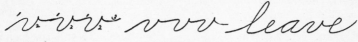

EXERCISE 75

pare this with the two review exercises. Be sure that there is not too much slant to the up-stroke. It should curve slightly inward. Give Exercise 76, *Yellow leaves fall from the trees*. Other words than those found in the 100 per cent list are now introduced, but they include letters already practiced. The word *from*, in Exercise 76, is an example of this. Wherever it seems desirable, practice these new words alone before using them in a sentence.

LESSON 2

Review Exercise 28, *n*. Give Exercise 77, *x*, *expect*, *X*, and Exer-

EXERCISE 77

cise 78, *box*, *six*. Give the *x* and show that the first stroke is just like the last part of the *n* and that the cross cuts the down-stroke in the middle. The children may make the *n* and erase the first stroke to get the curve. Have the children write Exercise 78; review words from earlier grades before writing the word in Exercise 77.

Show the capital *X*. This is very similar to the small *x*, and the children are likely to have little use for it, so that it is sufficient for them to know of its likeness to the small *x* and to practice it a few times. Because the capital begins with a short down-stroke the count is different from the small *x*.

LESSON 3

Give Exercise 79, *L*, *Leah*, *Louis*. This is a hard letter to make

L. L Leah Lewis

EXERCISE 79

and should be analyzed carefully. The loop at the bottom must touch the base line and the final stroke must touch the line and may extend a little below it. The down-stroke is a slightly compound curve, but if the children in this grade make it a straight slanting stroke and make the loops correctly, the work should not be criticized. After practice of any names that are appropriate, give Exercise 80, *Let Bert and Martin play ball now.*

LESSON 4

Give Exercise 81, *S, Susan, Stuart.* After having written the

S S Susan Stuart

EXERCISE 81

capital *S* on the board and discussed the count, erase the top of the letter and show how much it resembles the small *s.* Then let the children practice it and test their work by covering the upper loop to see if it looks like a small *s.* Then give the names — using any which come from the class. Give Exercise 82, *Susan sent Leah a picture by mail.*

LESSON 5

Prepare the papers as usual. Give Exercises 74, 76, 80, 82, 78. After papers are collected, practice the names with the metronome.

FIFTH MONTH. FIRST WEEK

This month we shall begin writing without the metronome part of the time. Give each exercise first using the metronome and then without, trying to keep approximately the same time and rhythm. Some allowance should be made for individual difference in rhythm. Use this method throughout the month unless definite instructions are given for a change.

The work of this month will consist in, first, completing the presentation of the capitals, eight of which remain to be studied; second, review of letters studied, giving new words which occur in the 100 per cent list for Grade 4A; third, drill in writing numbers of six orders both in columns and for the four fundamental processes; fourth, introducing some practice on composition forms.

LESSON 1

Set the metronome at 120, for all the work this month.

Give Exercise 83, *G, Gertrude*.   Give Exercise 84, *Gertrude and Winifred went to the Park to play.*

EXERCISE 83

LESSON 2

Review Exercise 41, *M*.   Give Exercise 85, *H, Homer, Harold, Horace*.   Make the first stroke just like the first stroke of *M*.   Call

EXERCISE 85

attention to the connecting stroke.   It should not be too low, but low enough so that when joined to the other letters the joining is at the one-space height.   Give Exercise 86, *How does John earn his money?*

LESSON 3

Review Exercise 85, *H*.   Give Exercise 87, *K, Kathryn, Karl.*

EXERCISE 87

The noticeable difference between these two is the mode of joining the strokes.   In the *H* there is a third stroke connecting the others, while in *K* the second stroke, itself, connects with the first by a decided break in direction at about the middle.   The second stroke of the *K* consists of two compound curves, but the teacher may be satisfied if the children of this grade make it well with slanting or slightly curved strokes.   Give the words.   Then give Exercise 88, *Kathryn came to school with me.*   The teacher may substitute any needed writing for the sentences given now, providing the work is done under standard conditions.

LESSON 4

Review Exercise 79, *L*.   "Notice the loop at the base line.   We have this same loop in another capital."   Give Exercise 89, *D,*

Donald, Dorothy, Dick. Practice the *L* several times and then give the *D.* After practice give the names and follow this by Exercise 90, *Do Donald and Harold like to play football?*

D Donald Dorothy Dick.

EXERCISE 89

LESSON 5

Prepare the papers as directed. Give the letters in Exercises 83, 85, 87, 89. Then write any two of the sentences given this week. Spend extra time writing the names first with, and then without, the metronome.

SECOND WEEK. LESSON 1

Give Exercise 91, *F, Flora, Fritz,* and Exercise 92, *T, Thomas, Tillie.* These two letters are so much alike that they should be

F F Flora Fritz F

EXERCISE 91

T Thomas Tillie T

EXERCISE 92

studied together. Give both letters before any words are given. The only difference is in the last stroke of the *F.* It is advised not to join the *F* to other letters. If it is joined, a cross stroke must be made on the stem. Care is necessary not to make the first stroke too long and to make such a slant in the down-stroke as will bring the lower curve farther to the left than the top horizontal stroke. After practice of both letters, give the names.

LESSON 2

Review Exercises 91, 92. Give Exercise 93, *Thomas and Fritz are good jumpers. They can run fast too.* Indent the first word and write in paragraph form.

LESSON 3

Review Exercise 43, *N.* Give Exercise 94, *U, United,* and Exercise 95, *V, Victory.* The capitals *U* and *V* are very little used,

U U U United U U

EXERCISE 94

V V Victory Victory

EXERCISE 95

but it is worth while for the pupils to become acquainted with the forms. If there are any names of children which can be used here, they should be made use of. After practicing these capitals, review Exercise 81, *S*, and give Exercise 96, *Victory for the United States*. This may be considered as a slogan, as it is not a sentence.

Victory for the United

States Victory for the

EXERCISE 96

LESSON 4

By this time the class should have gained some facility in rhythmic writing without the metronome. To-day we shall use all review work. Start the metronome for each exercise, but stop it as soon as the class is fairly started, perhaps after one or two words, and have them continue writing. It will be well to start it at intervals and see how many are keeping the swing. The same exercise should be written three times to give time to get a regular swing and to test it once or twice. If any one finds he is out of time, he should catch the metronome time without stopping more than one or two counts. Use Exercises 84, 86.

LESSON 5

Prepare the papers as usual. Give Exercises 91, 92, 93, 94, 95, 96, writing first all the letters, then the separate words, then the sentences. If more work is wanted, select one exercise that has given trouble and use it, testing the rhythm with the metronome as in Lesson 4.

THIRD WEEK. LESSON 1

Review Exercises 10, *b*, 12, *d*, 20, *c*. Give Exercise 97, *bill, add;*

act, club. Give drill in numbers from one to six orders in column form for addition. Some numbers requiring the use of ciphers should be given. Pay attention to the forms of the figures.

bill add act club

LESSON 2

Review Exercises 24, *f*, 27, *m*, 28, *n*. Use a free swing movement. Give Exercise 98, *feel, follow; became, become; been, need, cannot, woman.* There are several points of difficulty in these words so

feel follow became

need cannot woman

EXERCISE 98

that it seems desirable to spend most of the time to-day on them. The points of difficulty are, *f*, *b*, *w*, and the joining of the *b*, *w*, and *o*.

LESSON 3

Review Exercises 35, *z*, 48, *g*. Give Exercise 99, *dozen; among.*

dozen among

EXERCISE 99

The word *dozen* has been given before, but it can be practiced again with advantage. The teacher should choose from other subject-matter some material which can be used for paragraph writing. Such work should be given for the rest of the period to-day. This practice on outside material is Exercise 100.

LESSON 4

Review Exercises 49, *h*, 57, *y*. Give Exercise 101, *Chain, tenth, thought, without; copy, lady, maybe, young.* Give Exercise 102, *I thought the young lady had a gold chain.*

tenth thought without

copy maybe chain

EXERCISE 101

I thought the young lady had a gold chain

LESSON 5

Prepare the papers as usual. Use the metronome intermittently as has been done in the practice drills. Give some of the work written this week including the paragraph furnished by the teacher. If there is more time, review some of the words practiced during the week.

FOURTH WEEK. LESSON 1

Review Exercises 66, *s*, 67, *r*. Give Exercise 103, *cast, finish, question, seen, set, should, state, study, suit; bridge, clear, doctor, dollar, drill, hear, hour, matter, number, pair, price, print, reach, report, sir, sorry, story, teacher, there, write, wrote, yesterday.* Practice on

finish question suit

bridge should clear

price report sorry sir

write yesterday there

EXERCISE 103

selections from these words, introducing several of them into a sentence if possible. Return to this exercise for review until all these words have been given.

LESSON 2

Review Exercise 70, *k*, 75, *v*. Give Exercise 104, *alike, broke;*

cover, even, move.   Write numbers of six orders for subtraction examples and numbers of five orders for multiplication with a multiplier of two or three orders, according to the advancement of the class.

Lesson 3

Review the capital letters *A, O, J, N, D.*   Give Exercise 105, *April, October, January, November, December.* If this proves too much for one lesson, finish the exercise to-morrow instead of the work which is assigned.

Lesson 4

Give Exercise 106, *The teacher wrote a story yesterday.*   Most of the words are taken from Exercise 103.   If the teacher has context material that requires practice in writing, it should be substituted for this exercise.

Lesson 5

Prepare the papers as usual.   Give one row each of subtraction and multiplication examples such as were given in Lesson 2, and give Exercises 105, 106.

Sixth Month.   First Week

The work during the first two weeks will be in the nature of a review making new combinations of the old exercises or giving words which, while not included in the 100 per cent list, will be found to be of use.

Set the metronome at 132 for this month.

Lesson 1

Give Exercise 107, *January, February, March, April, May, June.*   Practice especially the names not studied this year and have these written in serial order.

Lesson 2

Give Exercise 108, *July, August, September, October, November, December.*   Use these in the same way as Exercise 107 was used. The teacher needs to be watchful of the position, grasp of pen, and the type of movement.   See that this last is easy and free from undue tension.

Lesson 3

Give Exercise 109, *Jan., Feb., Mar., Apr., Aug., Sept., Oct., Nov., Dec.*   Give these as the abbreviations of the months, writing each name in full once and following it by the abbreviation.

LESSON 4

Give numbers of six orders by dictation for short division and then for long division if that has been introduced. Check carefully the placing of figures. It is assumed that the teacher is doing this in the arithmetic work as well as in the handwriting period, and the result now should be quite satisfactory.

LESSON 5

Prepare the papers as usual. Give Exercise 110, *March, April, and May are the Spring months. June, July, and August are the Summer months. September, October, and November are the Autumn months. December, January, and February are the Winter months.*

SECOND WEEK. LESSON 1

Review *Monday, Friday,* and *Sunday,* which the children wrote in Grade 3. Then give Exercise 111, *The postman has something for you.*

LESSON 2

Give Exercise 112, *Tuesday, Wednesday.* Review the names of the days practiced yesterday and give the abbreviations, Exercise 113, *Mon., Tues., Wed., Fri., Sun.* After practice of this exercise, if there is time, write the names of the days of the week which have been studied once each, followed in each case by its abbreviation. Emphasize the fact that the period is a necessary part of the abbreviation.

LESSON 3

Give Exercise 114, *Thursday, Saturday, Thurs., Sat.* Then review Exercise 112 and give Exercise 115, *The days of the week are Sunday, Monday, Tuesday, Wednesday, Thursday, Friday, Saturday. We sometimes write them Sun., Mon., Tues., Wed., Thurs., Fri., Sat.*

LESSON 4

Dictate numbers for multiplication of four or five figures and a multiplier of three or two figures. Allow the pupils to solve these. Include some ciphers in the work and check carefully the accurateness of arrangement. If this is easily done now and more work is needed, review words from Exercise 103.

LESSON 5

Prepare the papers as usual. See that good page arrangement is planned. Use a free swing with the pen with no ink. Give Exercises 111, 115.

THIRD WEEK

A regular method of grading will be followed for the rest of the year.   This is based on the *Chart for the Diagnosis of Faults in Handwriting* and where possible the teacher should make use of this.

This week the teacher should study the Chart so as to be ready to begin the grading next week.   During the week when each category is being emphasized, that category alone should be graded; for example, when *letter formation* is being emphasized, it will be graded in terms of the Chart and will be rated 2, 6, 10, or the intermediate scores 4, 8.   Further information regarding the Chart can be obtained from *The Teaching of Handwriting*, by Frank N. Freeman (Houghton Mifflin Company), pp. 123-42.

The children should understand that the grading is in points, not in per cents as in other subjects.   When the marking is begun, the teacher should grade, in the special category for the week, the work done on the first day and on the last day.

The child should study his own work every day, not so much for the value of his estimate as to lead to a critical attitude toward his own work.

Only one or two specimens will be given for each week, with suggestions as to possible preliminary practice before writing the selection as a whole.   If the teacher thinks best, the verses given may be used for a book of poetry which should be made of the last copy of each verse written.   It has not seemed advisable to give written copies for all these selections.   If there is any question as to form of letters, refer to previous copies.

Do not increase the speed this year beyond 132 in the regular writing.   Where speed drills are suggested, select easier words from exercises that have been practiced and give them at the regular rate and then raise the rate a little at a time to see how fast the class can write and continue to do good work.   Do not allow a child to write at a rate that disorganizes the movement or gives poorer quality of writing.   Write each specimen with, and without, the metronome.   Use one or both selections for the week as seems best, but do not carry over work from week to week.   Select the most difficult parts of each verse for practice.   The use of poetry frequently from now on presents a new problem in arrangement. Discuss this with the class.   Compare the arrangement of prose and poetry in reading books, and draw conclusions.   Try different arrangements if there is an opportunity for choice.

Copies for the Week

Exercise 116:

> Do not look for wrong and evil —
> You will find them if you do;
> As you measure to your neighbor
> He will measure back to you.
>
> *Alice Cary.*

Exercise 117:

> Little things, yes, little things,
>   Make up the sum of life;
> A word, a look, a single tone,
>   May cause a calm or strife.

Unknown

Divide the work into periods as seems best for the class. For preliminary practice use the capitals and any words which are new to the class. In these verses the words which have not been studied are: *wrong, evil, measure, neighbor, sum, single, tone, cause, calm, strife.*

Fourth Week

This week we begin to give special attention to one category with grading on it as discussed in the general directions for the third week. Be sure that the pupils understand that the scoring is in points instead of on the per cent basis. The special category for this week is *letter formation.* Encourage each pupil to criticize the form of his own letters, to discover the best of his own work and try to make all his work as good. Suggest attention to writing in other subjects and that they try to write as well and in about the same time as in the writing lesson.

Take a few minutes each day for speed drill as explained in the discussion for the third week. Here the metronome may be run as high as the children can do good work, but do not be too ambitious about it.

Copy for the Week

Exercise 118:

> An owl once lived in a hollow tree,
>   And he was as wise as wise could be.
> The branch of learning he did n't know
>   Could scarce on the tree of knowledge grow.
> He knew the tree from branch to root,
>   And an owl like that can afford to hoot.

Oliver Herford.

Practice the capitals. The following words are new: *owl, hollow, wise, branch, scarce, knowledge, root, afford, hoot.* The word *learning* has not been given, but *learn* has. Not more than two days should be spent on preliminary practice before beginning to write the verse. In this case it can be divided into three sections of two lines each. Write the poet's name with the verse. It is worth while for the children to begin to give credit for copied material.

Seventh Month. First Week

Emphasize *spacing* this week. Consider both spacing between words and spacing of letters. Experiment a little to determine the best. It should not be cramped nor yet scrawly. Do not forget *letter formation*, but do the grading on *spacing*. Practice trying to write without the metronome after hearing the time given. Return to writing with it every few days.

Copies for the Week

Any teacher may now substitute for the copy given work that will correlate with other subjects.

Exercise 119:

MARCH

In the snowing and the blowing,
In the cruel sleet,
Little flowers begin their growing
Far beneath our feet.
Softly taps the Spring and cheerly, —
"Darlings, are you here?"
Till they answer, "We are nearly,
Nearly ready, dear."

"Where is Winter with his blowing?
Tell us, Spring," they say.
Then she answers, "He is going,
Going on his way.
Poor old Winter does not love you;
But his time is past;
Soon my birds will sing above you, —
Set you free at last."

Mary Mapes Dodge.

The poem *March* involves the use of quotation marks quite extensively, and may be related to the formal language work in this way. Select for practice any parts that seem likely to give difficulty. Keep good position and easy, free movement.

SECOND WEEK

The category for grading this week is *uniformity of alinement*. This refers both to position on the base line and to relative size of the letters.

By incidental suggestions keep both *letter formation* and *spacing* in mind. Use the metronome only to set the time, and to test the regularity, by starting it during the writing. If there is any difficulty in keeping the time, write a few minutes with the metronome. The speed drill may be given once or twice this week, and with this the metronome should always be used.

Copies for the Week

Exercise 120:

> What shall we wrap the baby in?
> Nothing that fingers have woven will do:
> Looms of the heart weave love ever anew:
> Love, only love, is the right thread to spin,
> *Love* we must wrap the baby in!
>
> *Lucy Larcom.*

Exercise 121:

> "Quack! quack!" says the Duck,
> "Was there ever such luck!
> Spring has cleared the pond of ice,
> And the day is warm and nice,
> Just as I and goodman Drake
> Thought we'd like a swim to take."

The last verse includes some difficult capitals and also continues the practice on quotation marks. There may now be some
composition work of the children's which can well be practiced.
Children of this grade should not be required to struggle with all
the problems of writing compositions at one time. The problems
relating to handwriting and arrangement should be met in the
handwriting period. For this reason it is suggested that the final
draft of a composition be made in the handwriting period.

THIRD WEEK

Emphasize this week *quality of line*. This refers to lightness or
heaviness of line and to smoothness instead of wavy appearance.
The factors contributing to good quality of line are: good pen and
ink; good position, which prevents cramping and undue pressure;
and keeping the rhythm which prevents wavy lines.

Copies for the Week

These two verses suggest illustrations which will help to make a
pleasing book of poetry.

Exercise 122:

> Oh, my delicate lily,
> Blossom of fragrant snow,
> Breathing on me from the garden,
> How does your beauty grow;
> Tell me what blessing the kind heavens give!
> How do you find it so sweet to live?
>
> *Lucy Larcom.*

Exercise 123:

> They'll come again to the apple-tree, —
> Robin and all the rest, —
> When the orchard branches are fair to see,
> In the snow of the blossoms dressed.
>
> *Margaret E. Sangster.*

FOURTH WEEK

This week emphasize *uniformity of slant* and grade on it. Lead the children to be critical of their own work. The slant should be quite good because it depends on position and rhythm. Recall attention to *letter formation, spacing, alinement,* and *quality of line.* Use speed drill occasionally.

Copy for the Week

Exercise 124:

> THE BEES THAT WENT UP TO THE SKY
>
> Fuzzy Wuzz, Buzzy Wuzz, Zippety Flop,
> All flew up to the cherry-tree top.
> "Pooh!" said Buzzy Wuzz, "this is n't high!
> Let us keep on till we reach the sky."
>
> *Mary Mapes Dodge.*

This verse is good because it interests the children and also gives practice on some of the more unusual letters and in the use of quotation marks. If more work is wanted, select from the optional work at the end of the chapter.

EIGHTH MONTH.   FIRST WEEK

This week emphasize and grade on *letter formation, alinement,* and *spacing,* summing the scores in each for the total points. Start an exercise with the metronome and then have it written two or three times without it. Start the metronome near the end and see how many have kept the time.

Copies for the Week

Exercise 125:

> May shall make the orchards bloom;
> And the blossoms' fine perfume
> Shall set all the honey-bees
> Murmuring among the trees.
>
> *Frank Dempster Sherman.*

Exercise 126:

> THE MELANCHOLY PIG
>
> There was a pig, that sat alone,
> Beside a ruined Pump,
> By day and night he made his moan:

It would have stirred a heart of stone
To see him wring his hoofs and groan,
Because he could not jump.

Lewis Carroll.

SECOND WEEK

Emphasize and grade on *letter formation, alinement,* and *quality of line.* So far as possible use the metronome only for starting an exercise and then do without. Give speed drill for a brief time during three periods this week. Suggest that good writing be carried over into other work.

Copies for the Week

Exercise 127:

BERRYING SONG

Ho! for the hills in summer!
Ho! for the rocky shade,
Where the groundpine trails under the fern-leaves,
Deep in the mossy glade.
Up in the dewy sunrise,
Waked by the robin's trill;
Up and away, a-berrying,
To the pastures on the hill!

Lucy Larcom.

Exercise 128:

Oh, the green things growing, the green things growing,
The faint sweet smell of the green things growing!

THIRD WEEK

Grade on the five categories this week. Try to have the class listen to the metronome in starting and then write without it. The writing should have improved very much in the last two months. If necessary emphasize *letter formation.* If more work is desired, select from the optional work at the end of the chapter.

Copy for the Week

Exercise 129:

WHERE DO ALL THE DAISIES GO?

Where do all the daisies go?
I know, I know!
Underneath the snow they creep,
Nod their little heads and sleep,
In the Springtime out they peep;
That is where they go!

Where do all the birdies go?
I know, I know!
Far away from winter snow
To the fair warm South they go;
There they stay till daisies blow,
That is where they go!

Where do all the babies go?
I know, I know!
In the glancing firelight warm,
Safely sheltered from all harm,
Soft they lie on mother's arm,
That is where they go!

Unknown.

FOURTH WEEK

This week a verse is given which is reviewed from Grade 3. If the class succeeds well with this, it may be used in speed drill. This is the only time context material is suggested for such work.

Copy for the Week

Exercise 130:

A DEW DROP

Little drop of dew,
Like a gem you are;
I believe that you
Must have been a star.

When the day is bright,
On the grass you lie;
Tell me then at night
Are you in the sky?

Frank Dempster Sherman.

NINTH MONTH

In the last month of school many occasions are likely to arise which demand writing. The proper time for such writing is in the handwriting period. For this reason it is suggested that a large part, if not all, of the work of this month shall be drawn from local school activities. These may be the writing of an invitation to a school festival or other event, letters of acceptance or of thanks for courtesies extended by others, reports of excursions for nature study or geography, organization of material such as dramatization of a story or experience for future use, etc.

Certain definite requirements must be met in this kind of work. The pupils should maintain the best position they have been able to reach. The writing should be free and rhythmical. Some allowance is to be made for individual rhythm, but some words should frequently be selected from the material being written, to use for speed drill where the class writes together with the metronome.

Do not assume that the freedom allowed here means that the handwriting lesson may be omitted at times nor that the time may be filled with *any* material without regard to its relation to the school activities. If such material as has been suggested is not available, the teacher should use the material given below. It is suggested that *one* of the poems be used as the basis of the work for the month. Each stanza may be studied for a week and the poem finally written as a whole. These poems suggest illustrations which may be made in the art period. Use some of the words for speed drills, and grade on the five categories, making the children critical of their own work.

During the third week of this month a two-minute test should be given following the directions on page 8. The scores of these papers should be compared with those on the test written at the beginning of the year.

A systematic review of all abbreviations taught during the year in other subjects should be made during this month. The following are suggested as some that may have been used. If there are others, they should be given.

A.M., P.M., U.S., yd., in., ft., pt., qt., gal., the Days, the Months, Mr., Mrs., Dr., yr., mo.

Copies for the Month

Exercise 131:

A HAPPY CHILD

My house is red — a little house,
    A happy child am I,
I laugh and play the livelong day,
    I hardly ever cry.

I have a tree, a green, green tree,
    To shade me from the sun;
And under it I often sit,
    When all my work is done.

My little basket I will take
    And trip into the town;
When next I'm there I'll buy some cake,
    And spend my bright half-crown.

Kate Greenaway.

Exercise 132:

WHERE GO THE BOATS?

Dark brown is the river,
Golden is the sand,
It flows along forever,
With trees on every hand.

Green leaves a-floating,
Castles of the foam,
Boats of mine a-boating —
Where will all come home?

On goes the river
And out past the mill,
Away down the valley,
Away down the hill.

Away down the river,
A hundred miles or more,
Other little children
Shall bring my boats ashore.

                    Robert Louis Stevenson.

OPTIONAL MATERIAL

These selections may be used if more work is needed, or may be substituted for those given in the exercises if they suit the teacher better.   They should be treated just as the assigned work is treated.   Optional material from lower grades may be used if desired.

Great, wide, wonderful, beautiful world,
With the beautiful water about you curled,
And the wonderful grass upon your breast —
World, you are beautifully dressed!

Be you to others kind and true,
As you'd have others be to you.

How doth the little busy bee
Improve each shining hour,
And gather honey all the day
From every opening flower.

                            Isaac Watts.

The wind one morning sprung up from sleep,
Saying, "Now for a frolic!   Now for a leap!
Now for a madcap galloping chase!
I'll make a commotion in every place!"

The lily has an air,
And the snow-drop a grace,
And the sweet pea a way,
And the heart's-ease a face, —
Yet there's nothing like a rose
       When she blows.[1]

---

[1] From Christina G. Rossetti's *Poems*, by permission of The Macmillan Company.

CHAPTER IX

EXERCISES FOR GRADE FIVE

OBJECTIVES

Content. With the advancement of vocabulary in content subjects should come an increased ability in independent writing and spelling. The following list of words illustrates the type of words which should be added during this year to the practice vocabulary:

deal	auto	between	quite	until
company	delay	duty	news	second
unless	knew	track	enjoy	jail
driven	everything	vacation	extra	collect
command	contain	office	engine	chief
police	public	reply	court	destroy
person	support	surprise	terrible	trust
provide	recover	several	view	visit

Capitals should be used habitually with any geographical name, and with historical or literary terms used. In arithmetic the child should be able to write any number, placing it in correct column form for any of the fundamental operations, including work in fractions and United States money. Forms of simple accounts should be familiar. In composition special attention should be given to spacing and to paragraphing. In correspondence formal and informal salutations and superscriptions should be used.

Movement. It is assumed at this time that the child has the habit of correct position and rhythmic movement quite well established. The chief point of emphasis in this grade is the still further extension of the fluency without the loss of the habits already established. The maintenance of a critical attitude toward the work is of great importance. A fluency of sixty letters a minute should be gained.

MATERIALS AND METHODS

Materials. Some latitude may be given in the choice of materials here, but the paper for drill should be of good quality and with three eighths inch ruling.

Methods. *A. Position.* Except in unusual cases this should not now require instruction from the teacher.

B. Types of exercises. 1. At the formal drill period the exercises should still be presented at the board by the teacher. The motivation will come from the child's recognition of the Grade Standard and his desire to reach it.

2. A complete "carrying over" of the writing ability to the work in other subjects should be the aim. This should be encouraged by occasional formal criticism and grading of the work done in other periods.

3. Speed drills are useful in increasing the fluency, providing the speed is not increased to the detriment of quality. After the exercises introducing the letters have been completed, the metronome should be used mainly to test the rhythm or to correct the lack of it, except in speed drills, where it should be used to measure speed and to encourage rapid writing as is consistent with satisfactory form.

C. Standards and criticism. The diagnostic chart should be the recognized standard. On the basis of this a graph should be made occasionally showing the per cent of the class who have reached the grade standard. This chart may also be used for purposes of individual comparison to assist those who have not done so to reach the grade standard. The standard in speed is sixty letters a minute. The standard is 18 on the Freeman Scale and 55 on the Ayres Scale.

First Month.   First Week

Lesson 1

A talk somewhat like this may be used to begin the work this year:

"We find good writing easier to read than poor writing, so we consider it a desirable thing. *Any one* can write well if he takes time enough and works hard enough. We shall try to learn to write so that we can write better with less effort.

"In order to do this, we must pay attention to these points: first, we must hold the pen loosely, without cramping the fingers; second, we must rest the hand on the third and fourth fingers instead of on the side, so that it will be easier to move across the page; third, we must have the paper directly in front, slanted about as we want the writing to slant. The position of the body is important, too, because if we bear much weight on our arms we tire much sooner than if they can move freely.

"Sit in an easy position with feet resting on the floor, then place the arms on the desk without bearing weight on them. Take the pen and hold it loosely." Explain the position as much as necessary. "Now slide across the paper and see how freely you can move. If your wrist is raised a little it will be easier.

"Now I will show you something to write." Give Exercise 1,

the over-swing, on the board. "Notice how I count it. We will make it all the way across the paper. Be sure you are ready for a good swing. Is your hand turned right? Are your fingers ready for the slide? Is your pen held right and loosely? Ready. Write.

EXERCISES 1 AND 2

One-two, one-two, one-two, one-two." Put it on the board again for comparison. Ask for self-criticism. "How many made too much curve? — too little curve? Try once more. Ready. Write. One-two," etc. (Four times.) "How many kept with the count? Class count softly as you do it. Ready. Write. One-two," etc.

Give Exercise 2, the under-curve, in the same way. Then give Exercise 3, *i*. Get a long free swing on the count. Then shorten

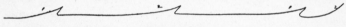

EXERCISE 3

it so that two or three groups can be written on a line. Recall the fact that in Grade 4 we tried to arrange the papers well and suggest that we begin at the very first of this year to watch margins and spacing.

LESSON 2

"What is most important in our writing now? Yes, position. The *way* we do it. Let us see how many can remember the right position. Good." Make corrections where needed, but not in a critical manner; as, "Turn your hand just a little more over, J." "Curl your two little fingers a little more, P." If there is any difficulty in hand position, have the class lay down pens. Show them your hand with the palm held toward them with the fingers curved as though holding a bird with its head toward the thumb. Hold it gently. Have them do this, looking at their hand and yours until they get the "feel" of the right position. "Now keep the hand in that position as you rest it on the desk. Take the pen in the left hand and place it carefully between the thumb and the first and second fingers of the right hand. You may slide without writing all the way across the page. Ready. Slide. One-two, one-two, one-two, one-two. Now we will make the sliding

exercise we had yesterday, first over and then under. Ready.
Write. One-two," etc.

Give Exercise 3, *i*, with long swing, with short swing. Then
give Exercise 4, *u*. "Make two curves close together and then

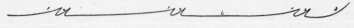

EXERCISE 4

make a long swing and then two more curves close together." Give
this first with the long and then with the short swing. Then give
Exercise 5, *it*. "Write the same two curves, but make one just as

EXERCISE 5

we have already made it and the next one nearly twice as high and
close to it. Write three groups of this kind across the page. We
need to be sure we have a good free swing in beginning this year's
work, so we will practice these exercises the whole period to-day.
You may count softly as you write. Write each one a few times."
Let this work be individual. It will be possible to determine
which pupils need help and which pupils can be trusted to work
independently by noticing how they succeed in counting for themselves in this work.

Lesson 3

"Show me the right position." If some are out, as is likely, call
attention to the points, as, grasp of pen, wrist nearly level, sliding
fingers curved in, thumb higher than first finger on penholder, etc.,
and see how many can make the needed adjustments. "Let
us make dots to mark the margin to-day and see if we can get a
well-arranged page. Now, without writing, take the long swing.
Ready. Slide. One-two, one-two. Does your arm rest on the
desk? Try to keep it so." Show Exercise 1 on the board.
"Ready. Write. One-two, one-two. We will put Exercise 2
directly under it. Ready. Write. One-two, one-two. Now write
these two with half-line swing. Ready. Write. One-two, one-
two."

Review Exercise 4, *u*, with long and short swing. Write Exercise 5, *it*, making long swings between the words. "Ready.
Write." Always give the count for the writing as it is given in the
written exercises in the Manual. Give this several times and then
give Exercise 6, *e*. "Let us see what an easy swing we can get here,

and how straight we can keep the down-stroke." Swing several lines, all writing to the same count.

"Now can you do the same thing but make the loop twice as

(handwriting exercise)

EXERCISE 6   EXERCISE 7

high?" Give Exercise 7, *l*. "Ready. Write." Emphasize the straight down-stroke of the *l*. If any fail to get this point, have them practice it for a time counting on both the up-strokes and the down-strokes so as to emphasize the long down-stroke. Drop this as soon as possible. Study the needs of your class this week with reference to grouping next week. Now give Exercise 8, *lee*, making it two or three times across the page according to the width of the paper.

(handwriting exercise)

EXERCISE 8

LESSON 4

"Position." Note carefully and correct where necessary at the beginning and throughout the lesson. "We will write Exercises 1, 2. Remember to make long swings and use your sliding fingers. Let the arm rest on the desk." Show the exercise once on the board. Exercise 1. "Ready. Write." Exercise 2. "Ready. Write." Review Exercises 5, *it*, 6, *e*, 7, *l*, emphasizing a free easy swing.

Give Exercise 9, *tell*, *little*, *lull*. Give these a few times, all following the count. Then let each write, counting independently

(handwriting exercise)

EXERCISE 9

for his own work. Give Exercise 10, *b*. "This is only slightly different from the *l*. Notice the pause before the connecting

(handwriting exercise)

EXERCISE 10

stroke is made. Get a free swing and emphasize the pause in the writing."

LESSON 5

To-day the class should write the first test of the year. Follow exactly the directions given on page 8, and use the material indicated for Grade 5.

There may seem to be too large an amount of material given for this week. The idea is to have only a short practice on any one exercise. Immature persons cannot give active attention to any one thing long at a time, and continued repetition without this is likely to confirm bad habits instead of establishing good ones. A frequent review of work which has been practiced, with the letters or words in varied combinations, is likely to result in more improvement than long-continued practice on one form.

SECOND WEEK. LESSON 1

The teacher should know now which of the class can be trusted to work independently and which need much help. It will facilitate matters if those who need much help can sit together during the handwriting period. During part of this period this group should work together while the others are directing their own work. This does not mean that any shall now be excused from writing, but that some shall not be required to carry on the organized drills so long as the others.

"The first thing of importance in good writing is good position. Show me your paper position. Your body position. Feet resting on the floor. Your pen position. Hands up so I can see; now hand position — fingers ready for sliding." Review Exercises 1, 2, with long and short swing.

Review Exercises 6, 7, 10. Give Exercise 11, *bell, but, bill*, all of

EXERCISE 11

which are review words from lower grades. Then allow the independent group to write Exercise 9, and any words containing only letters which have been practiced, while the practice group writes together to the teacher's count as many review exercises as there is time for, writing each two or three times. Lead this group to study their own work, finding the best and trying to imitate that.

LESSON 2

Give Exercises 1, 2, without ink, sliding across the paper with count. Review Exercise 10, *b*. Give *bell* which includes the three exercises having this swing. Give Exercise 12, *a*. "Notice the long swing at the top. Look again." Write it again. "Class,

EXERCISE 12

write. Some one did not make the swing at the top long enough and some turned the top down. Look." Show it again, emphasizing the upward tendency at the top of the *a*. "Now, again. Ready. Write." Note some who have improved and try again. Be sure that the top of the *a* does not turn down. We are laying foundations now and every point made right now will help later on.

"We will combine some of the exercises. Look." Give Exercise 13, *all*, *ball*, *at*, *tat*, all of which are review. Give each with

EXERCISE 13

count. See that there is a good swing with these. In order to give this, the words should be written with a spacing wider than is natural in these free exercises. Give Exercise 14, *d*, *dell*, *deal*, *lead*.

EXERCISE 14

This is just like the *a* except that the vertical stroke is extended. Some caution is necessary as to the first stroke's being kept up. After a little practice on the *d*, give the words. Then leave the independent group free to practice on word exercises at their own rate.

LESSON 3

Note position quickly and speak of changes needed. Swing Exercises 1, 2, without ink. "Ready. Slide. One-two," etc. (Four times each.) "We will write Exercise 12, *a*. Look. What are we to remember?" (Long swing, top up, closed at the top.) "Ready. Write. We will write the *d*." Give Exercise 15, *o*.

EXERCISE 15   EXERCISE 16

"There is a pause where the *o* closes just like the pause before the connecting stroke of the *b*. Notice, too, that there is the same kind of connecting stroke." After. practicing, combine the two letters in Exercise 16, *bob*, writing it with a long free swing.

Give Exercise 17, *auto, load, doubt, double*. Let the independent group write these trying to give a free swing while the practice

EXERCISE 17

group works with the teacher on the one word *auto* and on review exercises which need more practice. Emphasize the need of free swing. In developing this there may be loss in quality for a time, but if this is gained the quality will improve.

LESSON 4

"Position. Take the swing without writing. We will begin with Exercise 15, *o*. Make three across the line with a long swing. Ready. Write." Follow quickly with Exercises 12, *a*, 4, *u*, 17, *auto*, showing each and being sure that there is a good forward movement and that the time is kept. Make these with a short swing.

"We will take this" — Exercise 18, *w, between, wait*. Give the *w* alone. "Notice how much this is like the *u* except for the final

EXERCISE 18

swing which is like the final stroke of the *b* and the *o* and has the same pause. Notice the time." Write it for the class, counting as you do so. Then let the class practice it. "Does any one find any trouble with it?" Give the words one at a time.

LESSON 5

For the work every Friday use a clean sheet of paper, putting on it the pupil's full name, the grade, and the date. Preserve these papers for periodical comparison in the class in order to note improvement and so that they may be used as a record of progress throughout the year.

"Good position. Feet flat on the floor." Give preliminary swing. "Notice your margins. Write the name, grade, and date on the top line." This direction will not be printed hereafter, but should be given by the teacher. Give Exercises 12, 13, 14, 15, 16, 17, 18.

After collection of the papers, review some of the swinging exercises to give greater ease of movement and a definite rhythm. All should work together on this.

Third Week. Lesson 1

The teacher should determine as a result of last week's work whether there is need of shifting between the groups. No careless work should be tolerated in the independent group. While those in the practice group should be encouraged, be careful not to shift to the independent group before some stability in the habits being formed is gained. Do not relax at all attention to position and rhythm. The fixing of these things now is essential to the success of the work.

Begin with Exercise 1, 2, sliding only halfway across the page. Put two of the exercises on the line. Review Exercise 4, *u*, putting two groups of three each on a line. Repeat two or three times to get evenness of spacing, good forward movement and rhythm. Then give Exercise 18, *w*, in the same way, emphasizing the difference.

Give Exercise 19, *c*, *call*, *cow*, *coat*. The words are all review words. Call attention to the fact that the *c* does turn down at

Exercise 19

the top in distinction from the *a*. Review Exercise 12, *a*, and give *call*, paying special attention to this point.

Directions will not be given regularly about the separation of the groups, but the teacher should make this separation whenever and so far as she finds it to be for the good of the children.

Lesson 2

Give Exercises 1, 2, half-line swing. Review Exercises 12, 14, 19, reducing the spacing somewhat. Be sure that the top of the *a* does not turn down and that the top of the *c* does.

Review Exercise 7, *l*. Give Exercise 20, *f*, *awful*. Let the class see that the *f* is like the *l* except for the loop below the base line.

Exercise 20   Exercise 21

Practice the *f*, keeping exact count and making the down-stroke straight. Then give Exercise 21, *fell*, where all the letters have the same swing, and watch for straight down-strokes all the time. For further practice the class may write any simple words which contain only letters practiced. Such words may be found in the lists of previous grades following the exercise on the letter *f*.

Lesson 3

"Position. Hold pens loosely." Review Exercise 20, *f*. Be sure of the straight down-stroke and make the cross about halfway between the base line and the top of the letter.

Give Exercise 22, *q*, *quite*. Here the stem loop is just like that

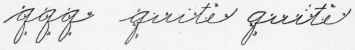

EXERCISE 22

of the *f*. See that it closes at the base line. The other part of the *q* is like the *a*. Do not allow a retracing of the first up-stroke.

After practice on the letter with the count, give the word *quite*. For more practice the word *quiet*, which is given in previous grades, may be used. Call attention to the page arrangement. Let several show their last page and discuss the good points and the points that need improvement. Recall the idea of indentation and suggest that when writing a page we indent the first line.

Lesson 4

Pass out to-day papers that have been corrected at an arithmetic period and discuss the work. "What figures have you made well? What others can you make better than you did? Is your work arranged well on the page? Is it too crowded or too widely spread out? Suppose each one decides how to make his page look best and then copies as much as will look well on one page in his very best way."

EXERCISE 23

Refer to Exercise 23 for the digits. Write these on the board so that the pupils may see how to make them. Then let each practice on his own work. Save these copied papers for comparison, so that the written arithmetic shall not fall below this standard, and for future reference upon points which need practice. This work should be individual or class work as is indicated by the faults to be overcome.

Lesson 5

Write Exercises 19, 20, 21, 22, 23. Collect the papers.

Devote the rest of the time to practice on some of the free swinging exercises.

FOURTH WEEK. LESSON 1

Do not forget position. By this time there should be little need to discuss it, but be watchful to see that every one regards it. Begin to notice evenness of slant and quality of line this week. Review Exercise 12, *a*. Give Exercise 24, *A*. Continue the regular form of command, "Ready. Write." Review with capital *A* any

[handwriting: A A bale of wool]

EXERCISE 24   EXERCISE 25

words that have been written with the initial *a*. Write any names of the class or any names used in the work which begin with *A*. Give Exercise 25, *A bale of wool*. This phrase writing is the first context writing of this year's course, but the children have been doing sentence writing for some time, so that they will need little special instruction for this.

LESSON 2

Review Exercises 1, 2, half-line swing. Review Exercises 6, 14. These early exercises will be repeated from time to time to keep up the automatic forward swinging movement that is easier to get with a comparatively rapid repetition of the same form. Give Exercise 26, *m*, and Exercise 27, *n*. These should be practiced

[handwriting: m m m n n n]

EXERCISE 26   EXERCISE 27

together with especial attention to the rounded tops of the parts. See that this is accomplished. Let each find the best he has made and try to make others like it. Then give Exercise 28, *until, don't, mind, none, turn, mountain, woman*. The last two are review words.

[handwriting: until don't mind]

[handwriting: none turn mountain]

EXERCISE 28

The others come from the Courtis 100 per cent spelling list for this grade.

LESSON 3

Review Exercises 12, 15, for swing. Notice position. After

swinging each once, review Exercises 26, 27, 22. Give Exercise 29, *queen*, *meal*. Write two or three lines. Give Exercise 30, *z*, *muzzle*, *nuzzle*. Review *Buzz*, *fizz*, *dozen*. If more work is needed, select a review exercise for practice.

EXERCISE 29

EXERCISE 30

LESSON 4

Review Exercises 12, 15, for practice in free movement. After giving each once, write the groups in alternation three to a line. This is to emphasize the difference in the connecting stroke, which is often disregarded.

Give Exercise 12, *a*, once alone. Give Exercise 31, *g*, *getting*, *gone*, *got*, *gold*, *game*. The first word is the only one from the 100

EXERCISE 31

per cent spelling list for the 5B class, but the others are either review or quite simple words.

LESSON 5

Give the preliminary swing without writing. Write Exercises 26, 27, 28, 29, 30, 31. Write the letters first as swinging exercises and then write the words.

SECOND MONTH. FIRST WEEK

Introduce the metronome this week.[1] The introduction of the metronome to give the rate has different purposes. It sets the teacher free to inspect and give suggestions to individual children. It gives an absolutely regular count for a continued period such as is impossible with the teacher's voice. Also it makes possible the

[1] If a metronome cannot be obtained for use, the voice count should be regulated so as to follow the rates indicated in the lessons as accurately as possible.

definite determination of the rate to be used at a particular time and the increase of the speed in a systematic way.

LESSON 1

Set the metronome at 120 for use all this month. This is lower than the rate at the end of the fourth year. If it seems too high, a lower rate may be used, but the rate should be brought to this as soon as possible and maintained throughout the month. Review Exercises 10, 12, 14, just to accustom the class to the use of the metronome. Give Exercises 32, *h, eight, change, enough, fifth, whole.* Be very careful that the *h* is not made in a slovenly way.

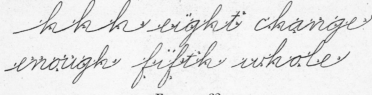

EXERCISE 32

Analyze it as much as is necessary to lead the children to cross the first stroke at about the middle, not to retrace the down-stroke, but to have a sharp turn at the bottom and a good curve at the top of the one-space part. The two down-strokes should be parallel. Give Exercise 33, *A fifth of the whole will be enough.* If there is trouble about getting the sentence with the metronome, write each word alone for one line and then combine them stopping after each word for an instant to get set for the next word. This delay should be lessened so that soon there is not more than a beat or two lost between words.

LESSON 2

Review Exercise 24, *A,* writing some of the words used. Give Exercise 34, *E, Edna, Edmund.* Write the capital first with voice

EXERCISE 34

count and then with the metronome. Write it several times on the board while the children count softly with the metronome and watch your writing. Call attention to the fact that we have parts of two ovals combined and that the lower one is larger than the upper one. Complete the ovals on some of the letters you have written, and when the children write let them test their work by attempting to complete the ovals. Give the words. Give Exercise 35, *Edna and Anne went home together*.

Lesson 3

Review Exercise 34, *E*. Give Exercise 36, *C, Claude, Cleo*.

C C Claude Cleo Cleo

EXERCISE 36

"Notice that the capital *C* is somewhat like both the capital *A* and the capital *E*. Let us make the three in succession keeping exact time with the metronome." If there is more time, write the words given with each.

Lesson 4

Note the position carefully. Give practice on Exercises 12, 24. Give Exercise 37, *p, point, apple*. See that the long stroke of the *p*

p p p point apple

EXERCISE 37

is well above the one-space part. The loop may be written either open or closed.

Give Exercise 38, *Apples are good food*. Here we have used two letters which have not been studied, *r* and *s*. This is justifiable in this grade because the children are writing these letters every day in their other work. They will later be used as letter exercises, when they will be studied.

Lesson 5

Good position. Free swing. Give Exercises 1, 2, without writing. Have the heading written with the metronome. Give Exercises 32, 33, 34, 35, 36, 37, 38. Group the letter exercises, word exercises, and the sentences. After collecting the papers, give selected exercises on which the children need drill.

Second Week. Lesson 1

The stress this week will be on capitals.
Review Exercises 24, 34, 36. Give Exercise 39, *O, Ohio*. "Here

O O O Ohio

EXERCISE 39

is the complete oval. Shall we make it just a few times just as an oval?" Do not swing the oval more than four times in retracing. The *h* in *Ohio* may need attention. See that it is well made.

Give Exercise 40, *O, Anne, call Edmund and Claude and come to me.* This gives practice on all the capitals that have been used. Each should examine his own work to find out what he needs to practice. Then individual work should be done following the metronome. The practice group should have the teacher's attention at this time.

LESSON 2

Give Exercises 1, 2, for swing without writing. Give Exercise 41, *B, Ben, Both, Big.* Be sure that the children get the correct

EXERCISE 41

idea of the count here and then keep to it. Any words that have been studied beginning with *b* may be used. Use any names which are available. Give Exercise 42, *Beans are good to eat.*

LESSON 3

"To-day we have one of the hardest capitals to make because it begins in the opposite direction from most of the other letters." Give Exercise 43, *I, Ina.* Use it as a word alone or in any familiar

EXERCISE 43

connection. See that the slant is right. This may be accomplished by the slant of the first stroke. That must be made so that the down-stroke has the slant of the other letters.

LESSON 4

Review Exercise 43, *I.* Give Exercise 44, *J, Julia, Janet, John.*

EXERCISE 44

This letter is much like the *I* and has the same direction of stroke, but the loop extends below the line. See that the long down-stroke is straight. Give Exercise 45, *I told Julia and John to go home.*

Lesson 5

Give the preliminary swing. Have the heading written with
the metronome each week now. Be particular about the position
of the body, hand, and pen. The sentence should be written in
time with the metronome. Give Exercises 39, 40, 41, 42, 43, 44, 45.
Group the exercises as suggested last week.

For extra time let each practice his name with metronome, raising
any difficulties he finds in letter formation or in time. The development of what may be called a "writing conscience" is desirable.
This consists in recognizing whether or not one knows what the
right form or movement is, and in the desire to learn what is right
when it is not known. This kind of attentive practice will do more
for the improvement of the writing than any other one factor.

Third Week. Lesson 1

Review Exercises 27, *n*, 31, *g*. Give Exercise 46, *y*, *company*,
delay, *duty*. The analysis of the *y* will help the practice group, and

Exercise 46

it may be needed by all, by way of emphasizing form and overcoming carelessness in the production of the letter. Give the words,
watching the letter formation and giving practice drills where
necessary.

The use of criticism here is somewhat different from that in the
lower grades. While adverse criticism should not be the chief type
used, habits have begun to be fixed by this time, and where a habit
is undesirable, it is sometimes necessary to call attention to what
is wrong about it. When this is necessary, do so in connection
with the right form and give immediate practice on the right form.

Lesson 2

Spend to-day in practice on numerals. It is best for each teacher
to use the type of arithmetic work being done just now in her own
class. As the work varies greatly in different places, what is given
here is only suggestive. Give practice on the correct placing of
the decimal point and dollar sign in expressing United States
money. Dictate a random list of different money values to be
properly placed in columns. Write a column on the board for
copy. Place numbers in correct form for addition and subtraction
of United States money.

When numbers are to be written in columns, it is very important that the children be shown how to do it correctly and that they be required to do it so thereafter in all such work.

When writing numbers in a column, each number should be separated from the number above it by a distance equal to one half the height of the figures. The columns corresponding to the different orders — units, tens, hundreds — should be separated by a space equal to the width of the figures.

The importance of attention to this from the beginning and all the time lies in the fact that the correct column placing of figures has been found to increase materially the accuracy of computation.

LESSON 3

Be sure the position is right and watch movement and time. Give Exercise 47, *s*, *swing*, *s*, *close*, *news*, *past*, *second*, *shall*, *slide*, *spend*, *stood*, *use*, *unless*. Give the free swing to get the slant.

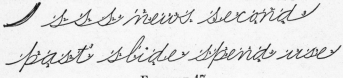

EXERCISE 47

Then give the letter and several of the words. Do not practice any exercise long at a time. Make the practice short and go back to it later. Give Exercise 48, *Company is coming to-day*.

LESSON 4

Review Exercise 6, *e*, and Exercise 47, *s*, for freedom of movement. Give Exercise 49, *r*, *address*, *afraid*, *another*, *board*, *carried*, *carry*, *father*, *forty*, *fourth*, *pleasure*, *raise*, *real*, *refuse*, *steamer*, *sure*, *third*, *throw*, *truly*, *under*, *understand*, *wire*, *wonder*, *worth*.

EXERCISE 49

Do not try to use the whole list to-day, but return to it for review until all the words have been used, as they are all from the

100 per cent spelling list.　From now on make use of words selected from this list which contain the particular practice needed.

Lesson 5

Give the preliminary swing.　Give Exercises 46, 47, 48, 49. Spend extra time on parts of review exercises which have not yet been practiced.

Fourth Week.　Lesson 1

It is not necessary to write all of every exercise, and it is not expected that all classes will do so.　Be sure, however, to give drill on all new work given in any lesson.　Wherever the words are indicated as 100 per cent words, all of them should be given either the first time or when the exercise is being reviewed.　Give Exercise 50, *M, Martha, Martin,* and Exercise 51, *N, Nathan, Nora.*　The *M* and the *N* should be taken together in this grade.　If the *M* is

EXERCISE 50

EXERCISE 51

given first, it may be pointed out that the last curve will be dropped in making the *N*.　The tops of the curves in each letter show a downward slant which helps to guide the making of the letter. After both letters have been practiced, give the names in both exercises or others which are more appropriate.　Review names beginning with the capitals already studied, or write names beginning with those capitals, including letters studied since those capitals were studied.　For example, Exercise 52, *Arthur, Arnold, August, Ernest, Edgar, Edith, Clara, Cora, Ora, Bert, Bessie, Benjamin, Isaac, Julius.*

Lesson 2

Review Exercise 41, *B.*　Give Exercise 53, *P, Pearl, Portland.*

EXERCISE 53

Show that the *P* is just like the *B* except for the lower loop.   The recognition of this likeness will make it easier to make.   Give Exercise 54, *Please bring Pearl and Arthur each a new book.*

LESSON 3

Be sure position and movement are good.   See that the arm rests mostly on the desk and that the rhythm is good.   Do not neglect to follow the prescribed directions in giving each exercise.   The definiteness of direction emphasizes the need of regularity in the activity.

Review Exercise 32, *h.*   Give Exercise 55, *k, knew, track, walk.*

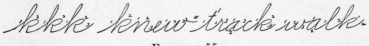

EXERCISE 55

The *k* is like the *h* except the last part.   See that this is made right.   The top should be just opposite the crossing of the loop, should not touch it, and should be very small with an opening left.   The last down-stroke should be parallel to the first down-stroke.   Give the words.   Give Exercise 56, *I knew John could walk around the track faster than Ned could run.*

LESSON 4

Review Exercise 46, *y.*   Give Exercise 57, *j, enjoy, jails.*   Let the pupils discover that *j* is the last part of the *y* with the dot added.

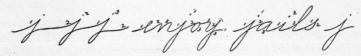

EXERCISE 57

Then practice the letter and the words.   Give Exercise 58, *Jack would not enjoy going to jail.*   If extra work is desired for to-day, allow each child to write his own name with the metronome, profiting by his study of form.   It is well to emphasize the fact that the name is an individual possession and being written often should be written well.

LESSON 5

To-day, instead of having writing, pass out the papers written on previous Fridays and saved for comparison.   Allow each child to compare his own papers and discover where he has made improvements.   Suggest the following questions: Is your writing of more even slant?   Do you keep to the base line better?   What letters do you see that you make better than you did? Is your spacing better? Are the letters too close now, too far apart, or about right? How about the words? Is your line more even and just light enough? Allow each to select an exercise he thinks he can improve, and write it with the metronome and compare it with the first writing. In this connection the *Chart for the Diagnosis of Faults in Handwriting* may be shown and explained and placed where the children can study it frequently.

THIRD MONTH. FIRST WEEK

LESSON 1

Set the metronome for the work this month at 126.

Recall the last lesson, in which a comparison was made of the writing done previously, and suggest that all try to remember the points discussed and make the writing better.

Review Exercises 27, *n*, 10, *b*. Give Exercise 59, *v, driven, everything, vacation.*

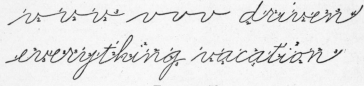

EXERCISE 59

The danger in writing the *v* is that the second up-stroke shall curve away from the down-stroke so as to make too wide an opening. See that it comes back about as in the *b*. After practicing the *v* with a long swing for several lines, give, before writing the words, the combination Exercise 60, *b o w, v o w,* first with a long swing,

EXERCISE 60

and then shortening it so as to put two groups on the line. This emphasizes the likeness of the letters in the pause before the connecting stroke.

LESSON 2

Write on the board the review words *fix, six, box, expect.* Call attention to the *x*. Give Exercise 61, *x, extra.* "Just where does

EXERCISE 61

the cross stroke come? What is the direction of the down-stroke?" Have the class write two lines of the *x*, making the letters separate, as this letter does not lend itself to the swinging form. If necessary show them its likeness to the *n*. Then let the pupils write the review words and give the word *extra*. Give Exercise 62, *Every auto should carry an extra tire*.

Lesson 3

Review Exercises 50, *M*, 51, *N*. Give Exercise 63, *W*, *Walter*, *Willard*. The first stroke of these three letters is the same, but in

Exercise 63

the *W* the turns are all sharp and the middle stroke is above the first, while the last stroke is shorter than any other. It is not a difficult letter to make, but it is important to see that it is correctly made in the beginning. Give Exercise 64, *Willard and Walter ran a one-mile race on the track*.

Lesson 4

Review Exercise 63, *W*. Give Exercise 65, *Z*, *Zebra*, *Zoo*. Relate the *Z* also to Exercise 30, *z*, as the stem is the same. After

Exercise 65

practicing this several times, give the words. Then give Exercise 66, *Zebras are wild animals somewhat like horses. There are two zebras in the Zoo*. Write this as a paragraph, indenting each time.

Lesson 5

Call attention to the proper arrangement of the margins. Select for writing words from Exercises 50 to 66, which have been practiced during the last two weeks. After papers have been collected, review some of these exercises which have not been written on the specimen paper.

Second Week. Lesson 1

Give drill on writing figures representing United States money for multiplication and division. See that the dollar sign and the

decimal point are correctly placed and be watchful of the figures
and the column placing. Give practice wherever needed either by
an individual or by the class.

LESSON 2

Review Exercise 65, Z. Give Exercise 67, Q, Queer, Quick. The
Q is like the Z in its curve, but is a little more rounded. Use any

EXERCISE 67

words which may interest the class with this letter. Give Exercise
68, *Queer things are found in the woods.*

LESSON 3

Review Exercise 51, N. Give Exercise 69, Y, Yesterday. The

EXERCISE 69

stem must be perfectly straight and not quite so high above the
base line as the first stroke. After practice give Exercise 70, *Yesterday Mabel and Pearl helped me with the work. You may help to-day.*
Write this in paragraph form with indentation and good arrangement and spacing. See that there is no crowding of the words to
get more on a line than will easily fill it.

LESSON 4

Review Exercise 53, P. Give Exercise 71, R, Robert, Rosalie.

EXERCISE 71

"How is the R different from the P?" (In the addition of the last
stroke.) Practice the letter and the names of pupils in the class.
Then review a selected exercise or one that is unfinished.

LESSON 5

Give two or three examples in multiplication and in division of
United States money. Give Exercises 65, 66, 67, 68, 69. For

extra work review the name exercise previously used. Practice the name of any one in the class whose name begins with the capitals practiced this week.

Third Week. Lesson 1

Introduce a study of correct correspondence form for an informal letter in connection with some class activity requiring the writing of a letter. It may be necessary to shift this lesson forward or back a little to connect with the other work. The lesson may be shifted, but do not omit it. A correct form is given in Exercise 72. This should so far as possible be developed by questions instead of being given to the class for copy. If the children understand a reason for a form they are more likely to remember it.

Exercise 72:

> 742 S. Clark St.,
> Chicago, Illinois,
> Nov. 17, 1920.

Dear Friend,

....
....
....

> Your friend,
> Mary Smith.

This form is not given for copy by the children, but as a suggestion as to the development of form. What the children write should be governed by local conditions and should be what they would be likely to use in a friendly letter. Such a letter might be to a sick classmate, to another class with regard to work to be done together, etc.

Lesson 2

Give Exercise 73, *L, Laurence, Louise.* The point of emphasis in the capital *L* is the loop at the base line and the succeeding stroke.

EXERCISE 73

See that the children follow copy here. If analysis is needed, refer to lower grade discussions. Give Exercise 74, *Look before you leap.*

Lesson 3

Give drill in writing numbers in correct column form from one to six orders, paying particular attention to long division, where the columns are much broken.

LESSON 4

Give Exercise 75, S, *Steven, Sarah.*

S S S Steven Sarah

EXERCISE 75

The capital *S* is very much like the small *s* in the lower part. After writing it, cover up the upper part and show the pupils that this is so. Practice the letter and names with a good swing. Then use material selected by the teacher from review exercises for drill for the remainder of the period.

LESSON 5

Write a short letter using the form in Exercise 72, and the work selected by the teacher. For extra work practice names with the metronome. These should be well written by this time.

FOURTH WEEK

We shall complete this week the first presentation of all the letters except capitals *U, V, X.* Are you watching the position carefully? Be sure you are keeping the writing exactly with the metronome.

LESSON 1

Give Exercise 76, G, *Georgia, Gerald.*

G G Georgia Gerald

EXERCISE 76

The *G* is very much like the *S,* but it is important that the difference be quite clearly brought out. The definiteness of count will be a great help in getting this letter right. Write it several times on the board, letting the children count it with the metronome as you write until they are sure they know just where each count comes. If there is difficulty, count it much more slowly until the children see how it is done. Give Exercise 77:

> Just to live is joy enough,
> Though where roads are dull and rough.
> Fill your cup and share it! Can
> More be done by flower or man?
>
> *Lucy Larcom.*

Review Exercise 51, *G*. Give Exercise 78, *H*, *Howard*. There is nothing hard about this except the cross. This must be at a

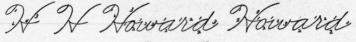

EXERCISE 78

height that will allow its connection with other letters at the one-space height.

Give Exercise 79, *K*, *Keep*, *Kate*. This letter is more difficult than the *H*, but its only difference is in its manner of connection. Here

EXERCISE 79

the second stroke makes the connection by a definite break at about the middle instead of there being an extra connecting stroke as in the *H*. This will require considerable practice, but it should be given at different periods rather than at one long-continued period.

Give Exercise 80, *Keep Harold with you until I come.*

LESSON 3

Review Exercise 73, *L*. "Here is another letter with the same loop at the bottom." Give Exercise 81, *D*, *Douglas*, *David*, *Dinah*.

EXERCISE 81

Practice the *D* and *L* until the class gets the loop swing at the bottom correct. The stroke must touch the base line always after the loop swing. After the words have been practiced, review the exercises given this week.

LESSON 4

Give Exercise 82, *F*, *Florida*, *Floyd*, and Exercise 83, *T*, *Theodore*,

EXERCISE 82

Texas. These two capitals should be studied together because the slight difference is not likely to confuse. The *F* must have the

EXERCISE 83

extra stroke for a cross if it is joined to other letters. Otherwise the cross is made on the end of the last stroke. The practice of these two capitals and the names will probably fill the period. If more work is wanted, review Exercise 79.

LESSON 5

The work to-day is to be graded. Be sure to follow the directions given on page 8 carefully and use the material indicated for Grade 5 in giving the two-minute test. First put the heading on right. Do not use the metronome at all for this test.

When the two-minute test is finished, write, on the other side of the paper if necessary, Exercises 77, 80, with the metronome. This is for the sake of determining whether the use of the metronome affects the writing in general.

FOURTH MONTH. FIRST WEEK

Set the metronome for this month at 132.

We have had direct drill on all small letters now and on all capitals except *U, V, X*, which will be given this week. The papers written at the last lesson and graded will help to show how far there has been success in getting the right results. There is ahead a problem fully as difficult, that of succeeding in making the correct methods of work habitual. This we shall attempt to do, first, by using relatively short and simple exercises combining all the letter forms with attention to rhythm, speed, alinement, slant, letter formation, quality of line, and spacing of letters and words, and later by the use of longer selections. Examples of different degrees of excellence in alinement, slant, letter formation, quality of line, and spacing can be seen in the Charts accompanying the book *The Teaching of Handwriting*, by Frank N. Freeman. The rhythm and speed, of course, cannot be illustrated. A single Chart containing all these illustrations can be obtained from Houghton Mifflin Company. It is desirable that in the upper grades the Chart be hung on the wall where the children can refer to it frequently.

LESSON 1

Allow the writing of each exercise with the metronome. After that use it intermittently, starting and stopping it irregularly. When an exercise consists of single words, write each six or eight times, to allow time to get well into the swing, so that the continuous rhythm will be felt before stopping. This irregular use of the metronome is preliminary to getting rhythmic writing without external stimulus.

Review Exercise 51, *N.* Give Exercise 84, *U, United,* and Exercise 85, *V, Virgil.*

U U U United United

EXERCISE 84

V V V Virgil Virgil

EXERCISE 85

In the *U* the up-stroke is somewhat shorter than the first downstroke. The turn at the base line in both letters is round. The second stroke of the *V* differs from that of the *U* in turning slightly inward and then turning out at the tip. It, also, is somewhat shorter than the first stroke. For additional work review some of the exercises given last week.

LESSON 2

Review Exercise 61, *x.* Give Exercise 86, *X, Xerxes.*

X X Xerxes Xerxes X

EXERCISE 86

This capital is seldom used, so needs little attention, but the children should have some experience with it. After practicing it half a dozen times, review Exercises 52, 56, 66, in whole or part.

LESSON 3

About this time give a lesson on a correspondence form for a somewhat formal letter. This may be to the Principal or Superintendent making a request or acknowledging some obligation. The form given in Exercise 87 should be filled in to meet the local situation.

Exercise 87:

Butte, Montana,
February 21, 1920.

Miss Frances Brown,
Principal of Lincoln School,
Butte, Montana,

My dear Miss Brown,

....
....
....

Very truly yours,
John Smith.

This lesson may be shifted forward or back to correlate with the need of the class, but should not be omitted.

LESSON 4

Give Exercise 88, *Horace and Kenneth were wrestling*. Note the special difficulties in this exercise and give the drill exercises needed. For variety, after a moment's rest of the hand give Exercise 12, *a*, first at the regular rate, 132, and then, increasing the speed one unit at a time on the metronome, let the children see how fast they can keep the time and yet keep the letter forms and slant and aline-ment good. As a game the children enjoy this and often do well.

LESSON 5

Remember the signal, "Ready. Write," after giving the time. Give Exercises 84, 85, 86, 87, 88. For the remainder of the period review exercises not completed; as, Exercise 49, *r*.

SECOND WEEK. LESSON 1

Continue using the metronome for first writing and then inter-mittently. Give Exercise 89, *Keep your mind on your work*, and Exercise 90, *Every pupil is present to-day*. Give the words with capitals several times alone. Then have the sentences written with good swing. Let each find in this writing the work on which he needs practice and devote himself to that. Allow questions about points not clear to the children. Near the end of the period write the sentence again and compare it with the first writing. There may be some in the class who should be excused from this practice and allowed to use the time for other writing in connection with their class work. Use this general method with the short-sentence work which is given in the following lessons.

LESSON 2

Give Exercise 91, *Sue took her sister to town*, and Exercise 92, *Did Edith and Frances come by here just now?*

Lesson 3

Give Exercise 93, *How many marbles have you, Bert?* and Exercise 94, *Were Ada and Mary at school yesterday?*

Lesson 4

Give Exercise 95, *Send Clara and Ora to the store for butter*, and Exercise 96, *Queer questions are sometimes asked.*

Lesson 5

Select three or four of the sentences written this week for writing. See that the arrangement is good.   If there is time, give speed drill using Exercise 15, *o*.

Third Week

This week emphasize *alinement* and *slant* especially.   Refer to the Chart in doing this.   A small sheet of transparent paper ruled about twelve lines to the inch helps in testing both these qualities. Continue to apply the general directions given last week.

Lesson 1

Give Exercise 97, *Xerxes was a great general*, and Exercise 98, *Zero weather makes good skating.*

Lesson 2

Give Exercise 99, *Green grass makes beautiful lawns*, and Exercise 100, *Paper plates are good for picnics.*

Lesson 3

Give Exercise 101, *Read your lesson quickly and quietly*, and Exercise 102, *You may call Laura, Ida, and Jane.*

Lesson 4

Give Exercise 103, *Violets blossom in the Spring*, and Exercise 104, *Theodore found your ball behind the hedge.*

Lesson 5

Select four of the sentences practiced this week to write.   Be sure the position of body, hand, pen, and paper is right.   If there is more time, write single words from the exercises practiced this week with increased speed for speed drill.

Fourth Week.   Lesson 1

Give Exercise 105, *No king rules over the United States.*   For variety, review some of last week's sentences.

LESSON 2

Give Exercise 106, *Zinnias grow in our garden*, and Exercise 107, *Never work too fast to do it well.*

LESSON 3

Give Exercise 108, *Have Mary and Anne found Kate?* Practice other words using these capitals and give speed drill with an easy exercise.

LESSON 4

Give Exercise 109, *Quarrelsome people are not good company.* The word *quarrelsome* is new and may need considerable practice. Give speed drill using Exercise 31, *g.*

LESSON 5

To-day instead of writing compare the work written last Friday with that written the first Friday of the third month; that is, just after the last comparison. It may be compared with any of the intervening lessons if desired. There should be quite marked improvement in uniformity of slant, in alinement, in letter formation, and in quality of line. The spacing between letters and words should have improved as a result of discussion on arrangement of the paper. While faults must be noticed and corrected sometimes, call attention particularly to the improvements made. Ask questions leading the class to find improvement. A very interesting exercise would be to have each write a brief statement of the improvement he has made, as an English exercise. This would give a good basis for context writing, would give point to the study, and give practice in clear, definite statements because the pupil wishes to make himself understood.

FIFTH MONTH. FIRST WEEK

This month we shall write without the metronome about half the time. At first the metronome should be used for the first writing of any exercise. Then allow the class to write it immediately once or twice more, without the metronome. Start it once or twice to test the rhythm. As soon as any who write irregularly have caught the rhythm, stop the metronome. The subject-matter for this month will be, first, the words from the 100 per cent list for Grade 5A, which have not been given. These will be presented in the same general order as that in which the letters were presented. Second, the writing of numbers which relate to the work being done in the arithmetic period. It is recommended that this month the writing of simple fractions be stressed.

Set the metronome at 144 for this month.

LESSON 1

Review Exercises 14, *d*, 19, *c*, 20, *f*. Give Exercise 110, *deal; collect; beautiful, fail, office.* After practice of all this work, use the rest of the period for speed drill on the exercises reviewed to-day.

LESSON 2

Review Exercises 27, *n*, 31, *g*. Give Exercise 111, *addition, command, contain, mean, engine.* Give Exercise 112, *Collect all the beautiful stones you can.*

LESSON 3

Review Exercises 32, *h*, 37, *p*, 46, *y*. Give Exercise 113, *chief, clothing, within; police, public; reply.* Give Exercise 114, *The chief of police is in his office.*

LESSON 4

Review Exercise 47, *s*. Give Exercise 115, *also, cities, dash, else, himself, itself, loss, sail, shed, since, size, sometimes, such.* This will be sufficient practice for this period.

LESSON 5

Give to-day selections from the exercises written this week so as to make about the usual amount. Then give speed drill on some of the letter exercises reviewed this week.

SECOND WEEK

Interrupt the metronome after the first writing of an exercise. Be very sure good rhythm is kept and good position. Where extra work is wanted this week, review some of the sentences in Exercises 88–107.

LESSON 1

Review Exercise 49, *r*. Give Exercise 116, *answer, clerk, court, daughter, destroy, during, enter, fair, friend, nearly, newspaper, offer, person, prison, reason, return, suffer, support, surprise, terrible, through, trouble, trust, weather.*

LESSON 2

Continue to-day the exercise given in Lesson 1. Give Exercise 117, *Ask the clerk not to destroy that newspaper but to return it to me.*

LESSON 3

Review Exercise 59, *v*. Give Exercise 118, *evening, navy, provide, recover, several, view, visit, vote.* After practice on these words, give Exercise 119, *We will visit the fair this evening and see several beautiful things.*

Lesson 4

Practice to-day parts of the exercises given this week that have not yet been studied. If there is not enough of this work to fill the period, use the review exercises of this week for speed drills.

Lesson 5

Select from Exercises 116 to 119, giving all the sentences and some of the words.

Third Week. Lesson 1

To-day study the writing of fractions in correlation with work which is being done in the class. If the children are making good figures now, they will have little trouble in putting the work into correct fractional form. For variation, write fractions for addition, subtraction, multiplication, and division. A review may be given of writing the symbols representing United States money if more variety is desired.

Lesson 2

For about a month now exercises will be given as sentences arranged to review all the letters, in context form, or in words which require the use of capitals, and which the children are likely to find use for frequently.

Give Exercise 120, *A quick brown fox jumps over the lazy dog.*

Lesson 3

Give Exercise 121, *Sunday, Monday, Tuesday, Wednesday, Thursday, Friday, and Saturday are the days of the week.*

Give as much practice as is necessary on the individual words.

Lesson 4

Give Exercise 122, *In the January thaw we often find butterflies in the woods.*

Lesson 5

Give a group of examples such as were studied this week and give Exercises 120, 121, 122.

Fourth Week

The work for this week will not be divided into daily lessons, and the teacher will select what is of most value to the group. For review use sentence exercises which need more practice. Speed drill may also be given.

Copies for the Week

Exercise 123: *February is the shortest month.*

Exercise 124: *March winds are often strong.*

Exercise 125: *April showers*
        Bring May flowers.

Exercise 126: *June is the month of roses.*

Exercise 127: *July fourth is Independence Day.*

Exercise 128: *August is usually a very hot month.*

Exercise 129: *In September school begins.*

Exercise 130: *The last night of October is Halloween Night.*

On Friday give the names of the months which have been practiced, and then allow each child to decide which sentences he will write. One or two sentences may be written.

Sixth Month. First Week

The type of work given last week will be continued. Follow the general directions. Set the metronome at 152. If this seems too high when studying an exercise, use last month's rate but raise it to 152 before the exercise is left.

Copies for the Week

Exercise 131: *Thanksgiving Day comes in November.*

Exercise 132: *December 25th is Christmas Day.*

Exercise 133: *December, January, and February are the Winter months. In these we have cold weather, snow, and coasting.*

Exercise 134: *March, April, and May are the Spring months. The snow goes away, the rain comes, and the flowers bloom. The birds come back and build their nests in the trees and bushes.*

Have these sentences written as paragraphs, indenting and giving proper spacing. Study page arrangement here.

Second Week
Copies for the Week

Exercise 135: *June, July, and August are the Summer months. Roses bloom, oats, wheat, and corn ripen, and some apples are ready to pick.*

Exercise 136: *September, October, and November are the Autumn months. During these we have the harvests and we get ready for the Winter.*

Use these as suggested for the exercises last week. Wherever need is evident in the quality of the writing or the movement, return to free letter exercises. Every day or two give a speed drill for a few minutes, using a single word and going as fast as the class can write without disorganization of the movement. Always make the advance gradually.

THIRD WEEK

A regular method of grading will be followed for the rest of the year. This is based on the *Chart for the Diagnosis of Faults in Handwriting*. Wherever possible the teacher should make use of this.

The teacher should study the Chart this week in preparation for its use next week. During the week that each category is being emphasized, that category alone should be graded; for example, when *letter formation* is being emphasized, it will be graded in terms of the Chart and will be rated 2, 6, 10, or the intermediate points 4, 8. Further information regarding the use of the Chart can be obtained from *The Teaching of Handwriting*, by Frank N. Freeman (Houghton Mifflin Company), pp. 123–42.

The children should understand that the marking is in points, not in per cent as in other subjects. When the marking is begun, the teacher should grade, in the special category for the week, the work done on the first day and on the last day.

The child should grade his own work by reference to the Chart, every day, not so much for the value of his estimate as to lead to a critical attitude toward his own work.

Only one or two selections will be given for each week, the most difficult parts of which should be used for preliminary practice. If the teacher wishes, these may be used as the basis of a booklet to be made in other classes. It has not seemed necessary to give written copies of all these exercises. If there is any question as to form of letters, refer to previous exercises.

Do not increase the speed above 152 this year except for speed drills. Attempt to stabilize the work at this rate. Use the metronome from now on only to set the time for an exercise and to test the rhythm by starting it occasionally during the writing. It should always be used in the speed drill which may be given at the discretion of the teacher.

Copies for the Week

Any teacher may substitute for the exercises given material which will correlate with other subjects. Where quotations are given, have the children write the name which shows the source. They should learn to credit properly what they use.

Exercise 137: *A man should never be ashamed to own that he is in the wrong; which is but saying in other words that he is wiser to-day than he was yesterday.*

Alexander Pope.

Exercise 138:

> Mine honor is my life; both grow in one;
> Take honor from me, and my life is done.

Richard II.

In the first selection the word *ashamed* is the only one which might be expected to give trouble.   In the second selection *honor* is the only difficult word.   It is not necessary for any class to use both exercises.

Fourth Week

We shall begin this week to emphasize a particular category and to grade at the beginning and at the end of the week as described in the general directions for the third week.   This week emphasize *letter formation*.   Pass out the last specimens saved for comparison and let each study his own to find good letter form and to find where improvements should be made.   Have each child grade his own work every day.   For this purpose the Chart should hang on the wall where the children can refer to it at odd moments.   Call attention to special points of difficulty in *letter formation*.

Copies for the Week

Exercise 139:

> Flower in the crannied wall,
>   I pluck you out of the crannies;
> I hold you here, root and all, in my hand;
>   Little flower, if I could understand
> What you are, root and all, and all in all,
>   I should know what God and man is.
>
> *Alfred, Lord Tennyson.*

Exercise 140:

> Some one we cannot hear,
> Some one we cannot see,
>   Shakes the baby,
>   Wakes the baby,
> Makes him laugh with glee.
>
> *Mary Mapes Dodge.*

Select the difficult words for practice.   Take no more than the class can do well.   The plan is to give more than some classes can do.   It is expected that the teacher will substitute work that is derived from other class activities for some or all of the material. In doing so she should be careful to keep the standard of quality and the method of writing high.

Seventh Month. First Week

This week emphasize and grade on *spacing*.   The attention on arrangement should have helped in this some.   This week emphasize it all the time.   Show the class how to write poems properly where more than one line is needed for a line of poetry.   Do not allow cramping but do not spread the letters and words too much. Reference to the Chart will help in determining a good proportion. Discuss especially the difference in the arrangement of prose and poetry.

Copies for the Week

Exercise 141:

> Give me of your boughs, O Cedar!
> Of your strong and pliant branches,
> My canoe to make more steady,
> Make more strong and firm beneath me!
>
> *Henry W. Longfellow.*

Exercise 142:

> Give me of your bark, O Birch-tree!
> Of your yellow bark, O Birch-tree!
> Growing by the rushing river,
> Tall and stately in the valley!
> I a light canoe will build me.
>
> *Henry W. Longfellow.*

Second Week

Emphasize *alinement* this week. All letters should rest on the base line. Regard also proportionate height. Do not let the one-space letters lie down on the line and make the loop letters a little more than twice as high. While doing this, try to keep good letter form and spacing; but do not call attention to these as strongly as to alinement. If the copies any week are too long, omit part of them. Give preliminary practice on any part that is likely to cause trouble.

Copies for the Week

Exercise 143:

Hiawatha's Childhood

> Then the little Hiawatha
> Learned of every bird its language,
> Learned their names and all their secrets,
> How they built their nests in Summer,
> Where they hid themselves in Winter.

Exercise 144:

> Of all beasts he learned the language,
> Learned their names and all their secrets,
> How the beavers built their lodges,
> Where the squirrels hid their acorns,
> How the reindeer ran so swiftly,
> Why the rabbit was so timid.
> Talked with them where'er he met them,
> Called them Hiawatha's Brothers.
>
> *Henry W. Longfellow.*

Third Week

Our point of emphasis this week will be *quality of line.* This depends upon good position, which prevents cramping and undue pressure; good pen and ink; and rhythm, which tends to give regularity instead of waviness of line. Call attention incidentally to the categories previously emphasized; but make this one the principal one for the week.

Copies for the Week

Exercise 145:

> Buttercup shareth the joy of the day,
> Glinting with gold the hours of play;
> Bringeth the poppy sweet repose,
> When the hands would fold and the eyes would close.
>
> *Eugene Field.*[1]

Exercise 146:

> Be noble! and the nobleness that lies
> In other men, sleeping, but never dead,
> Will rise in majesty to meet thine own.
>
> *James R. Lowell.*

Exercise 147:

> Have love! Not love alone for one,
> But man as man thy brother call,
> And scatter like the circling sun
> Thy charities on all.
>
> *Schiller.*

Fourth Week

Emphasize *uniformity of slant* this week. Because this depends on position and rhythm, it should be very good by this time. Try to get the pupils to carry over their writing form to their writing in other subjects. Lead them to be critical of their own work. Do not forget to have the pupils grade their own work.

Copies for the Week

Exercise 148:

> The union of lakes, the union of lands,
> The union of States none can sever;
> The union of hearts, the union of hands, —
> The flag of our union forever!
>
> *Geo. P. Morris.*

Exercise 149:

> The grass comes, the flower laughs where lately lay the snow,
> O'er the breezy hill-top hoarsely calls the crow,
> By the flowing river the alder catkins swing,
> And the sweet song sparrow cries, "Spring! It is Spring!"
>
> *Celia Thaxter.*

---

[1] Reprinted by permission from *The Poems of Eugene Field.* Copyrighted, 1910, by Julia S. Field; published by Charles Scribner's Sons.

Exercise 150:

SONG OF SUMMER

Up in the air, down in the ground,
High in the blue sky, far, all around, —
Nearby and everywhere, singing and humming,
Busily, joyfully, Summer is coming!

Mary Mapes Dodge.

EIGHTH MONTH. FIRST WEEK

We will now combine grading on the categories of *letter formation,* *spacing,* and *slant.* Sum the grades given to each for the total score. Be sure that the pupils understand that the score is in points, not in per cent.

Copies for the Week

Exercise 151:

OH NO!

If bluebirds bloomed like flowers in a row,
And never could make a sound,
How would the daisies and violets know
When to come out of the ground?
Then would wait and wait the seasons round;
Never a flower on earth could be found.

And what would birds and butterflies do
If the flowers had wings to fly?
Why birds and blossoms and butterflies too,
Would stay far up in the sky;
And then the people would droop and sigh,
And all the children on earth would cry.

Mary Mapes Dodge.

Exercise 152:

The sweetest song our whole year round,
'T is the first robin of the Spring!
The song of the full orchard choir
Is not so fine a thing.

Lucy Larcom.

SECOND WEEK

Grade on *letter formation, alinement,* and *quality of line.* Sum the grades as last week. This method of analysis of the writing to determine where changes are desirable should be helpful to the class. Urge that all writing be made in as good form as the work done in the writing period. Spend one day this week reviewing the work in numbers as a test to see whether further practice is necessary. If the teacher and children attend to this in the arithmetic period as

well as in the handwriting period, it should need no further practice at this period.

Copies for the Week

Exercise 153:

SPRING SONG

Spring comes hither,
　Buds the rose;
Roses wither,
　Sweet Spring goes.

Summer soars, —
　Wide winged day;
White light pours
　Flies away.

Soft winds blow,
　Westward born;
Onward go,
　Toward the morn.

George Eliot.

Exercise 154:

There is always hope for a man that actually and persistently works.
In idleness alone is there perpetual despair.

Thomas Carlyle.

Exercise 155:

Under the greenwood tree,
Who loves to lie with me,
And tune his merry note
Unto the sweet bird's throat?
Come hither, come hither, come hither!
　Here shall he see
　No enemy
But winter and rough weather.

William Shakespeare.

THIRD WEEK

Grade on all categories this week. Help each child to determine
which one needs the most attention and let each try to bring up
that one.

Copies for the Week

Exercise 156:

THE SHELL

See what a lovely shell,
Small and pure as a pearl,
Lying close to my foot,
Frail, but a work divine,

Made so fairly well
With delicate spiral and whorl,
How exquisitely minute,
A miracle of design.

Alfred, Lord Tennyson.

Exercise 157:

QUEEN MAB

A little fairy comes at night;
Her eyes are blue, her hair is brown,
With silver spots upon her wings,
And from the moon she fluttered down.

She has a little silver wand,
And when a good child goes to bed,
She waves her wand from right to left,
And makes a circle round its head.

And then it dreams of pleasant things —
Of fountains filled with fairy fish,
And trees that bear delicious fruit,
And bow their branches at a wish.

Thomas Hood.

FOURTH WEEK

Two short copies are given this week. If more work is wanted
select it from that which has been omitted in the previous exercises.

Copies for the Week

Exercise 158:

Rollicking Robin is here again.
What does he care for the April rain?
Care for it? Glad of it. Does n't he know
That the April rain carries off the snow,
And coaxes out leaves to shadow his nest,
And washes his pretty red Easter vest,
And makes the juice of the cherry sweet,
For his hungry little robins to eat?
"Ha! ha! ha!" hear the jolly bird laugh.
"That is n't the best of the story, by half!"

Lucy Larcom.

Exercise 159:

He gives only the worthless gold
Who gives from a sense of duty.

James R. Lowell.

NINTH MONTH

In the last month of school there is frequently an accumulation
of subject-matter which requires writing. The teacher sometimes

allows careless work here because of the press of work and lack of time to do careful work. The handwriting period should give relief at this time instead of being one thing more to add to the work. Any subject-matter which calls for writing may at the discretion of the teacher be written at the handwriting period.

There are certain stipulations with regard to such work. First, it should be done with the same care that would be used in a regular handwriting exercise, giving practice on any parts that need it; second, the position, movement, and rhythm should be up to the standard.

In case the teacher has not enough work which she feels is of enough importance to use in this way, she should use the material given below and follow the same general plan as was used in the eighth month.

During the third week of this month a two-minute test should be given according to the directions on page 8. This should be compared with the first test of the year so that both the teacher and pupils will appreciate what the progress has been.

At some time during this month a systematic review should be given of all the abbreviations which have been taught this year or of any which have been reviewed that were used before.

The following list is suggested for this grade. Any others which have been used should be added.

Names of States, *bl., bu., lb., cts., pk., cwt., etc., Geo.,* and other common abbreviations of commonly used names, *Mt.,* the directions, *No., P.O., R.R., Rev.*

Copies for the Month

Exercise 160, *An effort made for the happiness of others lifts us above ourselves.*

Exercise 161, *Education is a better safeguard of a nation than a standing army. — Edward Everett.*

Exercise 162:

> Swinging on a birch-tree!
>> This is summer joy,
> Fun for all vacation;
>> Don't you think so, boy?
> Up and down to seesaw,
>> Merry and at ease,
> Careless as a brook is,
>> Idle as the breeze!
>
> *Lucy Larcom.*

Exercise 163, *You can't mix oil and water.*

Exercise 164:

> The world's a bubble, and the life of man
> Less than a span.
>
> *Francis Bacon.*

OPTIONAL MATERIAL

The selections given here may be used as additional material at the end of the year or may be substituted for material given in the assigned lessons.

ONE MOTHER

Hundreds of stars in the pretty sky,
Hundreds of shells on the shore together,
Hundreds of birds that go singing by,
Hundreds of flowers in the sunny weather.
Hundreds of dewdrops to greet the dawn,
Hundreds of bees in the purple clover,
Hundreds of butterflies on the lawn,
But only one Mother the whole world over.

George Cooper.

A good man out of the good treasure of his heart bringeth forth good things. — *New Testament.*

Beautiful hands are those that do
Work that is honest, brave and true.

Dewdrops are the gems of morning,
But the tears of dewy eve!

Samuel T. Coleridge.

Every person is responsible for all the good within the scope of his abilities. — *Gail Hamilton.*

In kindly showers and sunshine bud
The branches of the dull gray wood.

John G. Whittier.

CHAPTER X

EXERCISES FOR GRADE SIX

OBJECTIVES

Content. The aim in this grade is to make the writing so efficient in other subjects as to make unnecessary further formal drill in writing after this grade.

All common rules for the use of capitals should be applied. In arithmetic all forms previously learned should be used without exception. Common business forms, such as receipts, bills, checks, should be used. In composition the simple composition and correspondence forms previously given should become habitual. The arrangement of material on the page should be studied with reference to all these forms. The writing vocabulary should now include all words used by the pupil.

Movement. The establishment of an individual rhythm which will make unnecessary the setting of an arbitrary rhythm, and will result in a thoroughly coördinated writing habit, is the aim of this year. The manner of writing should be fairly settled and automatic. A fluency of seventy letters a minute is the standard for speed.

MATERIALS AND METHODS

Materials. In this grade there should be considerable practice on unruled paper.

Methods. *A. Position.* A pupil who has had the training of the earlier grades should habitually assume a good writing position. Any who have not had this training should be helped by the teacher to acquire this habit.

B. Types of exercises. 1. Drills for free movement presented by the teacher and analyzed as to count should be given to those who need the formal drill. The motive here should be the desire to reach such a standard as to make formal writing drills unnecessary.

2. The aim in this grade is to bring all written work up to such a standard in speed and quality that further formal writing drill will become unnecessary.

3. The use of unruled paper necessitates special attention to the alinement and spacing.

4. Speed drills should be conducted on the plan of Grade 5 if a satisfactory standard has not been reached. The metronome should be used here only as a test or measure of rhythm.

C. Standards and criticism. The *Chart for Diagnosing Faults in Handwriting* is a basis for criticism and should be applied to all written work of the class, requiring the grade standard to be maintained. A formal test should be given three times a year — at the beginning, in January, and in April — which should be the basis for excusing from formal drill all who reach the required standard. It should be understood, however, that failure to maintain this standard in all written work will result in the return of any pupil to the formal drill periods in writing.

The standard in speed in this grade is seventy letters a minute. The standard in quality is 20 on the Freeman Scale and 60 on the Ayres Scale.

FIRST MONTH.　FIRST WEEK

LESSON 1

A talk somewhat like the following is suggested in beginning the work this year. It should be suited to the experience of the class:

"We find good writing easier to read than poor writing, so we consider it desirable. *Any one* can write well if he takes time enough and works hard enough. We shall try to learn to write so that we can do better writing with less effort.

"In order to do this, we must pay attention to these points: first, we must hold the pen loosely, without cramping the fingers; second, we must let the hand rest on the third and fourth fingers instead of on the side, so that it will be easier to move across the page; third, we must have the paper directly in front, slanted about as we want the writing to slant. The position of the body is important, too, because if we bear much weight on our arms we tire much sooner than if they can move easily.

"Sit in an easy position with the feet resting on the floor, then place the arms on the desk without bearing weight on them. Take the pen and hold it loosely." Explain the position as much as is necessary.

"Now slide across the paper and see how freely you can move. If your wrist is raised a little, it will be easier."

"Now I will show you what to write." Give Exercise 1, the

EXERCISES 1 AND 2

over-curve. "Notice how I count it. We will make it all the way across the page. Be sure you are ready for a good swing. Is your hand turned right? Are your little fingers ready? Is your pen held right and loosely? Ready. Write. One-two, one-two, one-two, one-two." Write the exercise on the board again for comparison. Ask for self-criticism, "How many made too much curve? How many, too little? Try once more.

"Now we will make the under-curve." (Exercise 2.) Show it on the board. "Ready. Write. One-two, one-two, one-two, one-two." Give Exercise 3, *i*. "Now let us make the *i* with a

EXERCISE 3

long swing. It is important that we begin our work this year with a free movement, so that all our writing shall be easy and not tiresome." "Write two curves close together with a long swing between the groups like this." Give Exercise 4, *u*.

EXERCISE 4

LESSON 2

"What is most important in our writing now? Yes, position. Let us see how many can remember the right position. Good." Make corrections where needed, but not in a critical manner. If there is any difficulty in position, show this again carefully. Refer to Grade 5 if necessary for discussion.

Give Exercise 1. "Slide 'way across the page. Ready. Write. One-two, one-two. Is it too curved? — not enough? — about right? Did you keep with the count?"

Give Exercise 2. "Go 'way across the paper. Ready. Write. One-two, one-two." Review Exercise 3, *i*, 4, *u*, with good free slide. Give Exercise 5, *it*. "This time we will make one curve just as we

EXERCISE 5

have and a second close to it, but nearly twice as high. Then make a long swing and repeat. Think more about the free swing than about the letters you are making. Ready. Write. One-two, one-two." Give Exercise 6, *tit*, for variety. These early exercises are to be given very largely to the establishment of a free, easy movement with good position, overcoming any laxity or tenseness that has come during the summer.

Lesson 3

"Show me the right position." If some have been out, as is likely, name the points of good position; as, clasp of pen, wrist nearly level, sliding fingers curved in, thumb higher than index finger on the pen, etc., and see how many can make the necessary adjustments. "Now, without writing, give a long slide. Ready. Slide. One-two, one-two. Does your arm rest on the desk? Try to keep it so." Give Exercises 1, 2, with the long swing and then repeat them swinging only halfway across the line. Review Exercises 3, 4, 5, 6, each once or twice with the free swing. "Here we have a somewhat different swing." Give Exercise 7, *e*. Have the class

Exercise 7

write it with a free swing. "Now can you make it twice as high?" Give Exercise 8, *l*. See that there is no ugly curve in the down-

Exercise 8

stroke and try to have it made on the same count as the *e*. When written independently the *l* will probably be given a little longer time than the *e*, but so long as we use the count for the purpose of developing rhythm in writing and a consciousness of the letter units, it seems best to give these the same count. Give Exercise 9, *let, little, lute*.

Exercise 9

Lesson 4

Note position carefully and correct at the beginning and throughout the lesson, wherever necessary. "We will write Exercises 1, 2. Remember to make long swings and use your sliding fingers. Let the arm rest on the desk."

Review Exercises 3, 4, 7, 8, swinging freely. Then give the same exercises with a shortened swing.

Give Exercise 10, *b, blue, built*. Call attention to the resem-

Exercise 10

blance of *b* and *l*, and to the difference. Make a definite pause before the last stroke of the *b*. The second up-stroke should curve a little toward the down-stroke, but should not touch it. Give the words in Exercise 10, after the letter has been practiced. Then review Exercise 9.

LESSON 5

The first test of the year should be given to-day. Follow the directions on page 8 exactly, using the material indicated for Grade 6. After the two-minute test is written, devote the remainder of the period to practice of the swinging letter exercises keeping position and count exactly.

It will be noticed that it is not suggested here, as in Grade 5, that at this time the class be grouped so that work may be assigned to meet individual needs. This plan is not used in this grade because the introduction of the letters is to be much more rapid than in the preceding grades with the idea of beginning as soon as possible the use of organized material as the subject-matter of writing. In this grade habits are relatively fixed, and it seems best to recall and give practice to all letter forms before any of the class is excused for individual work. An exception to this may be made in any lesson when review work is practiced after the introduction of new material if the teacher is reasonably sure that some of the class do not need the review. If this is done, other written work should be assigned and the work should be inspected to ascertain whether these pupils prove to be capable of independent work. As soon as all the letters have been introduced, those who have proved their ability to do so may be excused from the formal practice as long as their writing in other subjects continues to meet the standard for the grade, as stated in the general directions at the beginning of this chapter.

SECOND WEEK. LESSON 1

"The first thing in good writing is good position. Show me your paper position. Your body position. Your pen position."

Give Exercises 1, 2, writing them on the board once to count. "Ready. Write. One-two," etc.

Give Exercise 11, *a*. "Notice the long swing at the top. Look again. Ready. Write." Always give the count as shown on the

EXERCISE 11

written exercises in the Manual. After a second practice, note the improvements and try again. Be sure the top of the *a* does not turn down. We are laying foundations now, and every point made right now will help later on.

Give Exercise 12, *d*, *add*. The only new point here is the lengthening of the stroke, which should be written with the same count as in the *a*. As soon as the *d* has been practiced, give the word *add*,

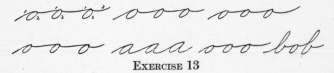

EXERCISE 12

which gives practice on the two letters and stresses the common points. Review with short swing the letter exercises which have been given.

LESSON 2

Give Exercises 1, 2, without ink, sliding across the paper and counting. Give Exercise 13, *o, ooo, aaa, bob*. Call attention to the

EXERCISE 13

fact that here the connecting stroke does not touch the line as in the *a*. These letters are often confused in writing them so that they decrease the legibility of the writing. Practice the groups in alternation. Then call attention to the fact that the connecting stroke is like that of the *b*, and have the children practice that combination, first with a long swing and then with a short swing.

Give Exercise 14, *w, bow*. "Here is a letter which combines a good many parts of letters we have studied. It is like the *i*, and *u*,

EXERCISE 14

in its curves, like the *b*, in its last up-curve, and like the *b* and the *o* in its connecting stroke." After practice, give the combination *bow* first with the long swing and then as a word.

LESSON 3

Note position quickly and note changes needed. Give Exercises 1, 2, without ink. "Ready. Write. We will write Exercise 12, *add*. What are we to remember?" (Long swing, top up, close.) Give Exercise 15, *allow*. This gives more varied combinations than

EXERCISE 15

any that has yet been given, and so requires careful attention.
"Do you see the count?" If any one is in doubt, write it again.
"Ready. Write. How many kept the *l*'s straight? How many
made the connecting stroke of *o* and *w* right? Try again, and this
time everybody right. Ready. Write."

The word *allow* is the first word given that comes from the Courtis 100 per cent Spelling List. None are given in that list for
Grade 6 which come earlier than this according to the classification
of letters which is used in this course.

Give Exercise 16, *c*, *could*, *came*. Don't allow the *c* to be carelessly made without the hooked turn at the top.

EXERCISE 16

LESSON 4

Give the swing without writing. Give Exercise 3, *i*. Follow
quickly with Exercises 4, 7, 10, 11, 12, showing each, and be sure
that there is a good forward swing, and that the time is kept.

Review Exercise 8, *l*. Give Exercise 17, *f*, *follow*, *feel*. Except

EXERCISE 17

for the loop below the line this is like the *l*. See that the down-
stroke is straight throughout its length. The crossing in the upper
loop should be at the one-space height. The closing of the lower
loop should be at the base line. Do not neglect these points of
letter formation.

LESSON 5

"Take clean paper. Good position." Give the preliminary
swing. "Write on the top line the name, grade, and date." Each
week in Lesson 5 these general directions should be followed, and
each week the papers written on this day should be saved for comparison throughout the year to show progress. These particular
directions will be omitted hereafter, but should be given by the
teacher.

Give Exercises 4, 7, 10, 12, 13, 16, one line of each, and Exercises
9, 15, two or three lines of each. Use any extra time in practice on
the free letter exercises to count and in good position.

THIRD WEEK.   LESSON 1

Do not relax at all on attention to position and rhythm.   The fixing of these things now is essential to the success of the work. Begin with Exercises 1, 2, sliding only halfway across the page. Put two of these exercises on a line.   Give Exercise 3, writing two groups of three each to the line.   Repeat two or three times to get evenness of spacing, good forward movement, and rhythm.

Review Exercise 17, *f*.   Give Exercise 18, *q*, *que*, *quite*, *quiet*.

EXERCISE 18

"The first part of the *q* is like what letter?" (*a*.)   "Notice that the loop is just the lower loop of the *f* and must close at the line.   Write it carefully.   Ready.   Write."   See that the pupils get the loop right.   Possibly no one will have trouble, but if any one has previously confused the *q* and the *g*, the direction of the curve will need special attention.   Any of the words may be used.   They need not all be used.

LESSON 2

To-day test the class on the writing of numbers.   Papers that have been saved from the written work in arithmetic should be used as the basis for the study of digits.   Refer to Exercise 19, for

EXERCISE 19

the digits.   After examination of the papers and discussion of the work has shown where the faults are, the practice should be mainly individual.

When numbers are to be written in columns, it is very important that the children should be shown how to write them correctly and that they should be required to do it so thereafter in all such work.

When writing numbers in a column, each number should be separated from the number above it by a distance equal to one half the height of the figures.   The columns corresponding to the different orders — units, tens, hundreds — should be separated by a space equal to the width of the figures.

The importance of attention to this from the beginning and all the time lies in the fact that correct column placing of figures has been found to increase materially the accuracy of the computation. The careful attention to the units column as guide to the placing for other columns is especially important where the class will be required to write decimals and whole numbers together. Choose numbers to be dictated or copied in this work as shall relate to the material required in the written work in arithmetic at this time.

Lesson 3

Give Exercise 20, *m*, and Exercise 21, *n*. Show these and write to count several times. Call attention to the round turn at the top

EXERCISE 20

EXERCISE 21

and have the letters practiced as swinging exercises with this point definitely in mind. Vary the practice by long swings, short swings, and alternating the letters.

Give Exercise 22, *omit; account, common, income, indeed, plain, unable, women*. In all this work call attention to the tops of the

EXERCISE 22

curves of *m* and *n*, as these are commonly written carelessly. The words in this exercise are all found in the 100 per cent spelling list and therefore should all be used.

Lesson 4

Review Exercise 11, *a*. Give Exercise 23, *A, C, O*. Because the *A*

EXERCISE 23

is like the small *a*, there is little difficulty. Show the *C* and *O* and call attention to the fact that they are all oval in general form.

Make three ovals on the board very lightly and change them respectively to *A*, *C*, and *O*. Let the children do this on their papers. After these have been practiced, give any names from the class which have these initials.

Lesson 5

Give Exercises 18, 20, 21, 22, 23. Have about a page written. Collect the papers. Devote the rest of the time to some of the exercises not yet entirely used, as Exercise 22.

Fourth Week. Lesson 1

Do not forget position. By this time there should be little need to discuss it, but be watchful to see that every one regards it. Begin to notice evenness of slant and quality of line this week.

Review Exercise 21, *n*. Continue the regular form of command — "Ready. Write."

Give Exercise 24, *z*, *zone*. This begins like the *n*. The lower

EXERCISE 24

loop is somewhat curved and turns to the left. The joining of these two strokes is somewhat peculiar and may require attention.

Give Exercise 25, *g*, *beg*, *gentlemen*. Call attention to the similarity of the *g* to the *a* and the *d*, and give practice for two or three lines on the combination *gad* with good swing. See that the tops of all these letters tend upward. Then give the words in Exercise 25.

EXERCISE 25

Lesson 2

Give Exercises 1, 2, half-line swing, and Exercises 7, 8. These early exercises will be repeated from time to time to keep up the automatic forward swing which can be most easily got with a comparatively rapid repetition of the same form.

Review Exercises 8, *l*, 21, *n*. Give Exercise 26, *h*, *death*, *machine*, *weigh*. The *h* is likely to give trouble. Get the class to be critical of their work and watch the points of the *h*. Let each find the best

hhh death machine weigh hhh hhh

he has made, and try to make others like it. If there is need of such help, refer to the discussion of *h* in Chapter VIII, Exercises for Grade 4, and use the analysis in class.

LESSON 3

Give Exercises 11, 12, for practice in freedom of movement. Review Exercise 23, *A*, *C*, *O*. "There is another capital much like these, but it has two ovals instead of one." Give Exercise 27, *E*.

E E E E E E E

Call attention to the two ovals by completing them and allow the pupils to do this.

Give names of children which begin with these initials or give Exercise 28, *Alice, Agnew, Claude, Callie, Ethel, Otto, Edna.*

Alice Agnew Claude

Callie Ethel Otto Edna

LESSON 4

Give Exercises 14, 16, for the swing. Notice position.
Give Exercise 29, *p, put, pit, pet, pat, pleat, plate.* Be sure that

ppp pit pleat plate

the top of the down-stroke of the *p* is well above the top of the one-space part. The one-space part may be closed or open as is desired. The words are only suggestive for rapid practice and variety. Review Exercise 28.

LESSON 5

Give Exercises 24, 25, 26, 27, 29, and any names which have been practiced. Review exercises which are not satisfactorily written yet, or give words from Exercise 22, which have not had sufficient practice.

SECOND MONTH. FIRST WEEK

LESSON 1

When the time is to be indicated, the use of the metronome is recommended from this time instead of the voice count because it can be absolutely regular in count, the rate can be definitely determined and the increase regulated, and it sets the teacher free to give more help to individuals than when she must give the count. If a metronome cannot be obtained for use, the voice count should be regulated to the count indicated in the lessons as accurately as possible.

Set the metronome at 144 for the work this month. If this proves too fast for the class to follow, it may be dropped to the rate that they can follow, but it should be raised as soon as possible to this rate.

Review Exercises 11, 13, 14, with attention to the metronome beat. Review Exercises 21, *n*, 25, *g*. Give Exercise 30, *y, anyway*. Be particular to see that the time given is kept. Call atten-

EXERCISE 30

tion to the likeness of *y* to both *n* and *g*. When the *y* is well made, it will make a good *h* if inverted. This comparison may help to overcome a common fault, the retracing the second up-stroke of the *y*. This comes about from disregard of the fact that the up-stroke is a curve and the down-stroke a straight line.

LESSON 2

Note position. Review words from Exercises 15, 23, in time with the metronome.

Give Exercise 31, *B, P, R*. If analysis of these letters is necessary, refer to Grade 5. Show the letters on the board, and before

EXERCISE 31

the children begin to write them call attention to any points which need emphasis. Give any names coming from the class in which these letters are used as initials or give Exercise 32, *Bob, Belle, Paul, Pete, Ruth, Ralph.*

Bob Belle Paul Pete Ruth R

EXERCISE 32

LESSON 3

Take to-day some composition work which the class has done as the basis for a review of good page arrangement. If this has been noticed when the pupils were preparing their compositions, the work will be right in general, and when this has been commended attention should be given to places where greater accuracy would improve the appearance. Lead the class to discuss desirable arrangement as to margins, indentation, spacing between letters, words, and lines, and to test their own work by their decisions on these matters.

Give the rest of the period to having each pupil prepare one page with the best arrangement he can make, copying from the paper he has studied as much as will look well on a page.

LESSON 4

Note the position carefully. Give rapid practice on Exercises 17, *f*, 18, *q*, keeping in time with the metronome.

Give Exercise 33, *s, case, instead, list, position, special, success, sudden.* These words come from the 100 per cent spelling list and should all be used.

sss case instead sss

list position special

success sudden

EXERCISE 33

Give the letter *s* first and practice on the slide as needed to get the right slant. Let the class see you write each word with the metronome until they are sure where each count comes. While these words are taken from the spelling list, the aim here is to get such a feeling for the letter units and their sequence that the correct spelling will follow. In this practice the pupil is developing the kinesthetic image which corresponds to the correct writing of the words.

Lesson 5

Give with free swing Exercises 1, 2, without writing. Suggest the problem of good page arrangement to-day. Give Exercises 30, *y*, 32, 33, making them conform to good page arrangement.

After collecting the papers, practice exercises in which parts have not yet been practiced or in which there is need for more practice.

Second Week. Lesson 1

The stress most of this week will be on capitals.

Review Exercise 33, *s*. Give Exercise 34, *r*, *arrest*, *center*, *comfort*, *direction*, *effort*, *factory*, *figure*, *forward*, *grant*, *history*, *importance*, *member*, *nor*, *order*, *perfect*, *power*, *present*, *press*, *rate*, *rather*, *remember*, *running*, *summer*, *term*, *their*, *tire*, *toward*, *wonderful*.

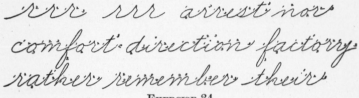

EXERCISE 34

The *r* and *s* are alike in having the tip above the first space. They are the only letters which have this. There is a perceptible pause at this point in each letter. See that the stroke following this tip in the *r* is a separate one, not merely a part of the down-stroke. Also see that this stroke is a slant instead of a curve, which makes an ugly depression in the top of the *r*. Practice some of the words of this exercise to-day. These all come from the 100 per cent spelling list and will furnish material to vary the work for the rest of this week and probably longer. Review some of the words from Exercise 33.

Lesson 2

Give Exercise 35, *I* and *J*. The two capitals differ from the

EXERCISE 35

other letters in the direction of their first stroke. Call attention to this and see that, aside from the general direction's being right, the slant of the first stroke is such that the down-stroke shall have the same slant as the other letters. In making the *J*, see that the down-stroke is straight throughout its length. Give any names which come from the class for these letters. ·

Give part of Exercise 34, *r*.

LESSON 3

Give Exercise 36, *M* and *N*. These are so much alike that they should be studied together and need very little separate practice.

EXERCISE 36

The tops of the curves in these letters give a slight downward slant. The recognition of this may give some help in the writing. Give any names from the class having these initials.

Give some words from Exercise 34.

LESSON 4

Review Exercise 36, *M*, *N*. Give Exercise 37, *W*, *Winona*, *Wallace*. Review exercises given this week that have been found difficult and give further work on Exercise 34.

EXERCISE 37

LESSON 5

Give the preliminary swing. Be particular about position of body, hand, and pen. Give Exercises 35, 36, 37, and some words from Exercises 33, 34.

THIRD WEEK. LESSON 1

Review Exercise 26, *h*. Give Exercise 38, *k*, *check*. There are three points about the k which need particular attention because

EXERCISE 38

of the danger of incorrect form. The second up-stroke must not retrace the down-stroke. (It cannot be so if made correctly, as the down-stroke is straight and the up-stroke is curved.) The final loop must be small, just one space high and open, and the second down-stroke must be parallel to the first. After practice give the word *check* and review any words from lower grades from the *k* list.

For extra work review Exercises 33, 34.

LESSON 2

Review Exercise 30, *y*, with attention to form. Give Exercise 39, *j*, *jazz*, *jolly*. Compare the *j* to the *y* and practice a few times. The words may be used for practice, though they are not required.

EXERCISE 39

Review Exercise 24, *z*. Give Exercise 40, *Z*, showing how much it is like the small *z*. Before having the class write this, give a

EXERCISE 40

review of Exercise 36, *N*, then give only the first stroke, making it slightly more curved than the *N* stroke. Have the pupils write the *Z* several times. This is a capital which is relatively little used, so that it does not need a great amount of practice.

LESSON 3

Be sure position is right and watch movement and time.

Review Exercises 10, *b*, 21, *n*. Give Exercise 41, *v*, *event*, *however*, *prove*, *serve*, *visitor*.

EXERCISE 41

Show that the *v* is like both the *b* and the *n*. Be particular about the up-stroke which curves a little toward the preceding down-stroke, and see that a brief pause is made before the connecting stroke. Practice with a free swing, first long, then short, the combinations *b o w*, *v o w*, which give all the letters having the elevated connecting stroke.

LESSON 4

Review Exercises 26, *h*, 38, *k*, for freedom of movement.

Review Exercise 40, *Z*. Give Exercise 42, *Q*, *Quebec*. This is another capital for which there is little use, but it is desirable for

2, 2 2 Quebec Quebec

EXERCISE 42

EXERCISE 42

the children to have some experience with it. The first stroke is like the first stroke of the *Z*, but a little rounder. After this is practiced, have the children write words from Exercises 33, 34, 41.

LESSON 5

Give the preliminary swing. Give Exercises 38, 39, 40, 41. Spend extra time on review work or give drill on free swinging letter exercises.

FOURTH WEEK. LESSON 1

It is not necessary to write all of every exercise. It is not expected that every class will do so. Be sure, however, to give drill on all new work given in any lesson except that the spelling lists may hold over as many periods as is necessary to introduce all the words from these lists.

Review Exercise 21, *n*. Give Exercise 43, *x*, *except*, *express*, *tax*.

x x x except express

EXERCISE 43

The *x* is a letter which often occasions considerable trouble. Have the class write the letter *n* several times separately. Then tell the pupils to erase the first curve and cross the down-stroke at the middle. They should think of the *n* stroke each time in making the *x* until they are sure of the form.

LESSON 2

Review Exercise 36, *M*, *N*. Give Exercise 44, *Y*, *Youth*. The up-stroke should be somewhat shorter than the down-stroke.

Y Y Y Youth Youth

EXERCISE 44

Make the comparison with Exercise 36, as usual. Review Exercises 23, 27, giving the capitals and any words written with them.

Lesson 3

Be sure position and movement are good.   See that the arm rests mostly on the desk and that the rhythm is kept.   Do not neglect to follow the prescribed directions in giving each exercise.   They develop a sense of regularity.

Give Exercise 45, *L, D*.   These two letters are alike in one point

EXERCISE 45

which distinguishes them from all other letters, the small loop at the base line and the return of the stroke to the base line.   Give *L* first, and after this idea is clear, give the *D*.   Then write names beginning with each, or give Exercise 46, *Loretta, Lorenz, Delia, Daniel.*

EXERCISE 46

Give Exercise 20, *m*, 21, *n*, for free swing.

Lesson 4

Give Exercise 47, *S, Saturday*.   Show the resemblance of this letter to the small *s* by covering the upper loop.   Practice it carefully.   Give names from the class with the initial *S*.

EXERCISE 47

Review Exercises 45, 46.   If extra work is desired, allow each child to write his own name with the metronome, profiting by his study of form.   It is well to emphasize the fact that the name is an individual possession, and, being written often, should be well written.

Lesson 5

To-day, instead of writing, pass out the papers written on previous Fridays and saved for comparison.   Allow each child to compare his own papers and find out where he has made improvement. Suggest the following questions: "Is your writing more even in slant?   Do you keep to the base line better?   Is your spacing any better? What letters do you see that you make better than you did? Is your line more even, and just light enough?" Allow each child to select an exercise he thinks he can improve, write it with the metronome, and compare it with what he did before.

THIRD MONTH. FIRST WEEK. LESSON 1.

Set the metronome at 152 this month.

Recall the last lesson in which a comparison was made of the writing done previously and suggest that all try to remember the points discussed and make the writing better.

Give Exercise 48, *G*. Emphasize the count in this letter because

ExERCISE 48

it will help especially in giving the form. The separation of this letter into units is especially important because of its many changes in direction. Have the class practice it until they get a good swing in making it, and fairly good form. Then give names, or words which may begin sentences. If more work is needed, review other capitals and names given with them.

LESSON 2

Review Exercise 36, *N*. Give Exercise 49, *H*, *K*. Compare

ExERCISE 49

these two capitals to the *N*. Then compare the second stroke of the *H* and *K*. In the *H* it is nearly straight and requires a third stroke for its connection. In the *K* the second stroke itself makes the connection by a sharp turn near the middle where it touches the first stroke. The two parts of the stroke are compound curves. The pupils in this grade should make these. Give any names of members of the class or names suggested by the class from geography, history, or literature.

Review Exercises 47, 48, with the names written.

LESSON 3

Give Exercise 50, *F*, *T*. The only difference between these two

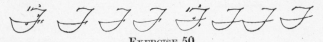

ExERCISE 50

letters is the cross on the *F*. The chief difficulty is likely to be in the proportion. Do not make the first stroke, the top line, too long, and see that the loop at the bottom extends farther to the left than the top of the letter. The down-stroke in each letter is a compound curve. The *T* may be directly joined to other letters. It is better to write the *F* without joining because of the cross. If joined, an additional stroke must be made for the cross.

Give practice on names given, or give Exercise 51, *Frederick, Frances, Theodore, Theresa.*

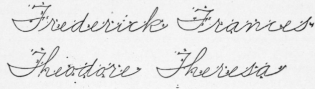

EXERCISE 51

LESSON 4

Review Exercise 36, *m*. Give Exercise 52, *U, V*. Neither of

EXERCISE 52

these letters is very commonly used as a capital. Make the comparison with *M*. Call attention to the fact that *U* is like *Y* in having the up-stroke a little shorter than the first down-stroke. The second stroke of the *V* is a slight compound curve. See that the curve toward the first stroke is not neglected. Review any capitals previously studied that need further study.

LESSON 5

Have the class write Exercises 48, 49, 50, 51, 52. Write all the capitals and some of the names practiced. If there is more time, review words from Exercises 34, 41.

SECOND WEEK. LESSON 1

Review Exercise 43, *x*. Give Exercise 53, *X, Xylophone*. Make

EXERCISE 53

it just like the small x except that the first stroke does not begin at the base line. The count is different because of the short down-stroke. The class will easily get it by writing the small x twice as high. Little time need be spent on this. Give the word *Xylophone*.

Review the capitals $M, N, W, Z, Q, H, K, U, V$, all of which have the first stroke made like the capital X.

Lesson 2

All of the letters have been introduced now. It will be noticed that there has been no use of phrase or sentence work in connection with this introduction, as in the lower grades. There are two reasons for this. First, it is assumed here that the class has a considerable amount of writing to do in other subjects which shows that the drill has practical application and gives incentive for practice. Second, in this grade the initial drill on the letters is made as rapidly as possible so that the effect of this work may be evident in the other writing as early as possible.

The remainder of this week should be given to review of forms which have been studied in previous grades.

To-day give examples in addition, subtraction, multiplication, and division, first from dictation and then from copy, to discover those who need practice of these forms. If the class has studied decimals, introduce some of these into the practice.

Lesson 3

Recall the forms for a friendly letter and for a simple formal letter. Discuss the difference and suggest the need of writing a still more formal letter in business relations; as, in applying for a position, getting information in regard to a trip, etc.

The planning of such letters with their motivation comes properly under composition work, but learning the correct forms and preparing them comes within the handwriting period.

For correct forms for these letters refer to Exercises 54, 55, 56.
Exercise 54, *Friendly letter:*

> 643 Chicago Ave.,
> Paris, Illinois,
> July 5, 1920.

Dear Jane,

....

....

....

Your friend,

....

Exercise 55, *Formal letter:*

> 567 S. Front St.,
> Lawrence, Kansas,
> September 12, 1920.

Miss Frances Johnson,
726 Kansas Ave.,
Topeka, Kansas,
My dear Miss Johnson,

. . . .
. . . .
. . . .

Very sincerely yours,

. . . .

Exercise 56, *Business letter:*

> 738 Georgia Ave.,
> Philadelphia, Penn.,
> August 20, 1920.

Taylor Mercantile Co.,
759 State Street,
Philadelphia, Penn.,
Gentlemen,

. . . .
. . . .

Very truly yours,

. . . .

State at the end of the lesson, "To-morrow we will discuss the making out of bills," and suggest that each look over some bills that have come to his house and be prepared to tell one way in which it is done.

Lesson 4

Have some bill forms to show to-day. Discuss the essentials in a bill. It must state the name of the article furnished or the service rendered, the quantity, the unit cost, the total cost. Let the class suggest bills which could be made out by local dealers, and each make out a bill to present to some member of the class.

Lesson 5

Let each child write to-day a letter of any of the types discussed this week. It should not be longer than the usual page for this lesson and should conform in all points to the standards set by the class for this work.

Third Week

We have had direct drill on all the elements which have been previously studied. There is ahead a problem fully as difficult as the presentation of these forms, that of succeeding in making the correct methods of work habitual. This we shall attempt to do by using relatively short and simple exercises combining all the letter forms, with attention given to rhythm, speed, alinement, slant, quality of line, and spacing of letters and words. Examples of different degrees of excellence in the last five may be seen in the Charts accompanying the book, *The Teaching of Handwriting*, by Frank N. Freeman. The first two cannot be illustrated. A single Chart called *Chart for the Diagnosis of Faults in Handwriting*, which contains all these illustrations, may be obtained from Houghton Mifflin Company. It is desirable to hang this on the wall for frequent reference in this grade.

Divide the class to-day into two groups, excusing from formal writing drill all those whose writing has kept up to the standard for the grade in the practice periods and in the written work in other subjects. Allow this group to carry on other work during the writing period which they may initiate. The other group shall receive the training needed, more or less individualized, to bring them up to the standard for the grade and stabilize the habits formed.

The work given will, for some time, consist largely of short sentences which shall serve to determine what practice is needed. Following this, each pupil of the practice group shall practice on his special difficulty and shall receive help from the teacher in this work.

Following an illustrative lesson in which the full procedure to be used is given, several lessons will be given in which the exercises are given without discussion, with the understanding that the teacher is to present them in the same general way. If any member of the independent group shows deterioration in writing he should at once be returned to the practice group.

LESSON 1

It will be understood from now on that these exercises are given to the practice group, and the independent group will be mentioned only at such times as they are to write tests with the practice group.

Give Exercise 57, *Queer things happen on Halloween.*

Exercise 58, *Zephyr yarn makes warm mittens.*

Have the group write the first sentence. Let each discover where his greatest difficulty is and give help at the beginning of the practice on that. This practice work should be done with the metronome at the regular rate. When any pupil has practiced the parts where he discovers the need for practice, he should write the sentence again and compare with his first copy. He should then compare it with the Chart and see where he stands. The second sentence may be used in the same way by those who need little practice on the first. It is assumed that the teacher will supervise so as to know that the work and criticism are accomplishing their purpose. Criticism by the teacher should usually take the form of questions which will lead the child to discover his own need.

Follow this general procedure in the lessons of the next few weeks.

LESSON 2

Give Exercise 59, *The more haste, the less speed.*
Exercise 60, *Many a mickle makes a muckle.*

LESSON 3

Give Exercise 61, *A rolling stone gathers no moss.*
Exercise 62, *Many hands make light work.*

LESSON 4

Give Exercise 63, *As the twig is bent the tree is inclined.*
Exercise 64, *If you want a thing well done, do it yourself.*

LESSON 5

To-day let each child choose four of the proverbs practiced this week to write, and before they are turned in, compare them with previous work to note improvement. Then have the group practice together several words for speed drill. Whenever any of the independent group wish to join the practice group in the writing for speed, they should be allowed to do so.

FOURTH WEEK. LESSON 1

Give Exercise 65, *Too many cooks spoil the broth.*
Exercise 66, *Birds of a feather flock together.*

LESSON 2

Give Exercise 67, *Two heads are better than one.*
Exercise 68, *Where there's a will, there's a way.*

LESSON 3

Give Exercise 69:

> Man wants but little here below,
> Nor wants that little long.

LESSON 4

Give Exercise 70:

> Early to bed and early to rise,
> Makes a man healthy, wealthy, and wise.

LESSON 5

Conduct the work to-day as it was done last week. If any children have individual difficulties which stand out especially, give them groups of words to write involving the element which causes the trouble.

FOURTH MONTH. FIRST WEEK. LESSON 1

Set the metronome during this month at 160. Allow the writing of each exercise the first time with the metronome. After that use it intermittently. When an exercise consists of single words, as when the child is practicing on special difficulties, write each six or eight times, to allow time to get well into the swing, so that the continuous rhythm will be felt before stopping. This irregular use of the metronome is preliminary to getting the rhythmic writing without external stimulus.

Give Exercise 71, *Nothing venture, nothing have.*

Exercise 72, *It's a poor rule that won't work both ways.*

LESSON 2

Give Exercise 73, *It's a long lane that has no turning.*

Exercise 74, *Half a loaf is better than no bread.*

LESSON 3

Give Exercise 75, *A word fitly spoken is like apples of gold in pictures of silver.*

LESSON 4

Give Exercise 76, *A merry heart doeth good like medicine.*

Exercise 77, *A stitch in time saves nine.*

LESSON 5

Have the children write Exercises 71, 73, 74, 77. After papers are collected, use Exercise 78, *have, lane, work, good,* for speed drill. For regular writing do not increase the speed beyond 160, but for speed drill it may be as high as possible without disorganizing the writing.

SECOND WEEK. LESSON 1

Give Exercise 79, *A bird in the hand is worth two in the bush.*

Exercise 80, *It's an ill wind that blows nobody good.*

LESSON 2

Give Exercise 81:

A man of words and not of deeds
Is like a garden full of weeds.

LESSON 3

Give Exercise 82, *Haste makes waste.*
Exercise 83, *Time is money.*
Review Exercise 78.

LESSON 4

Give Exercise 84, *Time and tide wait for no man.*
Exercise 85, *A penny saved is a penny earned.*

LESSON 5

To-day the whole class should take the two-minute test according to the directions on page 8, using the material indicated for Grade 6. These papers are to be graded by the standard scale, and on this basis the class may be regrouped as is found desirable.

After the test papers are turned in, a short business letter on an assigned subject may be written by each pupil. It is suggested that the teacher pass out advertisements clipped from a current newspaper which the children are to answer.

THIRD WEEK

The teacher may find it desirable to substitute for the exercises given some material from another subject. This is allowable, but the material so written should not be so extensive as to prohibit intensive practice where it is needed, and there should be frequent speed drills to encourage rapid writing without loss in quality.

This week emphasize *alinement* and *slant* especially.

Copy for the Week

Exercise 86:

THE SNOW-STORM

Announced by all the trumpets of the sky,
Arrives the snow, and, driving o'er the fields,
Seems nowhere to alight: the whited air
Hides hills and woods, the river, and the heaven,
And veils the farmhouse at the garden's end.
The sled and traveler stopped, the courier's feet
Delayed, all friends shut out, the house-mates sit
Around the radiant fireplace, enclosed
In a tumultuous privacy of storm.

Ralph Waldo Emerson.

Practice the capitals and words which may give trouble by their length or spelling, and then write the poem. It suggests illustrations which may be added at the art period. For the fifth lesson write the poem as a specimen to be saved or for a project planned by the class, if it is to be illustrated.

FOURTH WEEK
Copy for the Week

Exercise 87:

SLEIGHING SONG

When calm is the night, and the stars shine bright,
The sleigh glides smooth and cheerily;
And mirth and jest abound,
While all is still around,
Save the horses' trampling sound,
And the horse-bells tinkling merrily.

John Shaw.

If more work is needed, review some of the proverbs studied.

LESSON 5

To-day, instead of writing, compare the work written last Friday with that written the first Friday of the third month; that is, just after the last comparison. It may be compared with any of the intervening lessons if desired. There should be quite marked improvement in regularity of *slant*, in *alinement*, in *letter formation*, and in *quality of line*. The spacing between letters and words has been emphasized in study of arrangement, and if the rhythm and speed are good, this should show improvement. While faults must be noticed and corrected sometimes, lay particular emphasis here as before on the search for improvement. Ask questions leading the class to find improvement. A very interesting exercise would be to have each write a brief statement of the improvement he has made.

FIFTH MONTH. FIRST WEEK

Set the metronome this week at 168.

This month we shall write without the metronome about half the time. At first the metronome should be used for the first writing of any exercise. Then allow the class to write it immediately once or twice more, without the metronome. Start it once or twice to test the rhythm. As soon as any who are irregular have caught the rhythm, stop the metronome.

LESSON 1

Give Exercise 88, *Every cloud has a silver lining.*

Spend extra time on speed drill, taking the easy exercises in order. If the class has any trouble in writing at the rate set for this month, it will be well to use this rate for writing single words long enough to get the feeling of continuous writing.

LESSON 2

Give Exercise 89, *Familiarity breeds contempt.* Give speed drill.

Lesson 3

Give Exercise 90. *Fine feathers make fine birds.*
Exercise 91, *All is not gold that glitters.*

Lesson 4

Give Exercise 92, *Distance lends enchantment to the view.*
Give speed drill.

Lesson 5

Let each child decide what he will write and compare it with the same exercise written earlier in the week. Encourage the frequent comparison of work with the Chart.

Second Week. Lesson 1

Give Exercise 93, *Please all, and you will please none.*
Exercise 94, *Slow but sure.*

Lesson 2

Give Exercise 95, *Plodding wins the race.*
Exercise 96, *Don't count your chickens before they are hatched.*

Lesson 3

Give Exercise 97, *An ounce of prevention is worth a pound of cure.* Exercise 96, in review.

Lesson 4

Give Exercise 98, *Don't put all your eggs into one basket.*
Exercise 99, *The early bird catches the worm.*

Lesson 5

Give Exercise 96, 97, 98, 99. After these are collected, use for speed drill Exercise 100, *ounce, race, catches, bird.*

Third and Fourth Weeks

For the next two weeks use Exercise 101, Lucy Larcom's poem, *In Time's Swing,* as the basis of the work. Give practice on details, such as capitals and hard words, and discuss the proper spacing. If it is to be written all together, how much should be written on one page? If it is to be illustrated, how should it be placed? Make this a genuine study of arrangement where the children settle the matter on the basis of the study of good forms. The entire class may participate in this work even if some are excused from the intensive practice on details.

Exercise 101:

IN TIME'S SWING

Father Time, your footsteps go
Lightly as the falling snow.
In your swing I'm sitting, see!
Push me softly, one, two, three,
Twelve times only. Like a sheet
Spreads the snow beneath my feet:
Singing merrily, let me swing
Out of winter into spring!

Swing me out, and swing me in!
Trees are bare, but birds begin
Twittering to the peeping leaves
On the bough beneath the eaves.
Look! one lilac-bud I saw!
Icy hillsides feel the thaw:
April chased off March to-day;
Now I catch a glimpse of May.

Oh, the smell of sprouting grass!
In a blur the violets pass:
Whispering from the wild-wood come
Mayflowers' breath, and insects' hum.
Roses carpeting the ground;
Orioles warbling all around:
Swing me low, and swing me high,
To the warm clouds of July!

Slower now, for at my side
White pond-lilies open wide;
Underneath the pine's tall spire
Cardinal-blossoms burn like fire.
They are gone; the golden-rod
Flashes from the dark-green sod.
Crickets in the grass I hear;
Asters light the fading year.

Slower still! October weaves
Rainbows of the forest-leaves.
Gentians fringed, like eyes of blue,
Glimmer out of sleety dew.
Winds through withered sedges hiss:
Meadow-green I sadly miss.
Oh, 't is snowing; swing me fast,
While December shivers past!

Lucy Larcom.

Sixth Month. First Week

The words from the 100 per cent spelling list will be introduced now to give opportunity to practice on them. It will be worth while for the entire class to write these words, but the independent group need only prove their ability to write them independently.

Lesson 1

Set the metronome at 176 for this month.

Review Exercises 16, *c*, 17, *f*, 21, *n*. Give Exercise 102, *elect, fact, field, file, action, attention, diamond, intend, obtain*. After these are written correctly, use some of them for speed drill. There is an advantage in this for spelling as well as for writing, as the fluent repetition, if correct, tends to make recall more automatic.

Lesson 2

Review Exercises 25, *g*, 26, *h*, 29, *p*. Give Exercise 103, *oblige; though, which; population*. Review part of Exercise 102 and give speed drill.

Lesson 3

Review Exercises 33, *s*, 34, *r*. Give Exercise 104, *busy, cause, inspect, least, publish, suppose, thus, usual; aboard, appear, capture, contract, crowd, different, direct, district, either, honor, inform, liberty, manner, neighbor, perhaps, prepare, president, promise, proper, purpose, regard, remain, result, retire, royal, together, wear, written*.

Not all of these can be taken to-day. Return to this exercise for review until all are used.

Lesson 4

Review Exercises 38, *k*, 39, *j*, 41, *v*. Give Exercise 105, *o'clock; injure, judge, objection, subject; avenue, service, themselves, travel, vessel*.

Lesson 5

Write one line each of single words from the exercises practiced this week, making a particular effort on *letter formation*.

Second Week. Lesson 1

This week words from the exercises of last week are used in sentences. Other sentences accomplishing the same result may be used if these words have not been practiced. For additional work this week continue the practice of Exercise 102 and give speed drill on single words.

Give Exercise 106, *It is a great honor to be elected President of the United States.*

Lesson 2

Give Exercise 107, *A police officer directs the crowd on an avenue in the business district.*

Lesson 3

Give Exercise 108, *You may wear a diamond if you obtain it in a proper manner.*

Lesson 4

Give Exercise 109, *Inform your neighbor that I intend to fill the contract as usual.*

Lesson 5

Write the four sentences given this week. After the papers are taken, write single words for speed drill.

Third Week

A regular method of grading will be followed for the rest of the year. The grading is based on the *Chart for Diagnosing Faults in Handwriting,* and where possible the teacher should make use of this.

During this week teacher and pupils should study the Chart more than yet has been done. The grading will begin next week. During the week that each category is being emphasized, that category alone should be graded; that is, when *letter formation* is being emphasized, it will be rated in terms of the Chart, 2, 6, 10, or the intermediate points 4, 8. Further information regarding the use of the Chart can be obtained from *The Teaching of Handwriting,* by Frank N. Freeman (Houghton Mifflin Company), pp. 123–42.

The children should understand that the marking is in points, not in per cents as in the other subjects. When the marking is begun, the teacher should grade, in the special category for the week, the work done on the first day and on the last day.

The child should grade his own work every day, not so much for the value of his estimate as to lead to a critical attitude toward his work.

Only one or two specimens will usually be given for the week and the teacher should arrange for the detailed practice which is needed. It has not been thought necessary to give written copies for all this work. If there is any question as to form of letters, refer to previous copies. Use the metronome wherever there is difficulty in getting the time and for speed drill. Otherwise there should be little need for it except to set the time.

Copies for the Week

Any teacher may substitute, for copies given, material which will correlate with other subjects. Where quotations are given, the

name indicating the source should be written. It is important
that pupils learn to give credit for copied material.

Exercise 110:

> Day has put on his jacket, and around
> His burning bosom hath buttoned it with stars.
> > *Oliver Wendell Holmes.*

Exercise 111:

> Still sits the schoolhouse by the road,
> > A ragged beggar sunning;
> Around it still a sumach grows,
> > And blackberry vines are running.
> > > *John Greenleaf Whittier.*

FOURTH WEEK

Begin this week to emphasize a particular category. This week
emphasize and grade on *letter formation*. Pass out the last specimens saved for comparison and let each study his own for good
letter form and for improvements to be made. Lead each child to
grade his own work frequently. Call attention to special points
of difficulty in *letter formation*.

Copies for the Week

Exercise 112:

> From dewy morn to starry night
> > The birds sing sweet and strong,
> That the radiant sky is filled with light,
> > That the days are fair and long.
> > > *Celia Thaxter.*

Exercise 113:

> What is it that gives to the plainest face
> > The charm of the noblest beauty?
> Not the thought of the duty of happiness,
> > But the happiness of duty!
> > > *Celia Thaxter.*

Exercise 114:

> Flower in the crannied wall,
> I pluck you out of the crannies;
> I hold you here, root and all, in my hand;
> Little flower, if I could but understand
> What you are, root and all, and all in all,
> I should know what God and man is.
> > *Alfred, Lord Tennyson.*

SEVENTH MONTH. FIRST WEEK

This week emphasize and grade on *spacing*. If proper attention
has been given to the study of arrangement, the spacing should be

rather good.   Discuss with the class good arrangement in poems and what to do where more than one line is needed for a line of poetry.   Do not allow cramping, but do not spread the letters and words too much.   Reference to the Chart will help to determine a good proportion.

Copies for the Week

Exercise 115:

AWAKENING

Never yet was a Springtime
Late though lingered the snow,
That the sap stirred not at the whisper
Of the south wind, sweet and low;
Never yet was a Springtime
When the buds forgot to blow.

Margaret E. Sangster.

Exercise 116, *The will to do well is the next thing to having the power. — Charles Dickens.*

Exercise 117, *Set about whatever you intend to do; beginning is half the battle.*

SECOND WEEK

Emphasize *alinement* this week.   All letters should rest on the base line. Regard also proportional height.   Do not let the one-space letters lie down on the base line and make the loop letters a little more than twice as high.   While doing this, try to keep good form and spacing.

Copies for the Week

Exercise 118, *They laugh that win. — William Shakespeare.*
Exercise 119:

BIRDS

Birds are singing round my window,
Tunes the sweetest ever heard,
And I hang my cage there daily,
But I never catch a bird.

Richard Henry Stoddard.

Exercise 120:

A LULLABY

Sleep, my baby, sleep!
Over thy beautiful head,
Lightly, softly, and close,
Sweeter than lily or rose,
Thy mother's kisses are shed.
Sleep, my baby, sleep.

Celia Thaxter.

THIRD WEEK

Our point of emphasis this week will be *quality of line.* This depends upon good position, which prevents cramping and undue pressure; upon good ink and pen; and upon rhythm, which tends to give regularity instead of waviness of line. Call attention incidentally to the categories previously emphasized; but make this one the principal one for this week.

Copy for the Week

Exercise 121:

FOUR THINGS

Four things a man must learn to do
If he would make his record true:
To think without confusion clearly;
To love his fellow men sincerely;
To act from honest motives purely;
To trust in God and Heaven securely.

Henry van Dyke.

If more work is needed, use some preceding exercise which has been omitted or review one which the children liked especially.

FOURTH WEEK

Emphasize *uniformity of slant* this week. Because this depends on position and rhythm, it should be very good by this time. Try to get the pupils to carry over their writing form into their writing in other subjects. Lead them to be critical of their work.

Copy for the Week

Exercise 122:

THE SHIP OF STATE

Thou, too, sail on, O Ship of State!
Sail on, O Union, strong and great!
Humanity with all its fears,
With all the hopes of future years,
Is hanging breathless on thy fate!

Henry W. Longfellow.

Give speed drill this week and review an exercise selected by the teacher.

EIGHTH MONTH.   FIRST WEEK

We will now combine grading on the categories of *letter formation, spacing,* and *slant.* Sum the scores given to each for the total score. Be sure the pupils understand that the scoring is in points, not in per cents.

On Friday of this week the third two-minute test of the year should be given to the entire class to determine what pupils shall be excused from writing practice for the remainder of the year. The practice group *may* by this time be relatively small, and if so, very intensive training should be given on the particular difficulties. For lack of freedom of movement give time every day to the early free swinging exercises with little regard to form. If the trouble is with some element of letter formation, give part of the time each day to concentrated practice on the letters including this element, putting them in different combinations so as to give variety. Use the copies which are given so far as they give meaning to the practice and are helpful. Material from other subjects may be substituted if it gives opportunity for the drill needed.

Copies for the Week

Exercise 123:

> Truth crushed to earth will rise again;
> The eternal years of God are hers.
>
> *James R. Lowell.*

Exercise 124:

> One sturdy little violet peeped out alone, in March
> While cobwebs of the snow yet hung about the sky's gray arc.
> But merry winds to sweep them down in earnest had begun:
> The violet, though she shook with cold, stayed on to watch the fun.
>
> *Lucy Larcom.*

SECOND WEEK

Grade on *letter formation, alinement,* and *quality of line.* Sum the grades as last week. This method of analysis of the writing to determine where changes are desirable should be helpful to the class. Urge that all writing be made in as good form, speed, and rhythm as the work done in the writing period.

Copy for the Week

Exercise 125:

THE HUMBLE-BEE

> Burly, dozing humble-bee,
> Where thou art is clime for me.
> Let them sail for Porto Rique,
> Far-off heats through seas to seek;
> I will follow thee alone,
> Thou animated torrid-zone!
> Zigzag steerer, desert cheerer,
> Let me chase thy waving lines;
> Keep me nearer, me thy hearer,
> Singing over shrubs and vines.
>
> *Ralph Waldo Emerson.*

Third Week

Grade on all the categories this week. Help each child determine which one needs the most attention and let each try to bring that one up.

Copies for the Week

Exercise 126:

May

May shall make the orchards bloom;
And the blossoms fine perfume
Shall set all the honey-bees
Murmuring among the trees.

Frank Dempster Sherman.

Exercise 127:

Lo, here hath been dawning
Another blue day;
Think! wilt thou let it
Slip useless away?

Out of Eternity
This new day is born;
Into Eternity,
At night, will return.

Thomas Carlyle.

Fourth Week

Two short copies are given this week. Spend any extra time on speed drill with single words or groups of easy words.

Copies for the Week

Exercise 128:

All human race would fain be wits,
And millions miss to one that hits.

Jonathan Swift.

Exercise 129:

Heaven is not reached at a single bound.
We build the ladder by which we rise
From the lowly earth to the vaulted skies
And mount to the summit round by round.

Henry W. Longfellow.

Ninth Month

By this time a large part of the class should have reached the standard for the grade. If this is so, the handwriting period may be used for the preparation of any material connected with school activities which requires writing — compositions, letters, invitations, programs, etc.

If this is done, see that those who are in the practice group have the help that they need and still have some time for practice on details where it is necessary. Seating this group together during the writing period will facilitate this.

If most of the class is still in the practice group, as may be in some cases, or if there does not seem to be material that is desirable to substitute for what is given, use Exercises 130, 131, for this month, giving as much drill on details as is necessary and giving speed drills with the easier words. Exercise 131 is especially good, because, aside from its interest, it gives practice on fourteen different capitals and all the small letters except j, q, z, so that it gives opportunity for varied practice.

During the third week of the last month a two-minute test should be given to determine the progress made during the year and to provide a standard for the next year. No pupil in Grades 7, 8, should be allowed to use a quality of writing poorer than that used in Grade 6. If any pupil fails to reach the standard for Grade 6, it is recommended that regular writing drill be taken in Grades 7, 8, following the course for Grade 6.

There should be given during this month also a systematic review of all abbreviations which have been used during the year. These should be written for the sake of fixing the correct usage. The following are suggested as some which may have been introduced in connection with other subjects this year. See lists in the chapters on Grades 4 and 5, the ninth month, for others which may be given:

Capt., C.O.D., Col., Gen., Lt., Maj., Gov., O.K., names of foreign countries, *Sec.* (Secretary), *Sen.* (Senator), *sq., Supt., vs.*

Exercise 130:

A GREEN CORNFIELD

The earth is green, the sky is blue;
    I saw and heard one sunny morn
A skylark hang between the two;
    A singing speck above the corn;

A stage below in gay accord,
    White butterfly danced on the wing,
And still the singing skylark soared
    And silent sank, and soared to sing.

The cornfield stretched a tender green
    To right and left beside my walks;
I knew he had a nest unseen
    Somewhere amid the million stalks.

And as I paused to hear his song,
    While swift the shining moments fled,
Perhaps his mate sat listening long,
    And listened longer than I did.[1]

Exercise 131:

THE ELF AND THE DORMOUSE

Under a toadstool
    Crept a wee Elf,
Out of the rain
    To shelter himself.

Under the toadstool,
    Sound asleep,
Sat a big Dormouse
    All in a heap.

Trembled the wee Elf,
    Frightened, and yet
Fearing to fly away
    Lest he get wet.

To the next shelter —
    Maybe a mile!
Sudden the wee Elf
    Smiled a wee smile.

Tugged till the toadstool
    Toppled in two.
Holding it over him
    Gaily he flew.

Soon he was safe home,
    Dry as could be.
Soon woke the Dormouse —
    "Good gracious me!

"Where is my toadstool?"
    Loud he lamented.
— And that's how umbrellas
First were invented.

Oliver Herford.

Optional Material

These selections may be used where more work is needed or as substitutes for some of the assigned exercises. If they are used they should be treated in the same general way as the exercises which are assigned.

[1] From Christina G. Rossetti's *Poems,* by permission of The Macmillan Company.

THE OWL

When cats run home and night is come,
And dew is cold upon the ground,
And the far-off stream is dumb,
   And the whirring sail goes round;
   And the whirring sail goes round;
     Alone and warming his five wits,
     The white owl in the belfry sits.

Alfred, Lord Tennyson.

SNOW

Little white feathers, filling the air,
Little white feathers, how came you there?

"We came from the cloud-birds sailing so high;
They're shaking their white wings up in the sky!"

Little white feathers, how swift you go!
Little white feathers, I love you so!

"We are swift because we have work to do;
But hold up your face and we'll kiss you true."

Mary Mapes Dodge.

THE AMERICAN FLAG

Flag of the free heart's hope and home,
By angel hands to valor given;
Thy stars have lit the welkin dome,
And all thy hues were born in heaven.
Forever float that standard sheet!
Where breathes the foe but falls before us,
With Freedom's soil beneath our feet,
And Freedom's banner streaming o'er us.,

Joseph Rodman Drake.

CHAPTER XI

GRADES SEVEN AND EIGHT

IN Grades 7 and 8 a different procedure is followed. The increasing establishment of junior high schools makes an organic separation between these two grades and the grades below them. The general acceptance of departmental work here has also encouraged a different type of work.

There should be differentiation of aims according to the needs and the vocational interests of the class.

1. For the commercial group, including those who plan to take business or clerical positions, there should be special instruction leading to expert work in respect to both speed and quality.

2. For the poor writers special instruction should be arranged following the course outlined for Grade 6 and excusing them from the work on the same conditions that would excuse sixth-grade pupils.

3. For those aside from the commercial group, who have reached and maintain in all their work the grade standard, there should be no formal drill. There should be an occasional grading of the written work in other subjects to determine whether a satisfactory quality is being maintained, and two or three times a year a formal test should be given to measure speed and quality.

INDEX